```
977.311                              149615
  Pal
  Ros
        Ross.
        Silhouette in diamonds.
```

Learning Resources Center
Nazareth College of Rochester, N. Y.

DISCARDED

THE LEISURE CLASS
IN AMERICA

This is a volume in the Arno Press collection

THE LEISURE CLASS IN AMERICA

Advisory Editor
Leon Stein

A Note About This Volume

Bertha Honore Palmer (1849-1918) was a woman of great spirit and energy. When the Chicago fire destroyed much of her husband's fortune, she put her imagination and organizing ability to work, moving rapidly up the social ladder to become the social leader of the city whose people and problems she knew well. She could deal with businessmen and working people, dispense directives and charity. She played an outstanding part in organizing the important role of women in the Columbian Exposition of 1891. Reviewing this book in the *New York Times*, Cleveland Amory wrote, "Here is a book which should be read and reread by our present-day so-called *grandes dames*. In Mrs. Potter Palmer's league, they would be the bushers." And the *Library Journal* noted "marshalling her facts from vast and varied sources, Miss Ross capably and objectively has exposed a vitally interesting woman. For all libraries."

See last pages of this volume for a complete list of titles.

SILHOUETTE IN DIAMONDS
The Life of Mrs. Potter Palmer

BY ISHBEL ROSS

ARNO PRESS
A New York Times Company

New York / 1975

149615

Reprint Edition 1975 by Arno Press Inc.

Copyright © 1960 by Ishbel Ross
Reprinted by permission of Ishbel Ross

THE LEISURE CLASS IN AMERICA
ISBN for complete set: 0-405-06900-6
See last pages of this volume for titles.

Manufactured in the United States of America

———•◦⟨∞⟩◦•———

Library of Congress Cataloging in Publication Data

Ross, Ishbel, 1897-
   Silhouette in diamonds.

   (The Leisure class in America)
   Reprint of the ed. published by Harper, New York.
   Bibliography: p.
   Includes index.
    1. Palmer, Bertha (Honoré) 1849-1918. I. Title.
II. Series.
CT275.P319R6 1975   977.3'11'040924 [B]   75-1868
ISBN 0-405-06934-0

SILHOUETTE IN DIAMONDS

Books by Ishbel Ross

SILHOUETTE IN DIAMONDS
The Life of Mrs. Potter Palmer

THE GENERAL'S WIFE
The Life of Mrs. Ulysses S. Grant

FIRST LADY OF THE SOUTH
The Life of Mrs. Jefferson Davis

ANGEL OF THE BATTLEFIELD
The Life of Clara Barton

REBEL ROSE
Life of Rose O'Neal Greenhow, Confederate Spy

PROUD KATE
Portrait of an Ambitious Woman, Kate Chase

CHILD OF DESTINY
The Life Story of the First Woman Doctor

ISLE OF ESCAPE

FIFTY YEARS A WOMAN

LADIES OF THE PRESS

HIGHLAND TWILIGHT

MARRIAGE IN GOTHAM

PROMENADE DECK

SILHOUETTE IN DIAMONDS
The Life of Mrs. Potter Palmer

BY ISHBEL ROSS

ILLUSTRATED

HARPER & BROTHERS, PUBLISHERS, NEW YORK

SILHOUETTE IN DIAMONDS

Copyright © 1960 by Ishbel Ross
Printed in the United States of America

All rights in this book are reserved. No part of the book may be used or reproduced in any manner whatsoever without written permission except in the case of brief quotations embodied in critical articles and reviews. For information address Harper & Brothers, 49 East 33rd Street, New York 16, N. Y.

FIRST EDITION

I-K

Library of Congress catalog card number: 60-13443

➤➤➤➤➤➤➤➤➤➤➤➤➤ Contents

	Acknowledgments	ix
1.	A City in Flames	1
2.	Merchant Prince	16
3.	The Innkeeper's Wife	37
4.	Mrs. Palmer Invades Europe	58
5.	World's Columbian Exposition	82
6.	The Nation's Hostess	100
7.	Conquest of Newport	125
8.	Art Collector	147
9.	The Paris Exposition	164
10.	Edwardian England	190
11.	Chaliapin Sings for Mrs. Palmer	206
12.	Back to Nature	222
	Notes	255
	Bibliography	263
	Index	269

Illustrations

The following are grouped in a separate section after page 84

Mrs. Potter Palmer
Mrs. Henry Hamilton Honoré
Henry Hamilton Honoré
Bertha Mathilde Honoré as a young girl
Ida Honoré
The great fire at Chicago, October 8, 1871
Panic-stricken citizens rushing past the Sherman House
Mrs. Potter Palmer in 1893
Potter Palmer in 1868
The Grant-Honoré wedding in Chicago
Mrs. Potter Palmer with her sister, Mrs. Frederick Dent Grant, and Julia Grant, Honoré Palmer and Potter Palmer, Jr.
Mrs. Palmer with Honoré

Illustrations

Mrs. Frederick Dent Grant

Princess Cantacuzène

Mrs. Palmer shortly after her husband's death in 1902

Tropical Garden on the Roof, Palmer House, Chicago

Tally-Ho going to the Washington Park Derby in 1870

Woman's Building at the World's Columbian Exposition in 1893

View from the balcony of the Woman's Building

Potter Palmer mansion on Lake Shore Drive in 1890

Ballroom and picture gallery

Main gallery

Library

Mrs. Potter Palmer, wearing her famous pink pearl

Potter Palmer

The Oaks—Mrs. Palmer's house at Osprey, Florida

➤➤➤➤➤➤➤➤➤➤➤➤➤ *Acknowledgments*

Since Mrs. Potter Palmer was deeply involved in public as well as social affairs her correspondence covered a considerable range and the bulk of her papers are now in the Chicago Historical Society. Her official records of the World's Columbian Exposition in this collection were a valuable source of material for this biography.

Although some of her personal papers were destroyed and others were lost by fire many are still to be found in the Art Institute of Chicago, the Newberry Library and the Sarasota County Historical Commission. Intimate family records are kept in the Chicago offices of the Palmer Florida Realty Company. Occasional letters are scattered across the country in libraries and in historical societies or are privately owned. Art catalogues and pamphlets, in addition to the records of leading art dealers in New York, London and Paris, give ample evidence of Mrs. Palmer's importance as a collector.

I am deeply indebted to Mrs. Palmer's son, Honoré Palmer, for giving me his personal recollections of his mother, and to her grandson, Gordon Palmer, for allowing me to explore the family papers in the Chicago offices of the Palmer family.

Princess Cantacuzène, who traveled in Europe with her aunt and saw much of her in Chicago, Newport and Sarasota, gave a great deal of time and effort to sharing with me intimate recollections of Mrs. Palmer. I am indebted to her for many anecdotes and personal touches that serve to throw light on the subject of this biography. Major General Ulysses S. Grant, III, Mrs. Palmer's nephew, was generous in indicating sources of material.

I am deeply grateful to Daniel Catton Rich, director in turn of the Art Institute of Chicago and the Worcester Art Museum, for his expert comment on Mrs. Palmer as an art collector, and for the time he gave to discussing her life and work in general. Charles Durand-Ruel of Paris was good enough to supply me with old records of Mrs. Palmer's art transactions in the 1890's, when she was building up her collection of Impressionist and Barbizon paintings. Benjamin K. Smith, art appraiser in Chicago who had many dealings with Mrs. Palmer and knew her well, gave me the benefit of his recollections. William B. Colvin, of the Palmer Florida Realty Company, and Graham Aldis both gave me special help in Chicago.

John Mason Brown was kind enough to advise me on Louisville sources and Mrs. Dorothy Thomas Cullen, curator of the Filson Club in Louisville, was helpful on details concerning the early history of the Honoré family in Kentucky. I am indebted to the Convent of the Visitation in Georgetown for the school records of Bertha Honoré, later Mrs. Potter Palmer.

Mrs. Doris Davis, director of the Sarasota County Historical Commission, and Miss Louise Higel of Sarasota gave me valuable aid in rounding up material on the last eight years of Mrs. Palmer's life, much of which was passed in Florida. In Sarasota I had access to family papers dealing with her farming and ranching operations, her attitude to her employees, her ambitious plans for land development, and her day-to-day life with her family. A number of Sarasotans still have vivid memories of Mrs. Palmer and I am indebted to the following for their personal recollections of her: Mrs. Ralph Caples, Mrs. Walter J. Bryan, Dr. Joseph Halton, A. B. Edwards, Albert Blackburn, Charles W. Webb, Captain Frank Roberts and Benjamin H. Russell.

In writing this biography I have used the facilities of a number of libraries and historical societies across the country but I should like to cite, in addition to the main Chicago sources, the Library of Congress, the New York Public Library, the New York Society Library and the Frick Art Reference Library. Of scores of persons who have given me assistance I am particularly indebted to the following individuals: Miss Waltraut M. Van der Rohe, art research assistant, Miss Ruth E. Schoneman, chief of the Ryerson Library, Wasco Rogula and Anselmo Carini, all of the Art Institute of Chicago; Paul M. Angle, director, Miss Blanche Jantzen, Manuscript Division, and Mrs. Paul M. Rhymer, Curator of Prints, all of the Chicago Historical Society; Mrs. G. L. Woodward and Stanley Pergill, Rare Book Room, and Frederick Hall, Newberry Library; Dr. Elizabeth G. McPherson and Miss Kate M. Stewart of the Manuscript Division, Library of Congress; and Miss Sylvia Hilton, Miss Helen Ruskell and other staff members of the New York Society Library.

I. R.

1

>>>>>>>>>>>>>> *A City in Flames*

A brisk wind rustled the withered autumn leaves in the garden of Potter Palmer's country house on the outskirts of Chicago on the fateful night of October 8, 1871. The grass on the lawn was like tinder for it had been one of the driest summers in the city's history. Bertha Honoré Palmer, a bride of twenty-two, was passing a quiet Sunday evening by herself in the home she was about to leave to take up quarters in the newly finished Palmer House, her husband's wedding gift to her. Potter Palmer, millionaire merchant and real estate man, had gone east to attend the funeral of one of his sisters in upstate New York. It was Bertha's first separation from her husband since their marriage fourteen months earlier.

Soon after nine o'clock she became conscious of a yellowish glow hanging over the city. She studied the scene with concern. Fires were an everyday occurrence but before long she saw that this was no ordinary blaze. Shafts of flame shot across the skyline until it seemed as if most of the city were on fire. She thought anxiously of her parents, Mr. and Mrs. Henry Hamilton Honoré, who lived on Michigan Avenue, right in the path of the flames, which seemed to leap out in different areas, leaving no clue to their focus. It was not until some time later that the legend spread of Mrs. Catherine O'Leary's cow kicking over her kerosene lamp in a De Koven Street barn at milking time. But in any event this was where the fire began and a dry southwest wind funneled the flames to adjoining shacks. Soon homes, shops, churches, factories, were going up like matchsticks. The downtown business area was quickly enveloped. From the slums to La Salle Street devastation prevailed.

At first Mrs. Palmer had confidence that the new waterworks on the North Side would be equal to the situation, but when the fire jumped the river and set them ablaze, all hope of staying its demoniac course was ended. When she saw that things were completely out of control she went into practical action with her servants and neighbors. Although at a safe distance from the burning city they all began assembling their treasures and preparing their houses for the dispossessed. Bertha murmured prayers for her family as she busied herself around the house. There was no way of reaching them in the blazing city.

By this time the sky was an awesome yellow, streaked with vivid columns of crimson where fire flashed out in yet another section of the city. There was little smoke because of the speed and intensity of the conflagration. Here and there the blaze was sharp and clear, illumining the distorted motions of a frantic population. The streets were jammed with fleeing families, carrying babies, bundles, furniture and armfuls of clothes. They ran in all directions, shouting and crying, while cinders hit them like stinging hailstones and sparks danced before their eyes like twinkling stars. Embers seemed to rain from the sky. Jets of flame pulverized safes and buildings that had been pronounced fireproof. Synthetic granite walls seemed to offer little more resistance than wooden shacks.

The noise was unearthly. To one it sounded like the lake on a stormy night. To another the crackling murmur suggested an enormous bundle of dry twigs burning. There were sharp explosions as barrels of oil and paint were touched off by the flames.

For days and weeks afterward Bertha heard tales of the terrible scenes enacted in the streets that night. One little girl with flames licking her long golden hair ran screaming through the crowd. But silence followed when a distracted onlooker threw a container of liquor over her. It flared up and enveloped her in blue flame. Fire touched off the skirt of a woman who knelt in the street, praying with her crucifix. Her anguished face was long remembered by those who saw her and survived. A forgotten canary sang in its gilded cage in a hotel window which was brightly lit by the approaching curtain of flame. A bride with half-wrapped wedding presents in her arms ran frantically back and forth calling for her husband. Women dragged Saratoga trunks along the sidewalks. Wheelbarrows and perambulators were piled high with family possessions.

There were screams and shouts and curses, tears and voiceless despair. The slum sections tossed up thieves, footpads and murderers, who plundered and rioted as the city burned. All along Lake Street they ravaged the shops. Liquor ran in the gutters and many were drunk. But the most desperate scenes were at the bridges, where struggling masses converged while fire already licked the foundations and one after another of the structures went down. Human beings and horses were inextricably mixed in the jam as carriages and teams attempted to cross the river. The horses, half mad from the flick of cinders and the frantic crowding, trampled men and women. Scores of the trapped clung to the guard rails; some wound up in the river. The ships drifted like sagging ghosts as sails and masts caught fire. The sirens of tugs trying to get through added piercing blasts.

Before many hours had passed Bertha knew that the Palmer and Honoré fortunes had gone up in flames. Her husband's thirty-two fine new buildings on State Street, as well as the nearly finished Palmer House, were burned to the ground. Honoré Block, a magnificent building for its time, put up by her father, with walls decorated with colonnades of synthetic marble, was in ruins. Most of his other properties were burned, too. The Palmer House was one of the first large buildings to go, although its fireproof equipment had promised protection. Terrified citizens sought safety in its lobby, bringing their valuables with them. But liquor or explosive oils had been stored in the cellar by some of the refugees and a terrific explosion wrecked the building when the fire reached this area. Detonations were so frequent that night that Bertha never knew which one signaled the collapse of her wedding gift.

The new Grand Pacific Hotel, with five hundred rooms and a vertical elevator connecting all six of its floors, burned before it had opened its doors to guests. The glass dome of its porte-cochere crashed to the ground with a smashing effect, adding another variation to the strange cacophony of the night. The Tremont House fared no better after a period of panic when the elevator jammed and the screams of women trapped upstairs could be heard above the wind, the roar of the fire and the shouts in the street. Many had sought shelter in this popular hotel and the public rooms were filled with people in various stages of undress, screaming, moaning or sobbing. The sick lay about on floors and sofas. Some women hugged their ball gowns, furs and jewels in their arms as they looked frantically for a way of escape. John B. Drake, the manager, managed to save the money in his safe and stuffed pillowcases with some of the hotel silver.

The marble seven-story Sherman House shared the fate of the other big hotels. Crosby's Opera House dissolved like tinder. It was about to reopen with a Theodore Thomas concert. The orchestra leader arrived with his musicians to find that his train could not enter the smoldering city. The courthouse subsided at three o'clock in the morning, its great bell pealing weirdly as it crashed to the ground. The watchman in the tower had first spread the alarm for the fire that now destroyed it. The buildings of the Historical Society and the Academy of Sciences were blighted by flames. All but one of the banks were gone. The flames skipped madly from point to point, leaving whole areas untouched, then consuming others with appalling speed.

The members of the Chicago Club met for a champagne breakfast, intent on a defiant toast to their financial ruin. Before they could finish, the flames had reached their clubhouse. They picked up the red satin sofas from the lobby, took their liquor and cigars and moved to the lake front to complete the rite they had begun. Friends of the Potter Palmers were in this group, since the Chicago Club membership represented the wealth of the city.

Bertha heard later from Marshall Field how he and Levi Z. Leiter directed the fight to save their brand-new store. They hung wet blankets over all the windows and tried to douse the flames with hose sprays. Finally they gave up and moved what they could to an old horsecar barn on the South Side. Joseph Medill, another friend of the Potter Palmers, strove mightily to get out the *Tribune*, although a scarlet cloud hung all night over his plant. With a score of his men he worked with water and shovels, drenching and stamping out the flames. By morning the press rollers were melting and the basement was filled with smoke. He hurried then to a job printing plant on the West Side, pushed his men into further action and turned out a special fire edition that carried the first challenge to rebuild: "*In the midst of a calamity without parallel in the world's history, looking upon the ashes of thirty years accumulation, the people of this once beautiful city have resolved that Chicago Shall Rise Again!*"

And rise again it did, almost from the bleak moment twenty-seven hours after the outbreak of the fire when it was declared under control. It burned itself out on the bare fields close to Lincoln Park, where the tall oaks were already singed and charred. The ultimate reckoning was three hundred dead, ninety thousand homeless, seventeen thousand buildings destroyed, and property loss of nearly two hundred million dollars, or one-third of the wealth of Chicago. It was compared to the Great Fire of London. None more terrible had figured in American history.

Bertha joined her family as soon as she could find a conveyance to take her to Michigan Avenue. They were all safe but badly shaken and weary from hours of vigilance and physical labor. Their house was scorched and ruined but not altogether demolished. All night long they had carried their possessions to the lake front, where hundreds huddled on the sand. Mrs. Palmer's descendants today have some statuary, as well as J. C. Gorman's painting of Mrs. Honoré, all of which went through the fire. They were able to save a few of their inherited treasures but most of their furnishings were ruined.

The scene at the beach was one that Bertha never forgot. Men and women still ran back and forth with buckets of water from the lake, as mattresses and carpets smoldered all around them. Children cried for food as each family sat in its own little mound of personal property. Mrs. Honoré, worn out from the night's exertions, relaxed on an Empire chair with its legs half embedded in the sand. Her husband was already making plans to attend a meeting at which the restoration of the city would be discussed. For days afterward homeless families squatted on the beach, using charred boards for shelters and spreading carpets on the sand. They set up family mirrors and used their mattresses to sleep on, living the alfresco life until homes were found for them.

Chicago was still smoldering when Bertha received a telegram from her husband. News of the disaster had reached him as he journeyed east. He knew at once what it meant—total ruin for him, for the Honorés, for friends and business associates. But the immediate suffering to the population was the paramount consideration. His message to his wife was to be of good cheer, to give all the attention possible to the victims of the fire and to take in as many of the homeless as she could.

This was just what she had already done. She gave refuge to the Honorés and opened her doors to all who could be squeezed in. Her practical instincts came into full play in this emergency. She rounded up women and children, fed them, found them clothes and shelter. Most of the women she knew were equally busy. Louise de Koven Bowen, who lived on Michigan Avenue near the Honorés and, like Bertha, had attended Dearborn Seminary, had forty or fifty refugees sleeping on the floor in her home, which had escaped the fire.

Palmer hurried back to a scene of devastation. Sadly he surveyed the city that he had left only a few days earlier. He found Bertha and her family groping around with candles. The explosion of the gasworks had left the city in darkness. There was also a water famine, because of the ruin of the waterworks. His house was filled with strangers as well as with members of the Honoré family. He and his father-in-law talked in the semidarkness. Both men were equally involved. The office buildings that Honoré had put up on Dearborn Street were wiped out, but he had already resumed business in a shed and planned to rebuild.

Palmer was discouraged. All but five per cent of his new buildings were burned. His investments had been enormous and he had not enough income at the moment to meet his taxes. The task of rebuilding was beyond imagination. Both he and Cyrus H. McCormick thought briefly of pulling out. But Bertha stepped in at this point. "Mr. Palmer, it's the duty of every Chicagoan to stay here and help to rebuild this stricken city!" she announced decisively.

Its renascence took time but in the end was something of a miracle. Stunned at first, the population picked up the challenge thrown them by their leading citizens. Rich and poor were in much the same plight. S. H. Kerfoot, a real estate man whose place had been landscaped with artificial ponds, rustic bridges and greenhouses, set up a ramshackle hut and hung out a sign: "Everything gone but wife, children and energy." He had lost his elaborate home, his office and his fortune.

Help came fast as the nation's papers spread news of the disaster. Carloads of provisions arrived from different areas. Merchants in the East extended unheard-of credit. Building supplies arrived and barracks were put up for forty thousand of the homeless. The sum of four million dollars was raised by public subscription within three months. Money came in from different parts of the world. The burned-out banks reopened for business. Queen Victoria sent books for a new public library. Every day Bertha read in the paper of some new act of grace.

Joseph Medill was elected mayor a month after the fire. The merchants Field and Leiter, after a loss of three and a half million dollars, bought the car barns to which they had fled and opened a monster bazaar within two weeks. Bertha was one of their first visitors. The hay had been pitched out, the oats and harness removed. Flooring and walls were varnished and painted. Rough board counters had been set up. Goods were rushed from the East and women who had lost all the clothes that they owned trooped in to replenish their wardrobes. Soon the New York *Evening Post* commented on the irony of a "richly robed lady leaning across the counter and fingering costly laces where a horse manger had stood." They got ample credit but it was a period of austerity all round. In less than two years, however, Field and Leiter were back on their old site with a much more magnificent building than the first.

Meanwhile, Potter Palmer moved forward with all the powerful drive of which this self-controlled man was capable. His credit, always excellent, enabled him to borrow $1,700,000 from the Connecticut Mutual Life Insurance Company, the largest single loan made in the United States up to that time. He brought this up to three millions from mortgages and other sources, his good reputation serving him at every point. As he moved forward others took heart and followed suit. He put up larger and better buildings on State Street than those he had lost. Foundations were renewed or rebuilt. He started a new Palmer House and raced to finish it ahead of the new Grand Pacific, which had collapsed in eight minutes during the fire. Artificial lights were used to hasten construction operations by night as well as by day, an innovation at this time. He lost the race by a narrow margin but felt that he had built a better hotel.

These were busy days for Bertha. She took the greatest interest in her husband's construction operations and his business affairs. By this time she understood his meticulous concern for the smallest detail. He seemed to be occupied constantly with workmen of the various trades and with the problems of getting the right materials. Not satisfied with the local limestone he sent to Vermont for marble. Prices for a time were fantastic. He headed a committee that petitioned Congress successfully to abolish the duty on imported structural iron. He and his father-in-law played leading roles in helping to make Chicago a habitable city again and a commercial center of the first importance. Three months after the fire the *Land Owner*, a Chicago publication, commented:

Mr. Palmer . . . is now, more than ever before, entitled to the esteem of our citizens. . . . With Spartan energy he now calmly but firmly commences again, with faith in Chicago undiminshed. . . . He is the land man, *par excellence*, of Chicago. . . . A pleasant gentleman, a man of unimpeachable integrity, he uses his vast means wisely and well, and *always* for the city of his faith. . . .

From the time of the fire he also had a rare helpmate in his wife. The experience she had been through had matured the girl he had married and the rebirth of the city had quickened them all into phenomenal effort and sacrifice. But Bertha had always been bright, calm and ambitious. She was only thirteen when Potter Palmer first saw her, moving with grace against a background of ancestral French furniture in her father's house in Chicago. A mere schoolgirl, she wore a simple white muslin dress and black lace mitts. A plain gold ring circled the first finger of her left hand and a diamond-patterned belt girdled her waist. Her dark hair fell in long strands over her shoulders and was looped behind her ears with tiny bows.

Palmer had watched her all evening, charmed by her looks and manners. She was quick and intelligent, dashing and sure of herself. Years later he told his son Honoré that he had decided that night to make her his bride. He would wait for her to grow up. He was then thirty-six, Chicago's richest bachelor but a lonely man. His life had been one steady drive for success and he had not paused for marriage. From modest beginnings in upstate New York he had established the most talked-of store in the country, made millions in merchandising and real estate, and at the moment was amassing a fresh fortune with cotton he had rounded up for the Union Army.

Although he was not a romantic man Bertha Honoré struck him at once as being a girl of promise whom he could love and cherish, one who would be both hostess and wife. He knew that the daughter of Mr. and Mrs. Honoré would be schooled in the social graces, finely educated, and disciplined in her approach to life. Her great dark eyes, bright and responsive, also suggested that she would not be dull. Palmer was impressed and although he saw little of her until she made her debut this first flash of interest developed later into lifelong devotion. Its effect was dynamic, immediate and lasting. He had lived consistently according to plan. Each step had been taken with foresight. Now he looked to the future with the fixed conviction that Bertha Honoré would be part of it.

Potter Palmer was a man of reserve, stockily built, with dark

BOOK ORDER FORM

LIBRARY OF CONGRESS SUBSCRIBER NUMBER	HOLD CODE	ALPHA PREFIX	LIBRARY OF CONGRESS CARD NUMBER
536805	3		75-1868

CL. NO.

ACC. NO.

DLR ORD NO. Direct

AUTH ROSS, ISHBEL

TITLE Silhouette in Diamonds; the life of Mrs. Potter Palmer.

PLACE   **SBN**

YR 1960   **VOLS**   **PUBL** Arno Press

SERIES EDITION Leisure Class

LIST 18.00   **COST**   **COPIES** 1   Nazareth College Learning Resources

DATE ORD 9-17-76   **FUND** Soc   **REV. BY**   P. O. Box 3908 Rochester, New York 14610

DATE REC

SEP 16 '76

SUBSCRIBER NAME Nazareth College of Rochester   **VAR. IN EDITION** 0   **NO. OF COPIES OF CARDS WANTED** 2 SA 1

brown hair, a high forehead and keen blue eyes that dimmed when he lapsed into one of the long silences habitual to him. He exhibited a wry sense of humor in the social chitchat of the family circle on the night that Bertha first saw him, but mostly the talk was of war. The year was 1862 and John Wilkes Booth was playing Richard III in McVicker's Theater.

The Honorés were a Southern family of distinguished lineage who had moved from Louisville to Chicago in 1855. By the time Potter Palmer came into Bertha's life they were settled in a spacious house, with cupola and pillared porch, fronting on Reuben Street and standing in the center of a square. Bertha still had fresh recollections of Louisville and the house in which she was born on May 22, 1849. She remembered the cobbled streets, the trees and flowers, and the river lively with craft. Her impressions had the deepened dimensions of early childhood—the flash of discovery, the intensity of the colors, the tremor of butterfly wings and the songs of the birds in Jacob's Woods, an enchanted forest close to her home which the adult public viewed more prosaically as a public park.

The same story-book quality invested the six large wooden spoons that hung at Kendrick's jewelry shop, known as the "House of Spoons." It threw a veil of illusion over the massive trees on Fourth Street that all but meshed in an arch overhead, and the meadows fringing Daisy Lane along which Bertha drove in the Sunday parade of surreys and barouches headed for Cave Hill Cemetery. Masses of starry white flowers danced by the wayside like dolls in the breeze. Gravely attentive, she sat in a stiff pew in the First Christian Church on Sundays. There she first sang hymns in public and said her prayers as a child. These memories, like the lamplighter passing along the street at sundown, the peal of the milkman's bell at dawn, the shooting of sparrows at James Guthrie's imposing home nearby, all made their impression on little Bertha Honoré.

She accompanied her mother to Madame Ruhl's to buy ribbons and laces. She watched J. C. Gorman paint Mrs. Honoré's portrait. The long, aristocratic face, the wise eyes, the blue card case that her mother held in her hand, the black ribbon bracelet circling her wrist, the cameo brooch fastened to the lace collar of her black dress, took living shape on the canvas, to the wonderment of Mrs. Honoré's small daughter. Bertha chattered with her friends about these events in her home and they all shared in the grown-up interest lavished on Jenny Lind, who bewitched Louisville with her nightingale voice and thin, eerie face. But her rose-colored dress, pink stockings and pantalets were of more interest to the little girls who heard her than her voice. A never-failing delight to Bertha was a visit to her father's shop on Pearl Street. He imported hardware and cutlery and always had fascinating wares on his shelves.

But she was only six when her experiences in Louisville faded into the sharper outlines of life in Chicago. Her family moved there in 1855 and at the time it seemed a big uprooting from the familiar. Mr. Honoré had talked with enthusiasm of the young city since visiting it two years earlier. As he studied the prairies stretching to the west and the great lake lapping the shore he looked into the future and saw a busy metropolis with a mounting population. Chicago already had gaslight. The first of its banks was established. The Board of Trade was functioning. In a decade the city had grown from a little settlement of frame houses hugging the lake front, with prairie grass growing in the unpaved streets, to the bustling center of the grain and lumber trade in the West.

Six years before the Honorés moved to Chicago Fredrika Bremer had pronounced it the most miserable and ugly city she had seen in America, resembling a huckstress rather than a queen. But she found its people to her liking. They were "most agreeable and delightful—good people, handsome and intellectual; people to live with, to grow fond of . . . rare people."

Although the air over Chicago was clouded with dust she could see beyond the small log houses floating like little birds' nests on the ocean to the "prairie hen on the wing, the blue sky, the sun of purest gold."

Six-year-old Bertha was more alive to its picturesque qualities than she was to its squalor. She delighted in the glimpses she caught of the lake, dull as pewter on gray days and rippling with crimson as the sun set on hot summer nights. The sails of many craft swooped back and forth and the steam vessels outnumbered anything she had known in Louisville. By this time the riches of the plains were pouring into Chicago—wheat, cattle, hogs and garden produce. The grain elevators rose like massive blocks against the sky. Thirteen railroad lines were operating and the McCormick reapers were already whirling on the farms. Nine omnibus routes linked the scattered streets together. Drawbridges spanned the river every few blocks. There were sixteen newspapers, sixty clergymen, two hundred lawyers and the population had reached eighty thousand. Land sold on Michigan Avenue for five dollars a square foot and a good room at the Briggs House cost two and a half dollars a day.

Chicago was growing up and Bertha's father was one of its early expansionists. He bought and subdivided and built and improved property. He envisioned driveways, parks and developments for the boulevard system that girdles Chicago today. He invested heavily in real estate even before George M. Pullman, a pioneer from New England, began pulling the city out of the mud by raising buildings with jackscrews.

Bertha, by this time attending St. Xavier's Academy, listened attentively to her father's talk of the city's growth. He was a man of charm and persuasion, an imaginative planner with a highly developed community sense. From her earliest childhood she was conscious of the world beyond her home. Both of her parents had active minds and a zestful approach to their new environment. Her mother made the transition from Louisville with the greatest ease and soon drew a strong social circle around her. Fellow Kentuckians who had asked Honoré to invest in land for them moved to the growing city and settled around Reuben Street, which later became Ashland Avenue. They had spacious houses, with flowering grounds. They brought their household treasures and Southern ways into this quiet neighborhood and lived as a unit in the community.

There were six Honoré children in all. Ida was a tinier edition of Bertha, doe-eyed, dark and beguiling in manner. The four boys were Adrian, Henry, Nathaniel and Lockwood. They were a harmonious family, living with considerable style in a menage characteristic of their capable mother, who, before her marriage, had been Eliza J. Carr, the daughter of Captain John and Mary Dorsey Carr, of Oldham County, Kentucky. Through her mother's family Bertha was descended from Edward D'Arcy (later Dorsey), who settled in Maryland in the seventeenth century, built Hockley on the Hold and married Sarah Wyatt, of Virginia. Although Bertha had English, Scotch, Irish and Welsh strains in her blood, the dominant influence was French. Her great-grandfather on the paternal side was Jean Antoine Honoré, a Parisian who was an enthusiastic republican and a friend of Lafayette. He settled in Maryland in 1781 and a quarter of a century later moved to Louisville, founded a hardware business and developed a country estate near Bowling Green, Kentucky. Here he hunted and lived in the manorial manner, meanwhile promoting commerce and operating the first line of steamboats to run between New Orleans and Louisville.

Jean's son, Francis Honoré, inherited his father's taste for hunting. He and his wife, the accomplished Matilda Lockwood, passed on a heritage of dash and vitality to their granddaughter Bertha. Their children were Mary Ann, Benjamin, Francis, Jr., and Henry Hamilton Honoré, Bertha's father, who divided his time between his father's plantation and his grandfather's hardware business in Louisville. He was a member of the Louisville firm when his visit to Chicago fired his imagination and led to the family exodus.

Proud Mary Dorsey, a vivacious woman of independent views, who freed her slaves because of her conscientious scruples long before this became mandatory, watched her daughter Eliza leave for Chicago with a strong sense of the inevitability of fate but without much belief in what the city had to offer. Thus small Bertha, whose name one day would be synonymous with Chicago, found herself growing up with the city itself.

2

>>>>>>>>>>>>>> *Merchant Prince*

Like everyone else in Chicago Bertha Honoré was familiar with Potter Palmer's store. She often drove with her mother to shop there and after her meeting with the owner in 1862 she was always observed and personally escorted by him from counter to counter. With his tall hat shoved back on his head and his hands full of papers, he would drop everything to pull out bolts of silk for her inspection or seek diligently for the gloves that exactly matched a gown.

He had brought original ideas and great dash into the merchandising world. Shopping at Potter Palmer's soon was regarded as an entertaining pastime between social calls. Mrs. Honoré and all her friends discussed the fascinating practice he had introduced of exchanging goods and giving credit. This was an invitation to plunge and take chances. It brought carriages rolling up to the entrance in unprecedented numbers and encouraged spendthrift buying. The women in hoops and wide-brimmed bonnets who bumped one another in the narrow passageways could always be sure that Mr. Palmer had the latest from Paris in stock. Goods were presented with a flourish. His window displays drew applause. He advertised in an original and persistent way and insisted on a courteous approach to the shopper. When he staged a bargain sale in the basement the response was overwhelming. This was a novelty for Chicago and the results encouraged further ventures of the sort.

The first man to arrive in the morning and the last to leave at night was always Potter Palmer, who supervised the details in every department. He drilled his clerks in courtesy and showed them how to handle laces with loving care and to unroll carpets with dexterous ease. He went to Europe and brought back tapestries, curtains, veils, gloves and brocades that made news stories in the papers and drew Chicago's matrons to the store to buy. His fame spread and Bon Marché in Paris introduced his system of credit and exchange. R. H. Macy's in New York sent a representative west to see what Potter Palmer was doing. His rivals were skeptical at first, but soon had to copy his methods. Bertha heard much discussion in her home of his great success. Mrs. Honoré said that it was good to have such a merchant in Chicago.

All this had happened in a comparatively short space of time. He had moved west in 1852, three years before the Honorés arrived from Louisville. The first through train from the East had arrived in the city that year. The streets still were mudholes and the sidewalks loose planks. The business blocks were little more than rough wooden shanties. With capital given him by his father he opened a dry-goods store on Lake Street, only seventeen years after the first little frontier shop had set up for business in Chicago. Tobacco chewers loafed with their feet on top of the stove in the small frame building until Potter Palmer electrified them all with his dashing ways. Business mushroomed overnight when the word spread that he handed out little slips entitling the customer to get goods on approval and exchange them if not satisfied. He made $47,000 in the first year and won the undying approval of the good dames of Chicago. But he saw beyond the windowpanes of his store. Noting the growth of the city he began investing his profits in real estate. In spite of his inherent Quaker prudence he made bold moves and almost invariably came out with a profit.

This brought him into touch with Bertha's father and soon he was calling at her home. Honoré found him a keen trader. He noticed that Palmer trusted his own judgment entirely, and had an independent approach that was brisk and refreshing. These qualities, applied to the rising fortunes of the West, the diversified population, the growing interest in fashion, made an irresistible combination at the time. In his later years Palmer often said that he had never taken a business partner, but that Cissie, as he called his wife, had shared this side of his life to the full. She, in turn, always recalled him as a man of constructive ideas in any field he entered. When friends sought to credit some of his success to her, she quickly reminded them of the place where he already stood when she met him. She would never detract from the business acumen of Potter Palmer.

When the Civil War broke out, he foresaw the need for cotton wares. He borrowed heavily from the banks, crammed all the warehouse space he could rent with cotton and woolen goods, and in one fast operation bought up all the cotton held by A. T. Stewart, of New York; then later sold it back to him when the price of cotton soared. Most of it had never been moved from the warehouses. This new fortune was being built up when Bertha Honoré, by sheer chance, came into view and all at once became more important to Potter Palmer than the rising tide of wealth that was sweeping him into greater prominence.

By this time she had moved on to Dearborn Seminary, studying all the standard subjects of the day. The girls wore white frilled caps and devoted considerable time to hemming towels and making wax camellias, violets and japonicas. Bertha practiced on the piano for an hour a day and sang ballads and hymns with the rest of her class. She prayed devoutly and attended church regularly. Her family was not Catholic but her parents were active in the First Christian Church and all the Honoré children were drilled in punctilious religious observance. In later years Mrs. Palmer was noticeably tolerant of all religions and understood the Catholic ritual, but eventually she attended the Episcopal Church.

All entertaining was done in the home at this time and invitations were delivered by hand. Bertha often drove with her mother and sat in the family carriage while their coachman handed out notes. The Honorés gave receptions on New Year's Day and Bertha and Ida moved composedly among the guests, their bell shaped skirts swinging away from their ankles, their long hair streaming down their backs. The house was hung with Christmas greens. The crystal chandeliers glistened from recent washing. Madeira and eggnog were served in the Southern homes, and the fare invariably included chicken salad, roast turkey and scalloped oysters. Bertha's social sense was strongly developed from her earliest years.

The German cotillion had recently been added to the schottische, redowas and polkas and they all learned to dance. Picnics, skating and sleighing parties were popular for the young and Bertha and Ida, with their brothers, glided over the snow in a low sleigh with bright blue runners. Buffalo robes kept them warm and the floor was stacked with hay. They skated joyously on icy days, doing the double roll, the Dutch roll and even the figure eight. A wide, soft hood of scarlet velvet framed Bertha's customarily pale face, stung pink by the icy wind when she skated. In summer she liked to walk with her classmates on the breakwater that faced Michigan Avenue. There were clouds of dust on August days and rivers of mud in spring as she skipped up and down the plank ascents and descents that served as sidewalks, and was spattered with muddy water from passing wagons. On hot summer nights families sat on their porches while the breezes off the lake fanned their faces. The stockyards were busy by this time but Bertha knew that prairie flowers still bloomed on the city outskirts and all around her were large gardens, lawns, cows and horses. The scene close to her home was almost as pastoral as in Louisville.

National holidays were exuberantly celebrated, with dancing, excursions, horse racing and military drills on Washington's Birthday. There were circuses, tableaux and pageants, and Barnum's "Grand Colossal Museum and Menagerie" gave three performances a day, charging thirty cents for adults and fifteen cents for children. Bertha was eleven when Baron Renfrew, whom she would later know well as King Edward VII, visited Chicago. She shared in all the excitement that the older girls showed in this event. The depot was brilliantly illuminated but the crowd was only mildly responsive as he drove to the Richmond House, accompanied by the city fire department's floats, representing Chicago's industries. He visited the courthouse, the waterworks and the Chicago Historical Society, then in its infancy. He was tired and sullen by the time he reached the Prairie City and in the end the girls had trouble viewing him as a romantic figure.

Bertha developed an interest in politics at an early age. She listened attentively to the verbal battles that raged over the election of Abraham Lincoln. All Chicago was in a fever when he and Stephen A. Douglas began their campaigns with speeches from the balcony of the Tremont House. Joseph Medill, editing the *Tribune*, opposed Lincoln at first and backed William H. Seward, but after the nomination he climbed on the bandwagon and threw powerful support behind the man from Springfield. Bertha walked past the big wooden building called the Wigwam where the historic convention was held. She was old enough to have views of her own, particularly in a home where the leading men of the city foregathered and conversation was spiced with debate.

Then the war broke out and a dark cloud fell over the Honoré home. Patriotic fervor ran high. Vigilance committees were formed and Southern families were eyed with some suspicion. Courthouse Square was checkered with recruiting tents. Bertha and Ida saw Ellsworth's Zouaves parading briskly in their picturesque attire as Chicago made its first concerted military gesture. Bands played. Flags waved. The news of battles lost and won traveled west. Chicago was far from the scene of the fighting but it was sending its sons, and Lincoln was a link between East and West. Soon the Southern families formed committees to distribute food and clothing to the prisoners at Camp Douglas. All of the Honorés worked for the Sanitary Fairs of 1863 and 1865, and women everywhere scraped lint and made bandages. Sewing circles were formed and there was a steady demand for nurses. Life was suddenly strange and more intense to the growing Honoré girls with all these echoes of war. The social pace was slowed but their home was always open and hospitable to every good cause.

Chicago grew rough and rowdy during these turbulent years. Gambling flourished and sharpers moved in from the river landings and the Far West. Some were unctuous fellows in stagey trappings; others were rugged plainsmen who swaggered through the streets in frontier attire. Keno was introduced and stakes were high. Gambling palaces, saloons and brothels flourished and a nomadic population drifted in to batten on the by-products of war. Through it all ran the undertow of death, destruction and mourning. Soon the Honorés, like everyone else, were hearing of Ulysses S. Grant as the Union Army battered its way to victory.

Bertha's life was discreetly removed from the rowdy elements that swamped Chicago during these hectic years. She was living the cloistered social life that her family decreed for her. She studied hard and got top marks in school, as well as high praise for her deportment. She drove in the family carriage through the dirty streets and heard her father insist that one day Dearborn Street would be the office center of Chicago. He bought subdivisions of land around their home in the Ashland Avenue district and when the war was over he sold his house and moved to Michigan Avenue. His family soon were settled in a spacious house on a tree-lined street in the most fashionable area of the city at that time. All around were imposing-looking homes, built for the most part of a local limestone deceptively known as Athens marble.

No sooner had Chicago celebrated the end of the war than news of the assassination of Lincoln stunned the city. Illinois claimed him as its own and the funeral train passed through on its way to Springfield, black blankets with silver stars draping the boilers. The slow processional wound its way to the courthouse while three dozen high school girls scattered flowers before it. Doorways and windows were somber with crepe and thousands streamed in double file past the bier.

That autumn Bertha journeyed to Washington and entered the Convent of the Visitation in Georgetown. The leaves were faintly stained with color and the air was crisp as the girls converged from different parts of the country. Before leaving she had said good-by to Potter Palmer, who was going abroad for his health. Years of hard work had worn him down. Physicians told him he must rest. His fortune at the time was close to seven million dollars and he was not yet forty.

He sold his store on easy terms to the two young men, Marshall Field and Levi Z. Leiter, who were partners in the firm of Farwell, Field & Company. For a time the new firm was known as Field, Palmer & Leiter. Then in 1881 it became Marshall Field & Company. Palmer left the two young merchants to their own devices and had nothing further to do with the business except to give them the benefit of his credit for several years until they could assume full financial responsibility. Field's early history resembled his own. As a boy he had worked hard on his father's farm in the Berkshires and had clerked in a little Pittsfield store. He arrived in Chicago in the year that the Honorés moved north from Louisville. Field did not believe at first in Potter Palmer's credit and exchange system. When he took control of the store he and Leiter abolished it, but the women of Chicago had found it irresistible. They demanded a return to the genial ways of Mr. Potter Palmer and the new owners soon went back to pampering the customers.

"Silent Marsh" now waited on the Honorés with the same attentive manner as Potter Palmer but with less concentrated interest. Although prices fell off badly after the war the store was prospering greatly and its sales were the third largest in volume in the country, after A. T. Stewart's and Claflin's. By 1868 the store profits had reached a twelve-million-dollar yearly average and by 1881 this had risen to twenty-five millions, although the building was damaged by fire a second time. In the year before Marshall Field's death the store cleared $68,000,000, more than Potter Palmer had dreamed of when he founded his dry-goods establishment.

While living the cloistered life of the convent Bertha gave little thought to the merchant prince who had gone abroad. She had no inkling of his plans for her future. In all respects she conformed to the daily routine of the convent and was a favorite with Mother Mary Augustine Cleary. Except for occasional excursions to take in the sights of the capital, and holidays spent at home, she rarely left the grounds. She studied hard and seemed an ideal student. Only the faintest echoes of the brisk and reckless course things were taking in Washington after the war penetrated the convent walls. But Bertha was alive to political currents and she saw and read enough to make pointed comments in her letters home. She followed Andrew Johnson's swift decline in public favor and was alert to the new social currents stirring the capital. The South was in total eclipse. Long ago the Southern hostesses had deserted Washington, although some Kentuckians with family ties were in touch with her from time to time. Grant was the man of the hour. Sectional feeling still ran hot and strong.

Bertha watched new buildings go up and the scars of war declining. These were formative years for her. Life was less luxurious and more disciplined than anything she had known. She matured rapidly and had an opulent look, even in her simple convent attire. Her mouth took a steadier line. On graduation day she was a glowing beauty, the picture of health. By that time she was five feet five and well developed. Her eyes were her most arresting feature. They were large and velvety soft when she was moved. More often they were keen and sparkling, and could be cool and appraising when Bertha was studying a question or meeting a new acquaintance. Her voice was low and musical, a quality that stayed with her through the years, although her intonations became more decisive as she grew older and her word became law. She was orderly in her habits and practical in her outlook.

On the June day in 1867 on which she was graduated, she was one of six students who received the highest honors in the Senior Circle. A Crown and Gold Medal were conferred on this favored group for "uniform excellence of conduct." Prizes were then known as premiums and the records show an imposing number of awards for Bertha. She walked off with honors in such assorted subjects as profane history, ancient and modern geography, chemistry, meteorology, astronomy and botany, logic and intellectual philosophy, rhetoric, literature and composition, algebra and geometry, mantua work and domestic economy.

She showed special interest in her music lessons and took top honors in piano, harp and vocal music. She was one of the harpists in the Grand March and sang in a vocal trio and chorus. When she moved smoothly forward in a soft white silk dress to accept her diploma she had already established the pattern of success that was to characterize her all through life. She made many friends in the convent although she was aloof rather than demonstrative in manner. The nuns remembered her for her intelligence and tact.

That autumn she made her debut in the new Honoré home on Michigan Avenue, surrounded by the heirlooms of her French ancestors. The music of Strauss was much discussed at the time but Mrs. Honoré would not permit Bertha to waltz. The new dance was considered too daring and Continental for Chicago. Four years later it was wholly accepted and Ida waltzed when she made her debut. Meanwhile, Bertha danced the approved steps with grace and precision, wearing white satin slippers with crossed ribbons. Her long dark hair was now done up in little puffs. Her sloping shoulders gleamed white above the dropped line of her simple debutante dress. Chicago's most eligible young men viewed Miss Honoré with appreciation as she was committed to the social round of the day. Beautiful girls were scarce and she was a godsend for the Bachelors' Assembly Balls given at the Tremont House by the town's eligible young men who banded together to repay their hostesses for hospitality. There were concerts and picnics and Bertha was conspicuously attractive in her own home as she played the harp and sang for guests. But she continued to study and read, and men called her clever. She had a succession of beaux and everyone expected her to marry quite soon. However, she was slow to make up her mind.

On his return from Europe Potter Palmer saw that she had developed as flawlessly as he had anticipated. He no longer made any secret of the fact that he wished to marry her. He sent uniformed messengers with flowers and begged for engagements but she went serenely on her way, without giving him much encouragement. By this time he had changed quite perceptibly from the quiet shopkeeper in business clothes to a sporting figure, familiar at the races. While Bertha was in the convent he had acquired the reputation of being a man of the world. In Europe he had learned to enjoy the money he had amassed so strenuously, and also with such phenomenal luck. On his return he made trips to Saratoga and drove along Broadway in one of its finest turnouts. The antebellum visitors from the South were gone from the scene, but a new generation of politicians, gamblers and sports had appeared with their wives or their mistresses.

The quiet Quaker from Chicago surprised them all as he tossed his money around. Pretty girls rode in his coach and many tried to ensnare the wealthy merchant who knew so well how to buy the proper gift, select the perfect flower or jewel. But he went on his way unmoved, quite certain that Bertha Honoré would be his bride when the time was ripe, and her parents gave their consent. He bent all his energies to this end and saw more and more of the Honorés. He had close business dealings with Bertha's father. Both men were considered mad dreamers as they talked of the Chicago of the future, but they could speak with some authority, since they had substantial records behind them. H.H., as his friends called him, talked in quick Gallic bursts of enthusiasm. Palmer presented his views with precision and dry wit, concealing the Midas touch behind a frosty exterior. By this time he viewed State Street as the future commercial center of Chicago. It seemed a central and natural channel and it already had some streetcar lines when he bought a mile of frontage and proceeded to develop it. Lake Street, which had most of the retail stores at this time, was a narrow, dirty and ill-lighted thoroughfare, and although plate-glass windows had been in use since the 1850's it was a dingy shopping area for women who were becoming increasingly fashion-minded. Their carriages bumped in passing. The road was deeply rutted.

Palmer bought the land along State Street for two hundred dollars a square foot, then asked the other merchants to join him in setting back their property so that the roadway might be widened and paved in the interests of a spacious, well-lighted effect. They declined, so he went ahead and gave twenty additional feet of roadway on his own property, leaving some zigzag effects that were put to rights after the fire, when all the merchants were forced to widen the street before they could rebuild. He tore down ramshackle old buildings and put up thirty-two stores and business houses. The most spectacular was taken over at once by Field and Leiter for the unprecedented rent in Chicago of fifty thousand dollars a year. It was six stories high and stood at the corner of State and Washington streets. Soon the other merchants deserted Lake Street and moved into Potter Palmer's fine new buildings.

Bertha visited the new store and admired its marble columns, its good lighting and spacious aisles. Entire floors were devoted to classified goods. Everything from ball gowns to ottomans, from Persian rugs to Alexander's gloves from Paris, were sold by whiskered clerks, all of whom knew Miss Honoré by sight. By this time she had become a zealous shopper. She loved fine clothes and bought with discrimination. The Honoré girls were a familiar sight driving with their mother along Michigan Avenue on their way to the shops. New homes were being built on all sides by men who had grown rich during the war. Great fortunes were in the making in the booming Western city.

The prosperity that followed the war led to inflation. Then there were heavy losses but through it all industry moved forward with irresistible force. More than twelve thousand vessels came into port in 1870. Twenty-seven bridges spanned the busy river. Fifty-seven miles of streets had more than six thousand lampposts. Clean lake water now flowed through 154 miles of pipes, so pellucid that the day's newspaper could be read through a thick cake of ice, a change from the plague-haunted days when the water supply was a constant menace to life.

But the city still was rough and tumble in many sections, with shanties and ramshackle tenements marring the scene. Factories sprawled toward the prairie, and a great assortment of people made reapers, axes and plows, shoes and clocks and candles, whiskey, soap and cookstoves. The National Watch Company turned out fifty watches a day at Elgin. Pianos and melodeons were manufactured on a large scale for a music-loving population. Thousand of workers processed grain, or slaughtered pigs and cattle at the Union Stockyards with methods that made the sensitive shudder.

The horsecars were crowded every day with workers, while the more affluent rode in hansom cabs and victorias. By this time the city had more than 300,000 inhabitants and Bertha and her father watched the suburbs spread south, north and west in the year 1870. Carpenters put flimsy buildings together on the prairies with some of the zeal of the pioneers, but Potter Palmer's new buildings had marble fronts, mansard roofs and external decorations. The Palmer House was going up as he courted Bertha. She and Ida watched its progress when they went downtown. At last she had ceased to brush him off as one of her father's old friends. In some respects he looked younger than before he went abroad. His health had improved. He dressed in a more fashionable way. There was no dearth of entertainment at this time after the austere days of the war and he went with the Honorés to various functions.

The year after Bertha's return from Georgetown, Crosby's Opera House, all blue and gold, was the setting for a Charity Ball, the first public social event of note in Chicago and a form of entertainment with which the future Mrs. Potter Palmer's name would be closely identified in later years. Tickets were twenty dollars apiece. Gowns were ordered from London, Paris and New York, as well as from Field, Palmer and Leiter's. The hairdressers built up waterfall coiffures, and Bertha's puffs and curls took hours to arrange. Supper was served at John Wright's fashionable restaurant underneath the Opera House. The Honorés and other well-known families feasted on prairie chicken and quail patties, boned turkey and boar's head, followed by pyramids, pagodas and Swiss châteaux of ice cream and temples of nougat.

The public crowded into Crosby's Opera House and McVicker's Theater, grateful for the serious plays, the opera, the oratorios and concerts given by German orchestras and choruses. By this time grand opera was superseding minstrel shows and brass bands, and Beethoven, Mozart and Schumann were played on the new pianos as well as in public places. Although most entertaining was done in the home Bertha, properly chaperoned, could go to the ladies dining room in the Briggs House, to Henrici's, or to the Richmond House, where Baron Renfrew had stayed. But by this time Potter Palmer was assuring her that she would have the finest suite in his new hotel, a sophisticated hostelry being built according to Continental standards.

The Palmer House was all but finished when word leaked out through a society column that the bridal suite was being hurried along for the month of August, 1870, and that the bridegroom would be Potter Palmer himself. The news caused a sensation in Chicago, where the Honorés were known to be an extremely conservative family and Bertha was an outstanding member of the younger set.

However, she had finally turned her back on all her youthful suitors and chosen the man who had vowed when she was only thirteen that he would make her his bride and had quietly pursued his purpose for eight years. She was now twenty-one and had met enough men to know her own mind. He was forty-four. Her parents favored the match, for they admired Potter Palmer and felt that the farm boy who had revolutionized merchandising and carried through such bold real estate operations as to make over the face of Chicago, was of superior mettle and ambition. But they explored his family history before giving their consent and to please Bertha and her parents he was baptized in the First Christian Church a few days before his marriage.

Actually, Potter Palmer was a man of some complexity. He was descended from two colonial families, whose combined names he bore. He was reared in the tradition of Quaker reticence and quiet speech, and was descended from Walter Palmer, one of the small group who came from Britain to the United States in 1628 with John Endecott, first Governor of the Colony of Massachusetts. Potter's grandfather settled in New Bedford and suffered severely during the sacking at the time of the War of the Revolution. After seven members of his family had died at sea he moved to New York State and farmed at Potter's Hollow in Albany County, on the west bank of the Hudson River. There Potter Palmer was born in 1826, the fourth in a family of seven. His father was prosperous but young Potter had no taste for the land. He preferred trading and at the age of seventeen he left home with a promise from his father that when he had gained some experience he would give him capital to found a business.

An awkward youth, quiet, but with hidden drive, he clerked for a time in a combined store, post office and bank in Durham County. Then he opened a shop of his own in Oneida, which he ran for two and a half years before moving to Lockport in Niagara County for another year of clerking. Finally he decided to leave New York State and travel west. He thought at first of going to California but stopped halfway in Chicago. His father gave him five thousand dollars and his blessing when he struck out for himself.

Now, eighteen years later, another ambition had reached fruition. He was about to marry Bertha Honoré, the girl of his choice, and one who had seemed unattainable in spite of his wealth and standing. He knew that there was much gossip about his latest move. The skeptics viewed it as a worldly marriage promoted by the Honorés and felt that the Palmer millions had clouded their judgment. Although comfortably off they were much less affluent at this time than in later years, and the story persisted that Honoré was so deeply in Potter Palmer's debt through his land operations that he was anxious to mollify the millionaire. The talk was so widespread that the Chicago *Tribune*, in reporting the wedding on July 29, 1870, took public note of the criticism:

The engagement has been short—only two months. It is stated that the bridegroom, when going away recently, offered to settle a million dollars on his intended bride but she nobly and persistently refused. This may put an end to the bitter observations of envious or cynical persons inclined to stamp the marriage contract—so momentous to the high contracting parties—as a commercial transaction. No matter who married Mr. Palmer the same cruel and unjust remarks would be made.

Ignoring such gross imputations Bertha was poised and sure of herself as she took her wedding vows in her father's home at 157 Michigan Avenue. The Rev. J. S. Sweeney, pastor of the First Christian Church, conducted the ceremony. Potter stood at her side, impassive and tight-lipped. Her Paris gown of heavy white satin was veiled in rose-point lace, looped up with orange blossoms. A circlet of the wedding flower rested on her dark hair. The ceremony was held at six o'clock and the women wore evening gowns of the most fashionable cut.

A crowd had gathered to watch the guests arrive as late afternoon sunshine flooded the treetops. Forty relatives and intimate friends witnessed the ceremony but seven hundred filed in for the wedding supper that followed. H. M. Kinsley, the fashionable confectioner and restaurant owner, did the catering and the Honoré silver and crystal from France were in use. Flowers and ferns adorned the rooms and stringed music came from behind potted palms.

At eight o'clock the Palmers slipped away and left for the East, en route to Europe for their wedding trip. It was Bertha's first ocean voyage, her first glimpse of another land. Paris was out of the question with the Franco-Prussian War raging and the siege of Paris about to begin. But Potter Palmer knew his way around Europe. He was familiar with the capitals, the art galleries, the shops, the spas, the pleasure resorts. He understood every wrinkle of the fashion and merchandising world.

Wherever the pair went they ran into groups of Americans. Since the end of the war many had settled in London or were passing through. When they drove in Hyde Park Bertha was observed with interest as the beautiful American girl who had married the rich man twice her age. They saw the traditional sights and spent much time in the shops. They went to the theater, the races, and sampled the best hotels of the day. Potter bought jewels for his bride, the first of a lavish collection to come. They toured the Continent, omitting France and Germany, and picked up treasures wherever they went. Bertha's favorite purchases were two gilt Florentine wedding chests that became familiar to her friends in later years, for she always kept them in her more intimate rooms.

She returned to Chicago with new clothes, jewels and objects of art for her home. During these weeks her horizons had broadened. Some of her history lessons had come to life as she explored old British castles and stood on the Ponte Vecchio. Potter quite visibly adored her. His wedding gift to her was the $3,500,000 Palmer House. The years ahead seemed filled with promise. But the Great Fire cast its shadow over her married life almost as soon as it had begun, and Bertha came face to face with the first realities of her sheltered life. She had many friends in the city but there was little social life during her early married days, except for gatherings at a club appropriately named The Cinders. All around her people were trying to recover ground and get on their feet again. It was odd to go shopping through ruins, to see roads gutted and holes dug everywhere for fresh construction. The clank of the hammer was symphonic as she drove about, paying calls, doing errands, helping friends much worse off than herself.

The Honorés had saved what they could of their things and taken a house at Vincennes Avenue and Forty-seventh Street. It stood in ten acres of land and had a cupola, a railed enclosure on the roof and great bay windows. It was simply furnished at first with bamboo pieces and Swiss curtains looped with blue satin ribbon at the windows. No one was pretentious in the years after the fire. Bertha drove out often to see her parents and brothers. Ida was at the Convent of the Visitation by this time and Mrs. Honoré missed her two daughters.

The Palmers were just getting on their feet again when the financial panic of 1873 struck them hard. They were up to their ears in debt because of the huge loans that Palmer had initiated. But he held to his course and sold some of his land to save the greater part of it. He mortgaged more at high rates. He persuaded some of his creditors to give him time, and again the banks carried him, having faith in his probity and recuperative powers. Bertha watched these operations closely and was party to some of the mortgage transactions. It was an anxious period in their lives. Palmer slept poorly and worked day and night. But he kept paying off his debts and in time completed the reconstruction of State Street. Another big fire flashed through the city in 1874, sweeping away part of the business district and destroying some of the structures that had been rebuilt. But the Palmer House escaped this time and soon the Palmers were magnificently quartered in their own hotel.

On February 1, 1874, Bertha bore her first son and named him Honoré. Palmer was proud of his infant son. He was proud of his beautiful wife. This was a happy summer for her as she nurtured the romance that had developed between Ida and Frederick Dent Grant, oldest son of President Ulysses S. Grant. Her sister had just graduated from the Convent of the Visitation and spent much time with Bertha. She played the harp and piano and had a well-cultivated mezzo-soprano voice. At parties she was always a gentle foil for her sister's more vibrant personality. Her dark eyes were wistful, where Bertha's gazed on the world with calm and assurance. The Honoré sisters had the same dark hair, the same interests, the same good manners, but Ida was the more pliant of the two. She was enraptured when Fred's letters arrived from the Black Hills region, where he was on service with General George A. Custer. Messengers rode in with them from the plains to Fort Abraham Lincoln, where they were mailed to Chicago. But it took six weeks in all for the letters to reach their destination. Ida showed Bertha the wild flowers that Fred sent her and read out snatches of his graphic descriptions of the wild deer in the forest, of the Indians who peered at them from cragged ledges, and of the bear and wild buffalo he had shot. Fred was twenty-four, a sturdy figure with much history behind him. He had been through five battles with his father before he was thirteen and was wounded just before the assault on Vicksburg. He was under General Philip H. Sheridan's command in the Chicago district, and it was inevitable that he and Ida should have met at social gatherings.

She found him irresistible. After a short engagement they were married at the Honoré home on October 20, 1874, with Ulysses S. Grant and Mrs. Grant looking on. The President beamed happily on Ida, well satisfied with the choice Fred had made. His only daughter Nellie had just been married in the White House to Algernon Sartoris, the nephew of Fanny Kemble, but he had not wholly approved. Ida Honoré, however, seemed to be everything that a parent could ask for and he found her as "charming for her manners, amiability, good sense & education as she is for her beauty." Her sister, Mrs. Potter Palmer, had already won Ulysses Grant's respect. From this time on she would be hostess to the Grants on their frequent visits to Chicago, and would sometimes present a dazzling appearance in Mrs. Grant's receiving line at the White House.

Fred arrived for his wedding in an open wagon drawn by

four well-curried army mules with burnished hooves and bells on their harness. His brown hair grew crisp and thick around his deeply tanned face. He had his father's bright blue eyes, and also his gravity. General Sheridan rode up with his staff in dress uniform. The Potter Palmers arrived with all the dash that a Palmer equipage entailed. Like Ulysses Grant, Potter Palmer had a taste for fast horses. The men on the box wore the maroon livery that Bertha had chosen for her staff.

She was spectacular herself in pearl gray with facings of cardinal red. Her basque had a postilion back and her sash was gray with a cardinal fringe. There were fresh pink roses among the diamonds in her hair and she wore a lace veil over an elaborate coiffure of puffs and ringlets. Her jewels were pearls and diamonds. Potter matched her in a gray frock coat with gray topper and one perfect pearl in his gray cravat. But the star performer at Ida's wedding was little Honoré Palmer, eight months old, who was carried in on a satin pillow, wearing a long embroidered dress of white mull with a pale blue ribbon sash. He held his peace throughout the wedding ceremony and was much admired by the guests.

President Grant stood beside the stately Mrs. Honoré as the bride came into view. Potter Palmer had showered diamonds on his beautiful sister-in-law, including a cross and a pair of matching earrings. She wore the pearls that Mrs. Grant had given her and carried a lace handkerchief, a gift from Bertha, who had been chief adviser on all the wedding arrangements. It was a much more imposing ceremony than she had had when she married Potter Palmer, and the presence of Ulysses S. Grant drew national attention. The Potter Palmers had supplied the silver service for the wedding banquet and the guests could choose from stewed terrapin, escalloped oysters, sweetbread patties, turkey, snipe, chicken or lobster salad, boned quail in jelly, ices, charlotte russe, fresh fruits and frappéed champagne, port and sherry.

Ulysses S. Grant, II, commonly known as "Buck," was one

of the ushers. Among the guests were Mrs. Custer, the Cyrus H. McCormicks, the Charles B. Farwells, the A. E. Bories and many prominent citizens of Chicago as well as close friends of the President's family and an array of Civil War officers. It was an evening wedding and the guests came in full panoply, with magnificent gowns and the built-up coiffures of the period.

Bertha embraced her sister warmly as she left the family home. Contented in her own marriage, she was happy to see Ida become the wife of Fred Grant, who seemed to be as sincere, modest and persevering as his father. She was also not indifferent to the fact that Ida was now going to live in the White House while Fred was west in service. Her little sister had done well. Their parents' faces showed how satisfied they were. Bertha drove back to the Palmer House with her husband in a glow of satisfaction. Baby Honoré had been an angel throughout. The pattern of life, which had come unraveled after the fire, was settling into place again.

She had only to look around her to see that the shattered city was recovering. Although shops, homes, theaters, hotels, churches and factories had been wiped out, better ones were rising to take their places. Emergency frame buildings still gave an air of disorder to the scene, but this phase was passing. A solid city was rising from the embers. The stockyards had escaped the fire and twice as many hogs were now being butchered as ever before. Since trade records had been destroyed businessmen used mutual trust in their dealings and the citizens felt purified, reborn, revitalized. Between the year of Ida's wedding and the 1890's 68,000 buildings would go up at a cost of $300,000,000. The Potter Palmers would never know another setback. They would be part and parcel of the growth of Chicago.

3

➤➤➤➤➤➤➤➤➤➤➤➤➤ *The Innkeeper's Wife*

All Chicago talked of the new Palmer House in the 1870's and visitors from abroad carried home tales of its grandeur. Its owner welcomed the first guest to sign the register and then installed himself in a small office on the main floor with a window opening on the lobby. Here he could watch the world go by, but he kept in the background and few of the guests knew that the vigilant man in the little cage was Potter Palmer.

Of all the gorgeous women in rustling silks and ostrich plumes who strolled by, none in his eyes compared with his wife, who by this time lived on the premises. He watched her comings and goings with the greatest pride and kept close track of the engagements she made. The hotel was a focus of fashionable life. While Mrs. Palmer presided in her own suite upstairs its lobby, ballroom, reception and banquet halls were the backdrop for many gay gatherings. The bridal suite was in great demand, often for rich young men who had made fortunes in the West and wished to take their brides to the most discussed hotel of the day.

The guests were a show in themselves. Swaggering gamblers

and gold rush millionaires swapped stories at the sixty-foot bar with Wall Street giants, world travelers, showmen and Viennese opera stars. Buffalo Bill and Jean de Reszke, Rudyard Kipling and Edwin Booth all drank from an assortment of colored glasses that sparkled like the night's conviviality. Anyone with a cause who passed through the city sooner or later might be seen at the Palmer House. Anyone with a great name who visited Chicago was bound to dine in the shadow of its stately pillars.

When the Chicago Club balked at receiving Sarah Bernhardt on her first visit to the city, Potter Palmer welcomed her as if she were royalty. He gave her a suite of rooms running along one side of the hotel. A "five-glass landau" drove her around town. Her meals were prepared in her own rooms. Her favorite French dishes were on the menu. Mrs. Palmer refrained from flying openly in the face of convention, and she did not deliberately arrange a reception for her coming, but she believed that all honor was due Sarah Bernhardt, Madam Modjeska and other actresses of great reputation who stayed at the Palmer House. Presidents were welcome, too. When Benjamin Harrison visited the city in 1889 Palmer wired to Senator Charles B. Farwell, another dry-goods merchant who had come from New York State: "Please extend the compliments and hospitalities of the Palmer House to the President and his family while in Chicago."

European princesses and well-known authors, farm girls who had married money, suffrage agitators and big-time gamblers alike chose dishes from an illustrated menu that showed on one side a pigsty and hovel with the inscription "Chicago Forty Years Ago" and on the other a wonderful city, "The Chicago of Today." Meals were a challenge to the unsophisticated palate. Boned quail in plumage, blackbirds, and partridge served in nests were listed along with buffalo, antelope, bear and mountain sheep. The spun-sugar confectionery and ices dazzled the guests and the gustatory delights of the

Palmer House became famous. But the silver dollars inset in the tiles of its barbershop were its unique feature. This oddity became a Western legend. Boys growing up on the prairie dreamed of the day they would visit Chicago and view the Garden of Eden, as the tonsorial parlor was sometimes called in honor of its proprietor, W. S. Eden. The hotel was justly noted, however, for its steaks, its excellent Negro waiters and its Continental touches. In his travels Potter Palmer had studied the best hotels of Europe. He adapted some of their features to his own, but in addition he gave it the individual touch that he applied to all his properties. The Egyptian note was strong in the public areas.

The building was eight stories high and covered a city block. Its fluted pillars supported carved and frescoed ceilings. The rooms were large and luxurious. Flowers appeared on the dining tables, a novelty at the time. Elevators ran the guests upstairs. The fireproofing arrangements were widely advertised. Memories of the Great Fire died hard. It had left scars on the people of Chicago, since none who went through it could ever forget the burning city.

"It is more like an elegantly appointed home than a mere resting-place for such birds of passage as ourselves," wrote Lady Duffus Hardy after a visit to the Palmer House in 1879. She found each suite perfect in itself, with its private bath, its luxurious lounges and the "easiest of easy-chairs." The halls were lined with *fauteuils*, sofas and all the appointments of a handsome drawing room and it had an air of great luxury, in the opinion of this visiting Englishwoman.

But Rudyard Kipling, staying there while on his way home from India in 1889, could see no virtue in Chicago and still less in Potter Palmer's hotel. He thought the city was inhabited by savages, its air was dirty, its water was like that of the Hooghly. He found the Palmer House a "gilded and mirrored rabbit warren" and decided that a Hottentot would not have been guilty of having silver dollars inlaid in a floor.

His brief view of the hotel left him with an impression of a "huge hall of tessellated marble, crammed with people talking about money and spitting about everywhere. Other barbarians charged in and out of this inferno with letters and telegrams in their hands, and yet others shouted at each other."

But few shared Kipling's view. A compatriot wrote in the London *Times* that it was more of a public club in feeling than a hotel. He was much impressed with the "extensive parlours, reception, reading, writing and smoking rooms, lifts constantly running, electric call bells and lights, with complete attendance and messenger service." He took stock of the poolroom where noted champions played, the tenpin alley, the magnificent bar and its restaurants, wines and food. Most astonishing of all to this visitor was its aggregation of shops, its manifold service and its telegraphic ticker which signaled fresh profits and gave an air of excitement to its lobby.

Not the least of its attractions was the chance to catch a glimpse of Mrs. Potter Palmer as she stepped from her brougham, heavily jeweled and dressed in the latest from Paris. It was an era of bustles and trailing skirts, of flounces, *tabliers* and hats with the plumage of birds. Black Maltese lace trimmed her polonaise and her ball dresses were of silk and tulle, bordered with ostrich tips. She favored delicate colors and was particularly fond of blue. Silk hose was the rage. Her stockings, ordered from Paris, were topped with Valenciennes, Cluny or Duchess lace. They cost from seventy to a hundred dollars for a dozen pairs and were worn with gold-buckled garters and bronze kid sandal boots. When the wind blew off the lake on icy winter days she carried a lynx muff and wore lace-topped balbriggan hose.

But these were Mrs. Palmer's more domestic years. She was fully occupied with family affairs while her husband built up a new reputation for himself and a fresh fortune as a hotelkeeper. Their second son, Potter, was born on October 8, 1875, on the fourth anniversary of the fire. Potter Palmer had changed greatly since his marriage and the birth of his children. To the surprise of those who knew him best, he had settled into a domesticated pattern. His most contented hours were passed in their private quarters watching his beautiful wife playing with her small sons or presiding at table.

Bertha was a formidable, if also an equable wife, with the knack of getting her own way. She avoided fuss and her voice was never raised in anger. Potter was quiet but he was also stubborn and from time to time he showed flashes of jealousy where his young wife was concerned. He was deeply absorbed in his hotel but he had come to worship Cissie. Men admired her openly and some of the bolder patrons of the hotel paid her extravagant compliments. Ten-year-old Artie Ballard, attending a private school near the Palmer House in the late 1870's, often called on Mrs. Palmer with some of his classmates on their way home. She gave them fruit, candy and cake. Having grown up with brothers she had a genial way with small boys.

But one day when Artie got to her door she called out: "Will you do something for me? I am locked in and cannot get out. I'll slip a note under the door. Take it to my brother, Mr. Honoré, and see that no one else gets it or sees you give it to him and he will have me let out." Artie was convinced that Potter Palmer had locked her in.

However, Mrs. Palmer's course through life was so steady, her reputation so unsmirched, her devotion to her family so genuine, that any attempts to give romantic inference to her numerous friendly contacts with men died for lack of nourishment. It was soon forgotten that she was the very young wife of a much older man. Some thought her cold. Others were intimidated by her quiet forcefulness. But she was much admired by men, and even some of the business letters addressed to her still convey a sense of personal compliment and warm admiration not usually found in such correspondence. She deplored scandal, gossip and marital mix-ups. When the marriages of some of her Chicago friends went on the rocks she was sympathetic but nothing of the sort touched her own family circle until after her death.

Potter at times was a demon taskmaster. He drove architects and workmen to desperation with his demands when the hotel was going up. He had his own ideas about the way things should be done and he stubbornly enforced his wishes. The effect was sometimes chaotic. His passion for repairs and improvements kept him constantly involved with decorators, carpenters and plumbers. When a wholesaler delivered a large consignment of furniture that was supposed to be stuffed with horsehair, he ripped open the coverings with a knife, pulled out tow, and promptly canceled the entire order, although it represented a fortune to the manufacturer. Before he lived on the premises he would drive to the hotel at three o'clock in the morning to see that his orders were being carried out.

Although a modest man, who stayed in the background as he ran his hotel, he had a natural flair for publicity. He did dashing things in an offhand way, then sat back and watched the results with quiet satisfaction. It was all part of his wry sense of humor. At the time he married Bertha he astonished the town by driving around in a French charabanc with leopard-skin seats, and he tallyhoed to the Washington Park Derby with considerable flourish. But he seemed meek and mild in his little cage at the Palmer House, and later in his more imposing office upstairs. It was not in his nature to show exuberance or to greet his guests in the lordly manner of John B. Drake, who presided at the new Grand Pacific Hotel and was his chief professional rival. He demanded courtesy in his hotel staff, however, as he did in his store, and he functioned with the assurance of a man who knew his business. Decisions were swiftly made. Like Bertha, he never raised his voice, yet none questioned his authority. Both were inclined to be perfectionists in their own performance, and to be equally exacting in their demands on others.

They always referred to the hotel as a "home" or "house." Potter wrote to a friend, Charles Leland, on August 26, 1876: "I am taking the entire charge of my house which very thoroughly occupies my time from six in the morning to late in the evening. The business of my house is continually improving and promises are more than flattering for the future. I have a very fine restaurant connected with my home and much need a good man to take charge of it."

Bertha's brother Henry became the steward after this but Palmer held the master hand in matters large and small. He was constantly on guard for Drake's operations. Their two hotels shared the theater and opera stars, political figures of note, and the bankers and businessmen from the East who had ever tightening links with the Prairie City. Drake functioned in the grand manner. He initiated dances which he called assemblies. Johnny Hand, then in his prime, conducted the orchestra and the fashionable younger set danced decorously to his hotel music. He and Potter Palmer were the first to install electricity in their hotels. They ran neck to neck on all innovations. The Tremont House, which reopened in 1874, was another favorite stopping place for the people of the theater, and the Sherman House was always filled.

With their growing fortunes and native generosity the newly made millionaires of Chicago went in for philanthropy. The Palmers gave generously to all projects that might encourage the development of the city. When asked soon after the panic of 1873 to give funds for a new building for the Y.M.C.A. Palmer demanded: "How much from me?"

"A hundred thousand," he was told.

He smiled noncommittally. "What are *they* doing—all our fine friends?" he asked.

"Oh, they are giving large amounts."

He pondered for a moment. "Well, I've at last cleared the mortgage on this hotel. I'm in good shape. I'll give you the money."

Palmer was one of the early managers of the Y.M.C.A. and he organized the Chicago Baseball Club at the Briggs House in 1871, becoming its first president. Through the Citizens League he worked with Cyrus H. McCormick, Marshall Field, George M. Pullman, Franklin MacVeagh, Martin A. Ryerson and Ferdinand W. Peck to check crime and drinking among juveniles. He played the master role in laying out and beautifying Jackson and Washington parks and the connecting boulevards. The shrubs, the trees, the seeds brought from Kew Gardens to Chicago, all stemmed in part from the Palmer influence in the early days. His work as South Park Commissioner left an indelible stamp on the city's development.

Bertha was a stimulating force in all such projects. She encouraged him to talk of his work and his aims. A silent man in company, he grew quite eloquent with her. Big though his visions were, she sometimes lengthened the vista, for she had grown up in the shadow of lofty enterprise and she loved Chicago. No scheme seemed too grandiose to an Honoré daughter. When her husband came upstairs at night, exhausted from the problems of pleasing the guests, handling his staff and ordering supplies, she listened attentively to what he had to say. In later years she often remarked that she had learned all she knew of business during these early days of her marriage, when there was time to be closer to Potter and they discussed his operations in detail.

True, much of her time even then was spent in social interchange. She had endless resources at her command and made the most of them. But inevitably she was swept into the area of public work and philanthropy. While lending herself readily to the purely fashionable elements she did not overlook the growing influence of the women's clubs. She built bulwarks around herself by her zeal for the charitable enterprises of the day. Bertha was early on the side of the reformers, and although the Palmer House bar did a fashionable and booming business every night, she interested herself in the Woman's Christian Temperance Union, founded in Chicago by Frances E. Willard. Soon Mrs. Matilda B. Carse, who was president of the Chicago branch, learned that she could turn to her for support at any time.

Mrs. Palmer allied herself with Jane Addams when Hull House became a focus of social experiment. She was never indifferent to a good community cause and always gave practical aid. Although posterity might regard her as a social snob and jeer a little at her magnificence she was the first of the very rich women in America to give fighting as well as financial support to the cause of the working woman. She was years ahead of her time in her approach to such matters. But she gave slight consolation to the professional suffragists. She had no patience with Bloomerism, short hair or freak theories. She thought that women should play up all their God-given assets but hold out for equal standards. It was strictly a world where men and women should work together. Rough tactics offended her. Her instinct was to use the weapon at hand and the vote still seemed far off. "One hears so much about the 'new woman' that one is in danger of being bored by her unless she arrives quickly," she commented on one occasion.

Mrs. Palmer set a high price on brains. Her most consistent goals were the better education of women and the improvement of their economic status. She doubted that men could genuinely admire the "stupid, superficial fools they have trained us to become." Nor could she believe that clever women were intimidating to men. "However bright, no woman need be frightened by the thought that man may not admire and love her, for she feels that he can't help it," said Mrs. Palmer, with biological understanding and the assurance of a beautiful woman.

The theory of equal pay for equal work made excellent

sense to her and nothing aroused her more than hampering strings on the woman worker. Suttee and polygamy seemed less barbaric than denying women the right to better themselves by work, she said in one of her more spirited addresses. Her emergence as a strong champion of the working woman came about by a series of logical steps. The Fortnightly Club was her first venture into public view. It was founded by Mrs. Kate Newell Doggett and its professed aims were cultural. Its two hundred members were women of wealth and fashion who assembled to discuss the arts. Other clubs were founded after this pattern and Bertha became a leading spirit in the Chicago Woman's Club, which was established in 1876 primarily for the study of social problems. Its members held literary meetings and discussed reform, philanthropy, education, science, philosophy, home care and the arts. Working girls as well as social leaders belonged to the club. By this time Chicago had a formidable number of women employed in the business field as secretaries, accountants, cashiers, typists, saleswomen and clerks, and it was noted that the invaders were "gallantly assisted by all true Chicago men who have the native spirit."

This club brought Mrs. Palmer into touch with the leading social reformers and she became a prize catch in their midst, not only for her practical interest but for the generous financial aid that she and Potter Palmer were always ready to give. The club took up one civic project after another. "If funds were lacking for any good cause, or if we had to make up a quota, we just asked the Potter Palmers," commented Mrs. Carter H. Harrison, the Mayor's wife.

Soon Mrs. Palmer was holding meetings for factory girls at her home and was studying the conditions under which they lived and worked. She helped in the push for protective legislation and joined forces with such women as Julia Lathrop, Florence Kelley, Alice Hamilton, Mary McDowell and Louise de Koven Bowen. She became a patron of the

Women's Trade Union League and it was largely through her efforts that the millinery workers of Chicago were organized and their working conditions improved. She often had illustrated lectures at her home, impressing on her friends the conditions under which factory girls worked, lived and played. One of her own favorite receptions was for shopgirls and she made a point of pushing their interests. She could handle them just as well as she did the debutantes who flocked to her house to show their skill as cooks when a domestic science teacher from Columbia University gave a cooking demonstration under her aegis. Mrs. Palmer was inevitably a pace setter for her generation.

She gave money lavishly to most of the causes brought to her attention and her regular charitable outlay was estimated at twenty-five thousand dollars a year, irrespective of large family donations for special projects. She gave strong financial backing to the Chicago Woman's Club and had life membership in a number of philanthropic organizations. She belonged also to the Tuesday Art and Travel Club, the Onwentsia Club and Saddle and Cycle Club, an old and exclusive organization on the North Side. Mrs. Palmer worked with drive and sincerity at all the activities to which she lent her name. For a time she was a trustee of Northwestern University.

Meanwhile, her social rise went on without interruption. President Grant had offered Palmer a Cabinet post in his second administration but Potter had no wish to be Secretary of the Interior or to hold any other government office. He was essentially a businessman, not a politician. He liked Chicago and he abhorred the jungle of politics. His decision was reached after he had talked things over with Cissie. The Grant administrations were checkered with scandals, and tales of nepotism flourished. Interested as she was in public service, Mrs. Palmer recognized Chicago as home ground. Since Ida's marriage she had made a number of trips to the capital. Mrs. Grant gave one of the most brilliant receptions of her eight years in the White House for the tiny beauty who had married her oldest son. Mrs. Potter Palmer flashed into focus for Washington society for the first time on this occasion when she made a dramatic appearance with her sister. She eclipsed everyone else when she walked into the East Room and took a stand in the receiving line. The White House was Ida's home now and the two Honoré sisters were thought to be irresistible together, with their good looks, their style and bright conversation. Both were fluent linguists and could handle the diplomats with ease. Fred was frequently away on military expeditions but Ida was well established and Mrs. Grant considered her an asset in her receiving line. Occasionally Nellie, her own daughter, returned from England for visits and then the two young matrons added glamour to the scene, with Mrs. Palmer showing up occasionally at Mrs. Grant's side.

Fred returned home on leave in June, 1876, for the birth of his first child. Otherwise he would have been in the Custer massacre. Little Julia Grant was born in a white and turquoise room in the White House and Bertha rejoiced that Honoré and Potter now had a girl cousin. She weighed thirteen pounds at birth and at her baptism in the East Room members of her grandfather's Cabinet took stock of the new baby and their wives admired the long dress of mull and Valenciennes made by Mrs. Honoré. Bertha soon regarded her sister's child as a daughter, since she was never to have one of her own. When Julia was three she stayed with the Palmers in Chicago and shared in the excitement of the Grants' return from their two-year trip around the world. With her parents she joined the party at Omaha and was part of the triumphal entry into Chicago.

Mrs. Palmer was much to the fore in the great reception given the former President there. A third term was under discussion and politicians had converged from all quarters to mount the bandwagon. But it was Grant the soldier, not Grant the President, who was wildly cheered during the three-day celebration. The family stayed at the Palmer House and Bertha took charge of Mrs. Grant. The business of the city stood still for a monster parade with floats and banners bearing the names of the General's battles.

The streets were jammed for blocks around the hotel as long as he was there. The Palmers gave a private luncheon in the red parlor for their guests. At the public reception that followed the crowd got out of hand and the program had to be abandoned. The halls, the stairs, the reception rooms and parlors were jammed. Mrs. Palmer swept Mrs. Grant up to her suite and spread the word that the guests had retired. The climax of their visit came with the thunderous welcome given Grant in the banquet hall by veterans of the Army of the Tennessee, led by General William Tecumseh Sherman. Six hundred war veterans yelled themselves hoarse. The decorations were miniature cannon, rifles, carbines and Minié balls. The menus were midget tents. Mrs. Palmer arranged for Mrs. Grant and other officers' wives to sit with her in the gallery behind a curtain of smilax, through which they could see and hear all that took place. Mark Twain, an interested spectator, reported that the orators "emptied Niagaras of glory upon Grant" but that this had no more effect on him than if he had been a bronze image.

It was one of the more memorable evenings in Palmer House history, and doubly so for Bertha, whose sister now was so intimate a member of the General's family. That winter the Grants went to Mexico and small Julia was sent west to stay with her for Christmas. Candles burned on a great tree such as the child had never seen. She played around it with Honoré and Potter and opened wonderful gifts. She was now three and old enough to observe the glitter of jewels around her aunt's throat as she stood at the head of the staircase sparkling like a fairy princess.

When she was five Julia went west again to stay with the Palmers at their country house outside Chicago. At this time

Uncle Potter drove in to work every day. When he came home in the late afternoon he pruned the bushes until Cissie came out and took the shears from him. He liked to go to the stables and hose the carriages but again she would interrupt him and then he would play with the children. There were lawns for them to roll on, garden patches for them to cultivate, and merry games to be played by Julia, Honoré and Potter. Mrs. Palmer took them driving in her brougham on fine days. The horses had silver harness and two top-hatted men sat on the box. They could produce a brougham, a coupé, a landau or a victoria at a moment's notice for Mrs. Palmer's use. The children had their own little governess cart.

The summer sped along until July 4, when a son was born to Ida and Fred. They named him Ulysses S. Grant in honor of his grandfather. The year was 1881. Julia had eaten too many cherries in the garden the day before. She sickened and was put to bed in a little room next to her mother's. But in the night her Aunt Bertha walked in and took her in her arms, carrying her into her own room and tucking her into bed. In the morning Mrs. Palmer rounded up the three children and marched them into Ida's room. She told them to be absolutely silent and to walk out again at a signal. But first she let little Julia hold her new brother in her arms for a moment.

Ida was ill for a long time after that and Julia passed more and more time with her Aunt Bertha, who dressed her in ruffles and her sons at times in Little Lord Fauntleroy velvet suits, a fashion of the period. But they were not coddled boys. Eighty years later Honoré could still remember the wallopings that his mother gave him at this stage of his life. She had vigorous ideas about the upbringing of the young, insisting that they learn everything well and finish what they started. As they grew older she introduced a regime of physical training and strenuous sports. Potter was named "Min" by his governess because of his fragile air. Although servants surrounded them on all sides their mother took an active part in their training. She liked to read to them and listen to their chatter. Remembering her own upbringing she taught them to be considerate of others and to respect old age. Honoré was adventurous. He resembled his father in liking fast horses and taking chances. Potter was quiet and studious. When Julia Grant was with them, the little group was complete and the boys treated her like a sister.

With his sons growing up and his hotel prospering beyond all expectation Potter Palmer began to think of building a home worthy of his wife. By this time few evidences of the fire remained except for picturesque shells of suburban houses now overgrown with flowers or weeds, some ruined churches and wrecked factory foundations. The population of Chicago had reached the half-million mark and it was the fourth largest city in the country. Cable cars were replacing the city's horse-drawn streetcars. The more affluent owned their own carriages but there were plenty of livery stables for public use. The foliage in Lincoln Park had now grown thick and the little lakes and hillocks were bright with flowers and shrubbery. Its cricket club had 150 members. Eighty cyclists had their own bicycle club. The Chicago Yacht Club and the Farragut Boat Club were responsible for flocks of white sails on sunny days. Twenty railroad lines ran into the city and by 1886 five thousand telephones were in use. The newspaper world was lively and competitive with the *Tribune* and *Times*, the *Herald* and *Post*, the *Inter-Ocean*, *Journal* and *Daily News*. Corn poured through the huge grain elevators. There were two tunnels for traffic and a succession of drawbridges across the river. George M. Pullman was building Pullman City and ginger-whiskered Philip D. Armour, who had come from upstate New York like Potter Palmer, dominated the packing field, with Gustavus Swift, a cattle trader from Massachusetts, close on his heels. Twenty-nine large packing concerns brought further wealth to Chicago and spread their trade-marks around the globe.

The Honorés still lived on Michigan Avenue and close at hand were Charles T. Yerkes, the traction magnate of dubious repute from Philadelphia; Ferdinand W. Peck, whose interest in music and a more sophisticated city led to the erection of the Auditorium; James H. McVicker, whose theater gave Chicago its most distinguished drama, and a number of packers and brewers whose houses were a reproof to Potter Palmer. Bertha had only a modest country dwelling to house her, aside from her more impersonal quarters in the Palmer House. Mansions with cupolas and buttresses, pinnacles and towers were being built by the new millionaires when he selected the site for his.

As always, he did the unusual. Instead of building on Michigan or Prairie Avenue he looked around for a new area to develop. He owned three thousand feet of lake frontage that seemed to everyone else to be a watery, wind-swept waste, low-lying and bleak. This stretch had once belonged to John Jacob Astor and Palmer had picked it up for a song. From this wilderness of sand dunes, stunted willows and pools of stagnant water, where boys used to crawl through the reeds to shoot mallards, redheads and canvasback ducks, he created Lake Shore Drive. The youthful hunters scattered when a big scow came in view and a pump began to suck sand from the lake bottom and throw it on the shore. The entire marsh was drained and filled with clean sand which made a good foundation for the buildings Potter Palmer planned. When the city ran a roadway through this area, known first as North Shore Drive and then as Lake Shore Drive, Chicago had taken a big step forward toward magnificence.

Palmer decided to build his own house in the center of the reclaimed land, facing the lake, looking toward Lincoln Park to the north and the city harbor to the south. He bought additional lake frontage in large sections and sold only to men of his choice. This marked the migration of society from the South Side to the Gold Coast and the beginning of a blue ribbon colony to become famous in the nation's social annals.

Bertha approached the plans for the family castle with her usual concentrated interest. Henry Ives Cobb and Charles S. Frost, two rising young architects, were commissioned to design a three-story building that would cost about ninety thousand dollars. But before it was finished a million dollars had been spent and Potter Palmer finally told his bookkeeper to stop entering charges against his new home. He had no wish to know the final reckoning.

From 1882 to 1885 the work went on, while Honoré and Potter grew and went to school and their mother moved more deeply into the current of community affairs. When finished the castle was variously described as early English battlemented style, castellated Gothic, and Norman Gothic. It was built of Wisconsin granite with contrasting Ohio sandstone. This created a striped effect that greatly irked Mrs. Palmer until the patina of time and a lacework of English ivy toned it down to medieval mellowness. Its tower, with a spiral staircase, rose eighty feet high and was its most arresting feature.

"The age of Pericles seems to be dawning," commented the Chicago *Inter-Ocean*. But Boni de Castellane stared at the porte-cochere and dubbed the castle "sumptuous and abominable." By this time the people of Chicago had become rather fond of the gloomy building on the lake front and there was much speculation about its interior until Mrs. Palmer stepped from her carriage one day in 1885 and was led by her husband into the great octagonal hall, three stories high, with Gobelin tapestries on the walls and a floor of marble mosaic laid by imported Italian craftsmen. There were no surprises for Bertha, for she and Potter had worked on the castle both inside and out with all the zeal of their active, ambitious natures.

But when the doors were opened for her first reception her many friends had something to talk about for weeks. Nothing like it had ever before been seen in Chicago. They moved with a mixture of awe and amusement from room to room, after admiring the baronial hall, with its carved oak staircase, its slender Gothic pillars supporting the gallery, its Bengal tiger skin stretched on the mosaic floor. The Honoré coat of arms—three silver serpents intertwined with tails terminating in arrowheads—decorated the newel posts of the staircase. The drawing room was French, the music room Spanish, the dining room English, the paneled passage to the ballroom Moorish, and the library, extending across the front of the house, Flemish Renaissance with carved oak figures brought from an old European cathedral installed over the fireplace. Much of the woodwork throughout the house was hand-carved.

Mrs. Palmer's guests clustered in the drawing room, the first Louis XVI salon to be seen in Chicago. It was white and gold, creating a delicate background for its dark-eyed hostess. The tile floor was inlaid with pink roses. Gabriel Ferrier later added murals with an intricate pattern of roses and gold tesserae. Cupids drifted across the ceiling.

The combination ballroom and picture gallery added later on was to be the background for many of Mrs. Palmer's receptions. It was ninety feet long and forty feet high. The walls were hung with rose-red velvet and light was suffused through iridescent Tiffany glass chandeliers. South of the ballroom and up a few marble steps was the little balcony where the orchestra played. The dining room, which seated fifty with ease, had San Domingo mahogany paneling, inlaid floors and a great mahogany and crystal sideboard, at each side of which hung George P. A. Healy's paintings of Mr. and Mrs. Palmer. William B. Ogden had persuaded Healy to leave the court of Louis Philippe and return to Chicago. The artist became a good friend of the Palmers and often visited them. His portrait of Bertha was Palmer's favorite among many done of her. It was painted in her youth and had warmth and grace, as well as suggesting her intelligence.

The house as a whole was a melange of styles and as the

years went on Mrs. Palmer came home from Europe with fresh treasures to install, new pictures to hang on the walls, fine Chinese porcelains and antiques from many lands to enrich her collections. But at the first reception it seemed as if the castle could hold no more. Guests left with confused impressions of magnificent carvings; murals, archways and filigree; of brass chandeliers and garnet glass; of Venetian mosaic; of marble, stone and wrought iron; of onyx in the vestibule doors and huge fireplaces of marble and oak. There was comment on the absence of locks and doorknobs. Even Potter Palmer could not get into his citadel until a door was opened by a servant. Later on few guests left without a visit to the sixty-foot conservatory that was added to the house.

Mrs. Palmer's bedroom, on the second floor, was of Moorish design, done in ebony and gold, with a paneled wainscot and carved ceiling. Her arched windows with cathedral glass were copied from the palace in Cairo. Smyrna rugs lay on the inlaid oak floor and three Moorish arches led to her dressing room, which was decorated in black and gold. She washed her face in an oval basin inlaid with a mother-of-pearl flower design. She bathed in a sunken tub shaped like a swan. All the bathroom fixtures had delicate flower designs in pastel colors and the ceiling was painted French gray.

Bertha slept in a Louis XVI bed ten feet high with Nattier blue taffeta draperies. She received her intimates in a small French sitting room known as the White Room, and here she kept the gilded Florentine chests that she had brought home from her wedding trip. However late a function, she always glanced into her sons' room in their early years to see that Honoré and Potter were sleeping soundly. She took special pride in having designed a sturdy setting for them. The woodwork was Hungarian ash and their furniture matched it, with decorative panels inlaid with a white holly design on ebony.

No private home in Chicago's history was so much discussed. Visitors from distant points viewed it as one of the city's wonders and half a century later the site was pointed out to tourists. Cobb, the architect, disowned the massing of towers and Mrs. Palmer took care to tell her friends that she was away when the discordant sandstone was applied. This was one of Potter Palmer's building whims. There were many local jokes about the Palmer mansion but the era of rococo furnishings was in full swing, so that the effect was less jarring to contemporaries than it is today. Mrs. Palmer simplified her décor in her later homes.

With the opening of Palmer Castle, as it came to be known, a new era had begun in Chicago hospitality. The parties given there became legendary for their style, novelty and the diversity of the guests. She welcomed the protagonists of many odd causes under her roof as well as foreign princes, statesmen, notable figures in every field, and the dowagers of the United States. Ward politicians, reformers, cranks, labor leaders, shopgirls, and all manner of zealots trooped through her reception rooms at one time or another, as well as such particular catches of hers as Benjamin Harrison, William McKinley and Ulysses S. Grant, who saw it only in its chrysalis stage since he died the year it was opened.

The Potter Palmer house stood until 1950, when it was torn down to make way for a modern apartment house. It had long been in decline and was used as a Red Cross surgical dressing center during the Second World War, a use that Mrs. Palmer would have approved. Thomas Tallmadge called it the "mansion to end all mansions" in his *Architecture in Old Chicago*. "No citizen in Chicago or lover of her traditions or her beauty could see the towers of this castle overthrown without real sorrow," he commented.

But the year they took up residence in their new home was a sad one in their family. General Grant died that summer on Mount McGregor after a long fight with cancer. Ida and Fred were with him constantly during the last weeks of his life and Bertha got firsthand accounts from her sister while the papers day by day mirrored his march to the grave. Nellie had come home from England toward the end. His other sons, Ulysses S. Grant, II, and Jesse, were at his deathbed with their wives. Mrs. Palmer went east to attend the funeral services at Mount McGregor and in New York. She sat in the little parlor with General Sherman and Mrs. Grant while the Rev. Dr. John Philip Newman delivered the eulogy. Bertha had liked the General and had talked to him often on public issues. As an ardent Democrat she had taken issue with him on some of his policies but with unvarying courtesy. She had not always agreed with him about the men in whom he placed his trust. But his devotion to Ida and her own affection for Fred were mutual bonds. The General was less comfortable in the presence of Chicago's *grande dame* than he was with her sister Ida. But he liked to talk to her about Chicago and the Middle West and Mrs. Grant enjoyed the company of Fred's imposing sister-in-law. The military note was strong in Mrs. Palmer's circle—possibly because of the Grant connections. Generals were much in evidence at her gatherings. General Philip H. Sheridan was always an honored guest and on more than one occasion she led the main column of the Charity Ball on the arm of General Nelson A. Miles.

In the year following General Grant's death all Chicago was roused by the Haymarket riot, when the first anarchist bomb was thrown in America, killing one and wounding seventy-three. The police fired blindly in the dark. Radical centers were raided and hundreds were arrested. Eight anarchist leaders were tried and four were hanged. There was growing unrest among the workers. Socialism was spreading fast among them. The millionaires of Chicago had become a prime target for attack.

4

➤➤➤➤➤➤➤➤➤➤➤➤➤ *Mrs. Palmer Invades Europe*

Mrs. Potter Palmer drove through Hyde Park in a barouche with high-stepping chestnuts on a summer afternoon in 1891 and took cool surveillance of a scene of Victorian splendor. Her husband sat beside her, his gray topper tilted rakishly, his attention focused on the horses and equipages which were a sight in their ornate way. Gilded coaches did not drive through the parks of Chicago.

The rhododendrons were in full bloom and the scents of June were in the air. The Duke and Duchess of Teck were out driving in a state coach with Princess May. Lady Brooke, whom Mrs. Palmer would know later on as the Countess of Warwick, stepped out of her carriage and settled herself in a chair beneath a shady tree. She had not yet been converted to socialism and was noted chiefly at the time as a great beauty and the friend of the Prince of Wales.

Mrs. Palmer had a chance to observe her golden hair, her fragile complexion and magnificent bearing. It was her first glimpse of this famous beauty. Lady Brooke had silver buckles on her suède shoes and a veil dangled from her tilted pancake hat. Men on horseback drew up to chat with the fine ladies seated in the shade, most of whom favored cool white China silk carriage gowns with clanking chatelaines. But the Palmers drove on. They had little time for dalliance. Mrs. Palmer had come to Europe at the end of May as chairman of the board of lady managers of the World's Columbian Exposition. Her purpose was to invoke the support of foreign rulers and government officials in women's exhibits for the Fair. She viewed the role of women for this event in large and inclusive terms. Not only did she plan to round up the best arts and crafts for a stunning display in the Woman's Building but she planned to bring together women of all nations and draw attention to their status. It was a bold conception for the early 1890's.

James G. Blaine, Secretary of State, became seriously ill just as he was about to alert the ministers abroad that Mrs. Potter Palmer was heading across the Atlantic. However, she found it easy enough to push through her plans without his aid. She knew a number of the ambassadors personally and Robert Todd Lincoln, an old friend and the son of Abraham Lincoln, made appointments for her in court circles. With the sanction of the Prime Minister, Lord Salisbury, she won the support of Princess Christian, third daughter of Queen Victoria. She tackled the British Royal Commission, which had among its members Sir Philip Owen, Sir Henry Wood and Sir Richard Webster, the Attorney General. The Prince of Wales was its president. All had worked for the Paris Exposition of 1889 and they greeted Mrs. Palmer's proposals with cordiality.

She spent her days holding meetings and her evenings in Victorian drawing rooms, letting all and sundry know what Chicago planned. The season was in full swing. Her husband went to the races. He haunted the clubs. He accompanied Bertha to the theater and met the peers of Britain with all the quiet and reserve that settled on him when exposed to titles and an acknowledged aristocracy. He frequently said that he was not a "society man," and no one disagreed with this. Although he had sold ribbons and rented rooms in his time he had an independent spirit and a tough pride in his sound heritage. He was well aware that some of the dukes looked into space when he was around but he made no protest when his wife, who had more affinity for the peerage, insisted that he escort her to all the evening gatherings and saw to it that he was well primed on the political questions bound to come under discussion. Horses and racing made unfailing bait and the Chicagoan had a sure instinct for commerce. If he was not wholly at ease in the historic men's clubs of St. James's, where visiting Americans had to have special gifts or eccentricities to make headway, he was never at a loss at a function with Cissie at hand to spread her own inimitable aura of assurance.

Over the teacups she explained to Princess Christian what she planned for the Exposition. The Princess showed signs of alarm. She was opposed to extreme views of any kind and she saw at once that this dashing American was lending an ear to the dreadful women who were clamoring for something they called their "rights."

"Women should be trained only to care for their families, beautify the home and nurse the sick," said Princess Christian when Mrs. Palmer insisted that they should have a place in every profession and be paid as well as men. As the exponent of Queen Victoria's views she told Mrs. Palmer what she thought of the suffrage movement and said she could see no place for women in the learned professions. But she was willing to concede their right to better wages in the occupations traditionally identified with their sex, and to anything that tended to make them better wives and mothers. At this time she headed the South Kensington School of Art Needlework, the Hospital Schools for Training Nurses and a number of industrial movements affecting women.

In any event, the Princess was won by Mrs. Palmer's arguments and personal force. She promised to head her commission in Britain and they ended up good friends. Thus Mrs.

Palmer forged a firm link with the court, although her own outlook on life was anything but Victorian. She soon found a fellow spirit in the Countess of Aberdeen, who was busy developing the cottage industries of Ireland and Scotland and proposed setting up an Irish village at the Exposition. She had a letter from Frances E. Willard to Lady Henry Somerset, who was interested in the temperance movement in England and had established homes for wayward girls. Finally her committee was complete and was set up under the patronage of the Queen. Its members were Princess Christian, the Duchess of Abercorn, the Marchioness of Salisbury, the Countess of Aberdeen, Lady Somerset, Lady Brassey, Lady Knutsford, Mrs. Bedford-Fenwick, Mrs. Millicent Fawcett, the Baroness Burdett-Coutts, and Lady Jeune, who had once maintained a literary salon frequented by Tennyson, Browning and Matthew Arnold. Thus Mrs. Palmer had neatly worked in some suffrage leaders and bohemian spirits along with traditional Victorians.

Her diplomacy was even more successful in Paris, where she had good groundwork. The committee of women who had worked for the Paris Exposition had "basked in the full sunshine of official power," she noted, and they were eager to extend their field of operations to the United States. She addressed forty-two of the most influential women of France as well as senators and deputies. Wrapped in a plush mantle lined with apricot silk she attended the opera with President Carnot. She had a long interview with his wife at the Palace of the Élysée. She found her "sympathetic and charming" but, like Princess Christian, a conservative about suffrage and women flaunting their powers outside of the home. Again Mrs. Palmer had to use persuasive force to get her way. Madame Carnot had never served on a French committee but she finally agreed to head the woman's work in France for the Columbian Exposition. Bertha talked in turn to Madame Yves-Guyot, wife of the Minister of Public Works, and Madame

Bogelot, who had represented France at the International Council of Women held two years earlier in Washington.

But she made a quick kill with the statesmen of France. Both Jules Simon and Jules Siegfried, influential senators, listened to her attentively, as did their wives. Antoine Proust, who had been appointed French Fine Arts Director for the Columbian Exposition and was a member of the Chamber of Deputies, was much impressed. Her most significant quarry, however, was Jules Roche, Minister of Commerce. She and Mrs. John A. Logan tackled him together, two eloquent American women pitted against a Frenchman who could not see the validity of separate exhibits in a separate woman's building. Why should women stand apart from men in a matter of this sort?

Mrs. Palmer quickly whipped out some preliminary sketches for a woman's building and told him a few home truths in perfect French. She was not only convincing but she was the most fashionably turned-out woman who had ever sat in his office and discussed big plans with him in a businesslike way. M. Roche was stampeded. The ultimate result of this interview was the appointment of the desired woman's commission, and a government appropriation of 200,000 francs for its expenses —a larger sum than the board of lady managers had yet received from Congress.

The Palmers stayed at the Grand Hotel and Bertha took time to stock up on gowns with the ruchings, wide belts and glittering embroidery of the period. The new Medici collars suited her to perfection as they rose above her jewels with Elizabethan majesty. Her husband was welcomed back at Tiffany's. He never went to Paris without buying new jewels for Cissie and on this occasion the tiaras, parures and stomachers of the British peeresses had sparked off striking additions to a collection already well under way.

Theodore Stanton, the son of Elizabeth Cady Stanton, who was resident commissioner in Paris for the Columbian Exposition, opened many doors for his visiting compatriots but Palmer passed most of his time seeking art for the Fair. Before leaving home he had promised Charles L. Hutchinson, president of the Art Institute of Chicago, that he would scout for him. Although Mrs. Palmer gets the major credit for introducing modern art to Chicago, her husband was equally alert and potent in this undertaking. He was a merchant in art as in all else. Like others of his affluent associates in the Middle West he had cultivated an interest in pictures, and had decided views about what he liked. While Bertha was busy conferring with French statesmen he visited art dealers, galleries and studios with Sara T. Hallowell, who was his wife's liaison in Paris on all questions involving art for the Woman's Building of the Exposition. Sara was pushing the Impressionists and was an established agent operating on behalf of the artists and dealers. Well-off Americans were her natural quarry and she had already done some work for the Potter Palmers.

Before they left Paris Bertha commissioned Mary Cassatt and Mary Fairchild MacMonnies, wife of Frederick MacMonnies, to do two large mural paintings for the tympana at either end of the main gallery in the Woman's Building. The directors had voted six thousand dollars for this purpose. MacMonnies was already at work on his fountain for the Exposition and Sara Hallowell considered it "wondrously beautiful," an early impression later confirmed by the public.

From Paris the Palmers went to Vienna. Fred Grant by this time was the United States Minister there and he and Ida were in high favor at the Austrian court. Potter watched approvingly while his wife danced Viennese waltzes on home ground with gold-laced officers and was entertained by royalty. Julia was now a lanky girl of fifteen who spoke the Viennese patois as fluently as she did French. Little Ulysses was attending the Theresianum, founded by the Empress Maria Theresa.

Ida was immensely popular in the Viennese capital but it was not a propitious moment for Mrs. Palmer's mission. Austria had broken off relations with the United States over the McKinley tariff act. The pearl button makers who exported most of their product to the United States were thrown out of work in great numbers. Mass meetings were held and measures were taken to relieve their distress. Although anxious to advance the interests of the Exposition, Fred did not consider it the time to push the matter officially. But Ida introduced her sister to Princess Metternich and other women interested in the native crafts, who formed a commission to work for the Fair.

Mrs. Palmer's proposals were warmly received by Queen Marie Henriette of Belgium and Queen Margherita of Italy. Both agreed at once to head committees, and eventually Belgium sent over monographs and charts with such figures as had never before been compiled on woman's status in that country. This was just what Mrs. Palmer desired. Queen Margherita directed the work personally in Italy and offered her priceless collection of laces which had never been shown outside of the country. Some of them dated a thousand years before Christ and were taken from Egyptian and Etruscan tombs. It was agreed that the laces and crafts of contemporary Italian women should be well represented beside the ancient treasures.

Mrs. Palmer returned to London satisfied with the results of her negotiations on the Continent, and she and Potter attended the final musicale of the season, held at Mrs. Ronald's home in Cadogan Place. Nordica sang and Mlle. Thénier of the Théâtre Français gave a monologue. Mrs. Bradley Martin was present in turquoise blue silk with fringes of jet and a tiny bonnet of jet tipped with blue plumes. Mrs. John W. Mackay chatted with Mrs. Palmer, nodding her gold lace bonnet with lilac sprays in her hearty way as they exchanged American gossip. It was evident to all that the visitor from Chicago had made her presence felt in London society. English women noted how dashing she was, how smoothly she worked, how quickly she had won royal approval.

By this time she justly felt that she was better off working by herself than with the aid of the State Department, which would have functioned with less speed and daring than she had applied to her diplomatic negotiations. "Working as I did, through the people of the country, and making the direct appeal with and through them, the matter was only semi-official and we were, at the same time, much more strongly fortified," she reported back to her board.

Mrs. Palmer's operations had gone deeper than anyone realized when she stepped off the *Normannia* in New York early in July, 1891, and gave the ship news reporters a modest account of her successes. Her trip to Europe was followed by an avalanche of letters and circulars sent out in French, German, Spanish and English, and a close combing of notable women from Dublin to Tokyo. By the time forty-one countries responded favorably Mrs. Palmer was able to say to her board: "We are now possessed of the most powerful organization that has ever existed among women."

Japan had been slow to respond until the Empress took a hand and headed a committee. Denmark declined to participate at first but relented. The Empress of Russia personally assembled an exhibit of laces, embroideries and national costumes. It was all much more than Mrs. Palmer had expected and it surprised the officials of the Exposition. Her fellow commissioners had been doubtful that women around the globe, poor backward things, would respond. But fresh from her stimulating encounters abroad Mrs. Palmer crisply pointed out that American women had nothing like the political power of their English sisters; that Russia had numerous colleges and institutions of higher learning for its women; that Denmark had noted women scientists; that during the golden "cinquecento" Italy had women professors, doctors, lawyers and writers; that France was as far ahead in women's affairs as the United States and had noted women orators, and that Austria had prosperous institutions and industries founded by women.

She also wanted the world to know that although queens,

princesses and duchesses seemed to have caught the limelight, no one must think that the foreign committees represented only royalty and the influence of government. All classes were represented and many of the guiding spirits were women who had risen by their own unaided talents. She deplored the fact that Tunis, Syria and various Oriental countries could not participate because of the subjugation of their women and the lack of organization among them. But the harem veil was lifted by timid hands, and individuals signaled across the seas though their governments were silent.

Mrs. Palmer viewed the Exposition as something broader than a passing spectacle. She believed it could help to improve the lot of women around the world. She considered it a prime opportunity for every country involved to appraise its woman strength in statistics. She planned a worldwide survey of the actual status of women in industry, in education, in the arts and in business. From New York to Siam women soon were scurrying around trying to assemble hardtack information for Mrs. Potter Palmer, often where it had never before been garnered. "Oh, how she could drive us, day and night," commented one of her committee workers. "She not only worked herself but made others labor, too. As a committee chairman, I've never seen her equal."

Mrs. Palmer projected the thought that they would set back the clock half a century for women if they did not realize the solemn nature of the trust placed in their hands. "If we live up to the possibilities we shall open a new era for them," she added. "Can we forget ourselves, and our personal ambitions and littlenesses, and be worthy of the work we have been called to do?"

But she soon encountered a chilling dash of littleness in her own empire. She returned from Europe to find that a situation she had left smoldering had burst into flame again on her return. She had survived her first sharp tilt with women practiced in strategic intrigue when she fired the corresponding secretary, Miss Phoebe W. Couzins, who had all but broken up the board of lady managers. From the start Miss Couzins, a lawyer and prominent suffragist, had assailed everyone connected with the management of the Fair, and Mrs. Potter Palmer in particular. Finally the board dropped her on charges of misconduct and neglect of duty just before its chairman left for England.

Phoebe promptly brought suit in the Circuit Court and lost her case. But many of the leading suffragists were behind her and the breach brought headlines in the nation's press. Mrs. Isabella Beecher Hooker led the attack. This veteran fighter for women's rights had backed Clara Barton for the presidency and Mrs. John A. Logan for the vice presidency of the board of lady managers. When Mrs. Palmer was elected unanimously she bowed to the inevitable and conceded that perhaps it was a good idea to have a prominent Chicago woman hold this office. She even paid her a public tribute as a young woman inexperienced in public duty of any sort who had managed their "large, untrained, deliberative body with the firmness and skill worthy of an old parliamentarian" and had proved herself to be the peer of any man at the Fair in her capacity for business and enthusiastic devotion to her work.

However, Mrs. Hooker soon piped another tune. She criticized Mrs. Palmer's method of selecting committees. She accused her of being cavalier about accepting the advice of women seasoned in long campaigns. She thought the Southern states should have better representation on the committees. But above all she raged over the dismissal of Phoebe Couzins, whom she had backed for the secretaryship. In the midst of all the luxury and approval of her stay in London Bertha opened her mail one morning and found an insulting tirade from Mrs. Hooker. The board, which should have used its power to bring honor to all womanhood, had been "practically annihilated," wrote the aged suffragist. She would not criticize her in public, Mrs. Hooker added. She would simply resign and she had no wish to meet her face to face to discuss the situation, as Mrs. Palmer had proposed.

Bertha was mollifying at first, remembering that Mrs. Hooker was about to celebrate her golden wedding anniversary. But after a few more letters she grew indignant. To say that the board was "practically annihilated" was nothing short of ridiculous, she pointed out, when every day she had practical evidence that it was growing in power and prestige. She felt that she was in a better position than anyone to judge its status at that time. Mrs. Palmer assured Mrs. Hooker that she was well aware from the bylaws that she could be dropped from the board at any moment, and added: "I beg you to believe, my dear Mrs. Hooker, that you do me great injustice in thinking that I have one standard of justice for myself and another for others."

But the wrangling went on, with Mrs. Palmer sitting at the top of the tree and refusing to get herself entangled in the poisonous weeds of controversy. Mrs. Logan scolded her for indulging Mrs. Hooker, whom she considered the most dangerous element in their board, and "full of parliamentary trickery and dodges that she would not hesitate to use to further her peculiar notions." Mrs. Julia Ward Howe quickly came to Bertha's support, recalling some of her own bitter experiences when running the woman's end of the Cotton Exposition in New Orleans. The suffragists with whom she worked had always been against Miss Couzins, she told her soothingly, finding her "full of conceit, arrogance and assumption." She quoted the Apostle Paul on Mary Lockwood, the author who served on the history, literature and education committee of the board, as being a lady of "sounding brass." Mrs. Lockwood had backed Miss Couzins' appointment but her letters to Mrs. Palmer were aglow with flattery and applause.

Mary commented on the chairman's tranquil exterior during the uproar that prevailed at the September meeting in 1891, when Phoebe Couzins and other controversial issues came under discussion. Mrs. Palmer, who never in her life indulged in a public scene, had gone the length of saying in an outraged tone: "Certain ladies mortify me." A few of the board members had wept over the abuse leveled at their leader. In the midst of it all, one woman jumped to her feet, waved her arms toward Mrs. Palmer and cried excitedly: "You— our queen." The chairman of the board drove home that night quite clearly the victor.

In the midst of all this uproar Mrs. Palmer was hostess to Mrs. Ulysses S. Grant for the unveiling of the equestrian statue of the General in Lincoln Park on October 7, 1891. Together they watched the remains of the Army of the Tennessee march past as they sat under an awning on the Palmer porte-cochere. Flags floated from the tower and the stone walls were checkered with streamers of red, white and blue. When Mrs. Grant moved from her seat to get a better view of the ships on the lake which were firing salutes, the crowd came to life with a tremendous ovation.

The fourth division of the parade halted in front of the house and she and Mrs. Palmer rode the rest of the way with the soldiers, applauded all along the route of march. It was Mrs. Grant's first visit to Chicago since her return from her world tour with the General and there was great interest in the widow's appearance at the unveiling ceremonies. Afterward a reception was held at the Palmer House, with the veterans bowing one by one over Mrs. Grant's lace-mittened hand. Mrs. Palmer made it clear to all that no allusion should be made to the past, lest she break down. Potter Palmer drove her personally to and from the station when she came to share in one of Chicago's biggest memorial days.

By this time Mrs. Palmer's name was constantly in the papers. She had become a prominent national figure. Her board of 115 women included physicians, temperance workers, suffragists, business women, lawyers, artists, writers, community leaders and the wives of prominent men. It was a heterogeneous group difficult to fuse into a whole, and a number of the professional women were inclined to view their chairman at first as a wealthy dilettante until they felt the lash of her whip. She told them briskly at the outset that they must leave the narrow boundaries of their individual lives and give their hearts and minds to the aspirations of others. She wanted no drones in her camp. Anyone who could not give full time to the work must say so at once. As she saw it, they were all entering on a larger sisterhood.

They were soon aware that a formidable figure had risen among them—a woman who showed up at their meetings dressed in the height of fashion, with jewels, soft speech and a persuasive way when points had to be won, either from men or women. She was a new type for this sort of work and they expected her to bend under pressure. But she stood firm and worked harder than any of them. She mowed down opposition or zoomed over it with bland superiority. Many were seasoned campaigners but she had the advantage of a subtle approach and her husband's great fortune behind her. She quickly learned her own lessons in strategy and felt the power of her position. Temperamentally, she was ambitious, tireless and keen. But, above all, Bertha Palmer had radiant health and vitality. No one who knew her intimately ever heard her say that she had a headache, or felt depressed, or had aches and pains, until the last months of her life, when she lived in perpetual anguish. She was usually too busy to give much thought to minor ills affecting the body. It was her habit to be on the job, early and late, her attention focused on a thousand details. Others around her grew tired and faltered. But she pushed on and pushed them with her.

There were times when the commissioners as a whole wished that Mrs. Palmer and her board were at the bottom of the lake. She waged her battles so convincingly that she frequently put them in the wrong. She had to stand up to the National Columbian Commission, representing all the states, and to the

Directory, which built the Fair. Although conceding the necessity for a board of women, neither body was willing to share labors and honors with them, nor to grant them any but a decorative role. They were not given representation on the joint committee which actually governed the Exposition. No funds were allotted them at first. Their only privilege in the beginning was the right of representation on award juries. But Mrs. Palmer ignored the implications that the Woman's Building was a negligible quantity and set out to make it the most distinctive area of the Fair.

She had to wring every concession from this reluctant group, some of whom knew her well on the social front. Their soft-voiced hostess surprised some of the Fair's commissioners in defending the interests of women so vigorously. They found her shrewd, unyielding and imperturbable as she demanded places on the award committees, more space for exhibitors, independence of action, larger funds and full recognition for the Woman's Building. She went to Springfield in the teeth of the gale over Miss Couzins and talked the legislators into an appropriation of eighty thousand dollars. She went to Washington and blitzed the Congressional Investigation Committee of the Fair. Mrs. Logan had warned her that Congress did not "receive suggestions from ladies favorably." But she charmed Senator J. W. Candler, chairman of the Fair committee, and his fellow Senators with her eloquence and pragmatism. She talked fluently of the utility and value of the women's plans; of the worldwide interest they would create through bringing exhibits from every country and presenting evidence of woman's status throughout the world.

When Mrs. Potter Palmer walked into an office, in molded bodice and trim hat, with all her vitality, dash and soft-voiced eloquence, she overrode opposition. After two meetings with the committee, the site and an appropriation of $200,000 were voted for a woman's building. When questioned by Daniel Burnham, chief of construction for the Fair buildings, about her wish to have a woman architect design their section, she whipped out a silver pencil and rapidly sketched the interior arrangement of a building two hundred by five hundred feet. A contest was soon under way to find the woman architect.

One of her toughest battles was fought over awards. She thought the artisan should be recognized as well as the manufacturer. Excited exhibitors called on Mrs. Palmer to expostulate. The official heads of the Exposition united to protest and objections were forwarded to Congress. She wrote to members of both Houses explaining the motives for her stand. The commissioners were then forced to beg an audience with her. They were arguing the matter when a telegram arrived for her from Washington.

She let the commissioners talk on. They insisted that Congress should await their pleasure on the issue. At last she quietly announced: "Well, gentlemen, it seems impossible for us to agree on this point, and there is really no need of further discussion, for I am informed that the proposed measure is now a law." She handed the commissioners the telegram she had been holding. In the end the "diploma of honorable mention" for which she had fought resulted in great popularity among the workers for the board of lady managers.

Soon after that she was able to report to the board on the advances made in the first year. Congress had given a liberal appropriation. The Directory had approved their building. The Fair Commission had given them the right to take entire charge of all women's interests, whether in their own building or elsewhere. By this time they had more scope and power than they had expected. The seeds that Mrs. Palmer had planted in Europe were bearing fruit, too. Theodore Stanton wrote to her just before Christmas, 1891, that Proust was working hard for her and that her work would be discussed at a banquet Frederic Bartholdi was giving at the Hotel Continental for Whitelaw Reid.

She urged George P. A. Healy to try his persuasion on the

Queen of Rumania on behalf of the lady managers. Healy said he would but wrote to Mrs. Palmer: "We are told not to put our trust in Princes, but this lady, like yourself, is an exception to all rules." She invited the Archduchess Maria Theresa of Austria to come to the Fair. She called from time to time on President Benjamin Harrison to keep his interest alight in the doings of the lady managers. His daughter, Mrs. J. R. McKee, always welcomed her cordially at the White House, which at that time was overflowing with women relatives of the Harrison family. The President's daughter-in-law, Mrs. Russell Harrison, was on Mrs. Palmer's board and they were good friends.

The lady managers functioned from a utilitarian office in the Rand-McNally Building. Mrs. Palmer was in her element, directing operations and keeping a sharp eye on the larger issues. She was a good executive and with a quick flick of her pen would delegate work where it belonged. The board was flooded with requests of every kind, but Bertha adopted a tough policy in selecting personnel for the state committees. She sounded out their capacities and tastes. Women wrote of their knowledge of floriculture, horticulture, needlework, the domestic arts, music, letters, ceramics, laces and handicrafts in volunteering for state committee work. They professed a little knowledge of French, of German, of drawing, of carpentry, of cooking, of products done in wood, stone, glass, marble and granite. Nearly all limited their choice to three or four committees, involving philanthropy, decorative art, music or education. Mrs. Palmer was delighted when one woman showed an interest in the Department of Fisheries and another volunteered for work in the electrical division.

She pleaded for fresh thought and ingenuity instead of the time-worn type of exhibit. She was cold to benevolence in selecting offerings. She wanted the best of everything and a solid showing. The sentimental and charitable point of view, she told her board, must be subdued to marked excellence, "without reference to the private sorrows of the producers." Otherwise the Woman's Building would represent the incapacity rather than the competence of their sex.

All too many wrote about inherited laces, about linen spun by their mothers and tatting done by Great Aunt Matilda. Indigent ladies with good family connections sprang up from everywhere. Friends, relatives, strangers, pulled every string to get in on the wonders of the Fair. "Thank very much for picture sent very good of all of them—shall value it highly and it was very kind of her to send it," Mrs. Palmer wrote in her dashing script across the back of an envelope for the benefit of her secretary. Susan B. Anthony begged for more floor space for the suffragists and got it. "I knew if it were in your power you would give us room commensurate with our proportions," Miss Anthony wrote approvingly. She and Anna Howard Shaw were two of the suffrage leaders who worked well with Mrs. Palmer. Mrs. Margaret F. Sullivan objected to the lady managers being presented as holding Queen Victoria in "deep and universal esteem and admiration" in connection with the Countess of Aberdeen's cottage industries. She, for one, felt that the Queen had "not been helpful to women although England is ready to follow any lead in that direction."

Mrs. Palmer settled each request with a quick decision. She was urged to make speeches, to travel to different places. Soon she was the focal point of a growing empire. Saint-Gaudens selected the seal used by the board of lady managers from designs sent in by women. He also approved the official badge bearing the motto "*Juncti valemus* (United we prevail)." There was trouble about the Isabella coin, however, for the women felt that a kneeling figure, with a distaff in her hand, was not in the spirit of the contemporary woman.

But Mrs. Palmer's great triumph was the Woman's Building itself. It overlooked the lagoon and was designed in the style of the Italian Renaissance, with balconies, loggias and touches of gold to relieve its snowy interior. The winner of the contest was Miss Sophia G. Hayden, a graduate of the Massachusetts School of Technology. This young woman was the first of her sex to design an important public building in the United States and when she had changed some of her original plans and added a roof garden at Mrs. Palmer's request, Richard M. Hunt, president of the Society of American Architects, was enthusiastic in his approval of the Woman's Building. The board had voluntarily relinquished the chance to have it designed by Hunt, in order to show their confidence in the ability of their own sex.

The building was two stories high and had land and water entrances. Its Hall of Honor, unbroken by supports, rose seventy feet in height and was inscribed in gold with the names of women great in art, in music, in science, in stagecraft and in letters. Side by side with the sovereigns of Europe— Isabella, Elizabeth and Victoria—were the names of the workers, the seers, the pioneers.

It was Mrs. Palmer who suggested the general plan of the interior and entrusted its decoration to women sculptors and painters. A girl of twenty-two made the models of the caryatids supporting the cornice of the roof garden, and women decorators, wood carvers and other specialists were invited to submit their work to the board. Mrs. Palmer thought she was particularly fortunate in having the brilliant Mary Cassatt do one of her murals. Her name was quite unknown in the United States at this time although her reputation among French artists was growing. She was a rich American girl who had shed the conservatism of her Philadelphia home and gone abroad to study art in Italy. By this time she was part of the artistic set in Paris and the friend of Degas. The sight of one of his pictures in an art dealer's shop window had changed her life. "I saw art then as I wanted to see it," she wrote to Mrs. H. O. Havemeyer. After that she worked hard to get the paintings of the Barbizon school and the Impressionists into the drawing rooms of affluent Americans. She and Degas quarreled and made up, and argued and admired each other's work, and between them gave modern art fresh impetus.

Mrs. Palmer had no hesitancy about giving Miss Cassatt the commission. An American woman artist endowed with real talent made an irresistible combination to this quick-witted impresario. Not having space like Frederick MacMonnies, who was using four studios to make his fountain for the Fair, with scaffolding and a score of assistants to help him put through his colossal project, Miss Cassatt built a large glass-roofed building at her summer home. Rather than work on a ladder she had the canvas lowered into an excavation in the ground when she wished to work on the upper part of her painting.

Sara Hallowell was so sure of Mary Cassatt's technique that she let her alone to work as she wished. "Since Miss Cassatt makes no sketch, it is all right to leave her work to my approval, but so far as Mrs. MacMonnies is concerned, I think it better for her to submit a sketch since she makes no objection to doing so," Sara wrote to Mrs. Palmer.

In the end Miss Cassatt's mural was called *Modern Woman* and Mary MacMonnies' *Primitive Woman*. There was some apprehension among board members about the Cassatt contribution. Would it be freakish, or shocking, or an offense to the conventional-minded? In the end there were no raised eyebrows over the flat, inconspicuous figures adorned with pastoral symbols. Miss Cassatt's mural has since been lost to view.

Twenty-five of the panels in the Woman's Building were the work of American women and they were among the most discussed features of the Fair. The building was finished for forty thousand dollars less than the appropriation. This sum was then absorbed for interior finishing. When the National Commission, out of funds, sought to apply the woman's surplus to general use Mrs. Palmer appealed to the Treasury Department, which promptly gave her board full control of its appropriations, including the hundred thousand dollars allowed for awards. By this time her business acumen had become an irritant to the directorate.

As the building approached completion the caryatids and pediments done by women were placed in position and Mrs. Palmer reported to her board on October 18, 1892: "While our building is smaller and less expensive than most of the others, its scholarly composition, beautiful proportions, refined and reserved details, hold their own, even when considered in comparison with the ornate creations of the great architects represented on the Exposition grounds. It is remarkable as being the first creation of a young girl."

All around the Woman's Building other snowy edifices were going up. The Greek motif had been agreed on for the Exposition, so that a White City rose like a mirage along the lake's south shore. It covered an area of 586 acres in Jackson Park. The Midway, a narrow strip of ground a mile long, connected it with Washington Park. Frederick L. Olmsted and his partner, Henry Sargent Codman, directed the landscaping and soon winding walks, drives and waterways, avenues, statuary, fountains and bridges spread over the waste area. Aquatic plants lined the waterways. A citrus grove, a peach garden and a cranberry patch became part of the scene.

The nation's leading architects, sculptors and painters worked under the direction of the dynamic and businesslike Burnham in putting together the Columbian Exposition. As she went to the grounds to study the progress of her own building Mrs. Palmer had many friendly exchanges with Richard M. Hunt, Louis H. Sullivan, Charles F. McKim, William R. Mead, John Wellborn Root and William Le Baron Jenney. Being artists they were all interested in what the lady managers were up to, and no one at the Fair was likely to ignore Mrs. Potter Palmer. They dined at her home. They listened to her views. Sometimes they told her frankly what they thought of her building. There were those who said it was too clearly a copy, but she stood behind Miss Hayden until

Hunt led the chorus of applause. The sculptors whose work embellished the buildings and grounds included Saint-Gaudens, Frederick W. MacMonnies, Daniel Chester French, Paul W. Bartlett, Karl T. F. Bitter and Lorado Taft.

Saint-Gaudens called it "the greatest gathering of artists since the fifteenth century" when they all assembled at Kinsley's. They worked through blizzards and summer storms, only half-believing that the buildings could rise in two years from the sand dunes, wild-oak ridges and icy swamps that they first surveyed in January, 1891. Root died almost as soon as the work began. The others lived and slept for the Fair and had a summer camp where they clustered in groups suggestive of the Latin Quarter. Eighteen workmen were killed and there were seven hundred accidents before the domes and towers of a dozen exhibition halls and more than two hundred smaller buildings were ready for dedication. Saint-Gaudens pronounced the Palace of Fine Arts, designed by Charles B. Atwood, the "greatest achievement since the Parthenon." It later became the home of the Field Columbian Museum and in 1933 the Museum of Science and Industry.

Next to the Woman's Building rose the Children's Building, also largely the work of the board of lady managers. Mrs. Palmer threw open her home in December, 1892, for the Columbian Bazaar of All Nations, organized to raise funds for this extra edifice. The bazaar in itself was a miniature fair. For three days the public trooped through the rooms of the Palmer mansion and a good many silver spoons went out with them. The sum of $35,000 was raised for the cause, however. Mothers and educators all over the country worked for this building and every child who subscribed received a printed certificate stamped with the gold seal of the board.

The dedication ceremonies for the Exposition as a whole were held on October 20, 21 and 22, 1892, and began with a great ball and banquet at which Mrs. Palmer presided like a queen, gowned in yellow satin and velvet. A watchful reporter of the period wrote that she rose like a calla lily from puffs of velvet, gleaming with crystal and gold embroidery. Ropes of magnificent pearls hung from her throat. Her dark hair was crowned with a diamond tiara. She led a parade of patronesses who trooped in to the "Coronation March" played by Sousa's Band. The procession was a long and brilliant one, with the colors of Ferdinand and Isabella in flags, in costumes, in lights. Edison's invention was still a novel plaything to the crowds.

Next day was gray and cloudy as General Nelson A. Miles led a great parade to Jackson Park. School children marched with Civil War veterans. Bands played and the streets were alive with color. Stores had massive tableaux on their fronts celebrating in one way or another Columbus' discovery of America four hundred years earlier. The buildings were only half-finished and the Fair grounds still looked chaotic when the main dedication ceremony was held in the Manufacturers Building. Cardinal Gibbons blessed the Exposition. Chauncey M. Depew delivered the Columbian oration with a graceful bow to the lady managers. "It was a happy omen of the position which woman was to hold in America," he said, "that the only person who comprehended the majestic scope of his plans, and the invincible quality of his genius, was the able and gracious Queen of Castile."

A chorus of five hundred had just thundered the "Hallelujah Chorus" and the "Columbia March" when Mrs. Potter Palmer was presented by the director general of the Exposition. Great applause burst out as she stood before them, not tall, yet quite impressive in her bearing. She picked up Chauncey Depew's theme and smartly made the point that inspired though the visions of Columbus might have been, he needed the aid of an Isabella to transform them into realities. The crowd listened in absolute silence as she announced in low melodic tones that official representation for women on so important an occasion was unprecedented. The group she represented was worldwide in scope. Its basic intention was to create public sentiment in favor of woman's industrial equality with man. Mrs. Palmer's speech was neither high-flown nor rhetorical. She confined herself to simple statements of fact, finishing with a slight nip and a note of challenge: "Even more important than the discovery of Columbus, which we are gathered together to celebrate, is the fact that the General Government has just discovered woman."

The Woman's Building was duly blessed in its white sanctity and the crowd of 75,000 scattered. Chicago by this time had more than a million inhabitants, with the German element predominating. But twenty-seven other nationalities were present in the crowd that surveyed the rising buildings of the Fair. The city had been growing up in the days since Bertha Honoré first saw it in 1855. Thirty-seven years had passed and she had watched many changes. The Woman's Temple of red granite and brick now towered at La Salle and Monroe streets. The Pullman building was a landmark, and the Rookery, eleven stories high, had thirteen thousand people moving through its doors each day.

Chicago by this time had more than two thousand miles of streets and covered nearly eighteen thousand acres. There were seventy-five miles of drives and the boulevard system that Henry Honoré had fostered circled the city, with many handsome parks interlocking. Lincoln Park stretched along Lake Michigan for at least two miles and its drives, its walks, its monuments, its inland lake, palm house, mineral spring and racing boulevard, drew thousands every month. There were open-air concerts, with Verdi, Strauss and Wagnerian music to delight the crowds that gathered. Charles T. Yerkes' electric fountain tossing sprays of prismatically illuminated water was still a nine-day wonder. The city had thirty-two good theaters, and concerts and lectures were given at the Central Music Hall. Opera was an accepted fact by the population and there was growing interest in art.

Michigan Avenue, where Bertha had lived when she married Potter Palmer, was a blaze of color as carriages bowled along it on the day of the dedication ceremonies. It was still a fashionable thoroughfare but as she drove under her own porte-cochere on Lake Shore Drive she had little doubt that the Exposition would further speed the development of Chicago and add to the city's fame. It would also give luster to the name of Mrs. Potter Palmer.

5

⟫⟫⟫⟫⟫⟫⟫⟫⟫⟫⟫⟫ *World's Columbian Exposition*

President Cleveland pushed an electric button at the Columbian Exposition on a May morning in 1893. The flags of forty-seven nations broke out simultaneously and whipped briskly in the breeze off the lake. The standard of Castile flew over the Administration Building beside the Stars and Stripes. The White City quivered with life. The Mac-Monnies fountain, with its rowing maidens, gushed sparkling water. Draperies slipped from the Statue of Liberty, leaving the colossal gilded figure in high relief. Guns boomed from warships in the harbor. Foghorns and sirens blasted through the triumphant music of the brass bands.

A massive flood of energy was let loose by the President's simple gesture. The crowd that filled the Plaza and Grand Court cheered as wheels began to revolve and life to possess the leviathan Fair. Launches darted under the bridges. Gondolas filled with passengers rocked on the lagoons. Doves wheeled through a flood of sunlight that split the banks of gray clouds.

Half a million people had crowded into the grounds to see the Exposition officially opened on May 1. They had come by train and ship, by carriage, wagon and streetcar, by horseback and on foot. The domes and turrets of the miraculous city loomed pearly gray through the heavy fog that lifted at the crucial moment of the opening. Sailors on the roofs who had controlled the outbreak of flags and banners relaxed. The crowds began to flow through the buildings, with quick impact as the wonders of the Fair were disclosed, from the Liberty Bell brought by special train from Philadelphia to the Queen of Italy's ancient laces in the Woman's Building.

Mrs. Palmer had driven to the grounds with the Duchess of Veragua. She was in the twentieth carriage on a day heavy with officialdom. President Cleveland headed the procession in Cyrus H. McCormick's monogrammed carriage, driven by chestnut and light bay horses with gold-plated harness. Harlow N. Higinbotham, president of the Columbian Exposition, rode with him, his lean bearded face already a familiar sight to the people of Chicago. Potter Palmer's two most magnificent carriages came next, with the Duke of Veragua and his entourage.

Gray-coated park policemen on big horses kept the crowd in order. Bugles blew as the troops swung into line, with capes thrown back to show yellow facings. Sabers were drawn for the salute and thousands cheered as the entourage moved along the Plaisance and up to the platform in front of the Administration Building. Umbrellas were folded as the sun came out and Mrs. Palmer, with Lyman J. Gage and Ferdinand W. Peck, escorted the Duchess to her place.

After the opening ceremony a luncheon was held indoors in a hall decorated with palms and Easter lilies. The guests sat at a circular table with Mrs. Palmer facing President Cleveland and the Duchess at her right. Toasts were drunk to the visitors from Spain. They lunched on consommé, soft-shell crabs, julienne potatoes, cucumbers, filet mignon, French peas, broiled snipe, celery and potato salad, strawberries and cream, cheese and crackers, Roman punch and champagne. But before cheese and coffee were served Mrs. Palmer whispered to the Duchess that they must move on for the formal opening of the Woman's Building, which was to follow the general ceremonies. The women rose in a body, creating confusion. Guests thought the luncheon was ended but the President sat down again to enjoy his cheese and coffee as Mrs. Palmer led her guests in a solemn parade to the Woman's Building. The dairymaids and salesgirls from the Irish village in the Plaisance waited to give the President a blackthorn stick and Lady Aberdeen produced a lace handkerchief made by the Irish girls for Mrs. Cleveland.

It was now Mrs. Palmer's turn to preside. The Duchess of Veragua was accompanied by Señora Dupuy de Loma and Señorita Maria del Pilar. Britain was represented by the Countess of Aberdeen, Mrs. Bedford-Fenwick and Mrs. Roberts-Austen. Princess Schahowskoy brought greetings from the Empress of Russia and Phra Linchee Suriya from the Queen of Siam. All the contributing nations had sent women of note to the Exposition. Their costumes and assorted languages gave life to the gathering.

The main gallery was not large enough to hold those who crowded in for the dedication. The Theodore Thomas orchestra played a jubilate composed for the occasion by Mrs. H. H. Beach of Boston, since the board had decreed that all offerings must be the work of women. A silver laurel wreath was handed to Mrs. Palmer, along with a gold nail to hammer into the building for the "golden touch." When withdrawn the nail made the crossbar of a brooch given her by the women of Montana, with such state symbolism as the official seal, a mountain, a waterfall, a farmer, a prospector, a rake and a pick.

"The day of fruition has arrived," said Mrs. Palmer, looking around at the imposing gathering of women. She wore a Paris gown of heliotrope and black crepe, studded with jet nailheads and threaded with gold passementerie. Her hat was

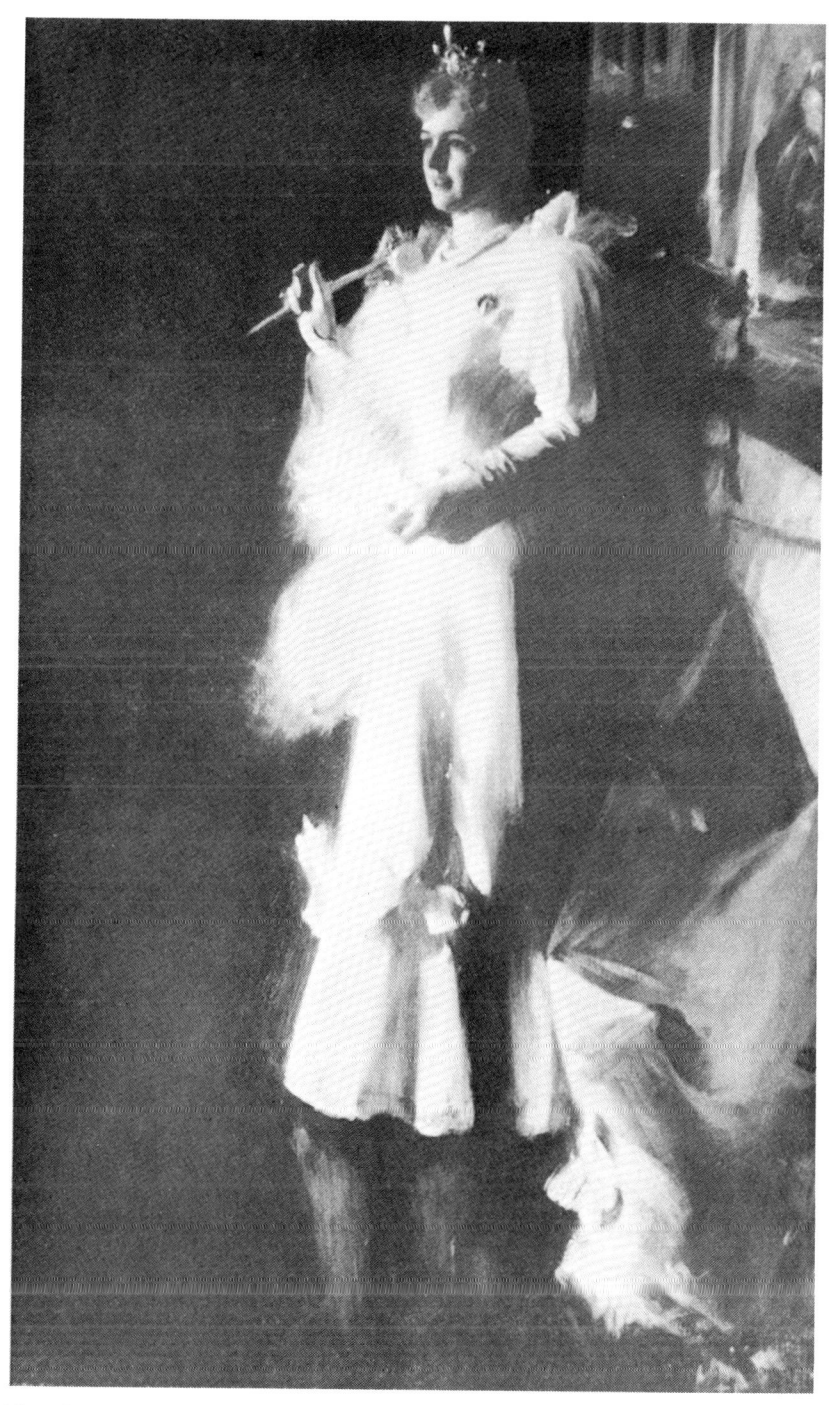

Mrs. Potter Palmer. (Portrait by Anders Leonard Zorn. Potter Palmer Collection, Courtesy of The Art Institute of Chicago)

Mrs. Henry Hamilton Honoré, mother of Mrs. Potter Palmer. (Portrait by J. C. Gorman. Courtesy of Major General Ulysses S. Grant III, Frick Art Reference Library)

Henry Hamilton Honoré, father of Mrs. Potter Palmer. (Engraving, courtesy Chicago Historical Society)

Bertha Mathilde Honoré as a young girl. (Courtesy Chicago Historical Society)

Ida Honoré, sister of Bertha, who later became Mrs. Frederick Dent Grant. (Courtesy Chicago Historical Society)

The great fire at Chicago, October 8, 1871. (Currier & Ives, courtesy Chicago Historical Society)

Panic-stricken citizens rushing past the Sherman House, carrying the aged, sick and helpless, and endeavoring to save family treasures. (*Frank Leslie's Illustrated Weekly*, October 28, 1871, courtesy Chicago Historical Society)

Mrs. Potter Palmer in 1893, as chairman of the Board of Lady Managers of the World's Columbian Exposition. (Courtesy The Art Institute of Chicago)

Potter Palmer in 1868, shortly before he married Bertha Honoré. (By John Carbutt, courtesy Chicago Historical Society)

The Grant-Honoré wedding in Chicago; center, above, residence of the bride's parents where wedding took place; below, left, the wedding reception; below, right, the wedding supper. (Sketches in *The Daily Graphic*, New York,

Mrs. Potter Palmer (right) with her sister, Mrs. Frederick Dent Grant, at the Palmer country house outside Chicago. Children, left to right: Julia Grant, Honoré Palmer, Potter (Min) Palmer, Jr. (Courtesy Major General Ulysses S. Grant III)

Mrs. Palmer with Honoré in Little Lord Fauntleroy suit. (By Steffins, courtesy Chicago Historical Society)

Mrs. Frederick Dent Grant. (Portrait by George P. A. Healy, courtesy Major General Ulysses S. Grant III. Frick Art Reference Library)

Princess Cantacuzène in 1907, the year in which she and her aunt, Mrs. Potter Palmer, were being entertained at Biarritz by King Edward VII.

Mrs. Palmer shortly after her husband's death in 1902. (By Steffins, courtesy Chicago Historical Society)

Tropical Garden on the Roof, Palmer House, Chicago. (Lithograph, about 1873, courtesy Chicago Historical Society)

Tally-Ho going to the Washington Park Derby in 1870. Potter Palmer sits on the box seat in front. (Engraving, courtesy Chicago Historical Society)

Woman's Building designed by Sophia G. Hayden for World's Columbian Exposition in 1893. (By C. D. Arnold, courtesy Chicago Historical Society)

View from the balcony of the Woman's Building. (Painting by Francis Coates Jones, courtesy Chicago Historical Society)

Potter Palmer mansion on Lake Shore Drive in 1890, when it was only five years old and had not yet been softened by ivy and the patina of time. (Courtesy Chicago Historical Society)

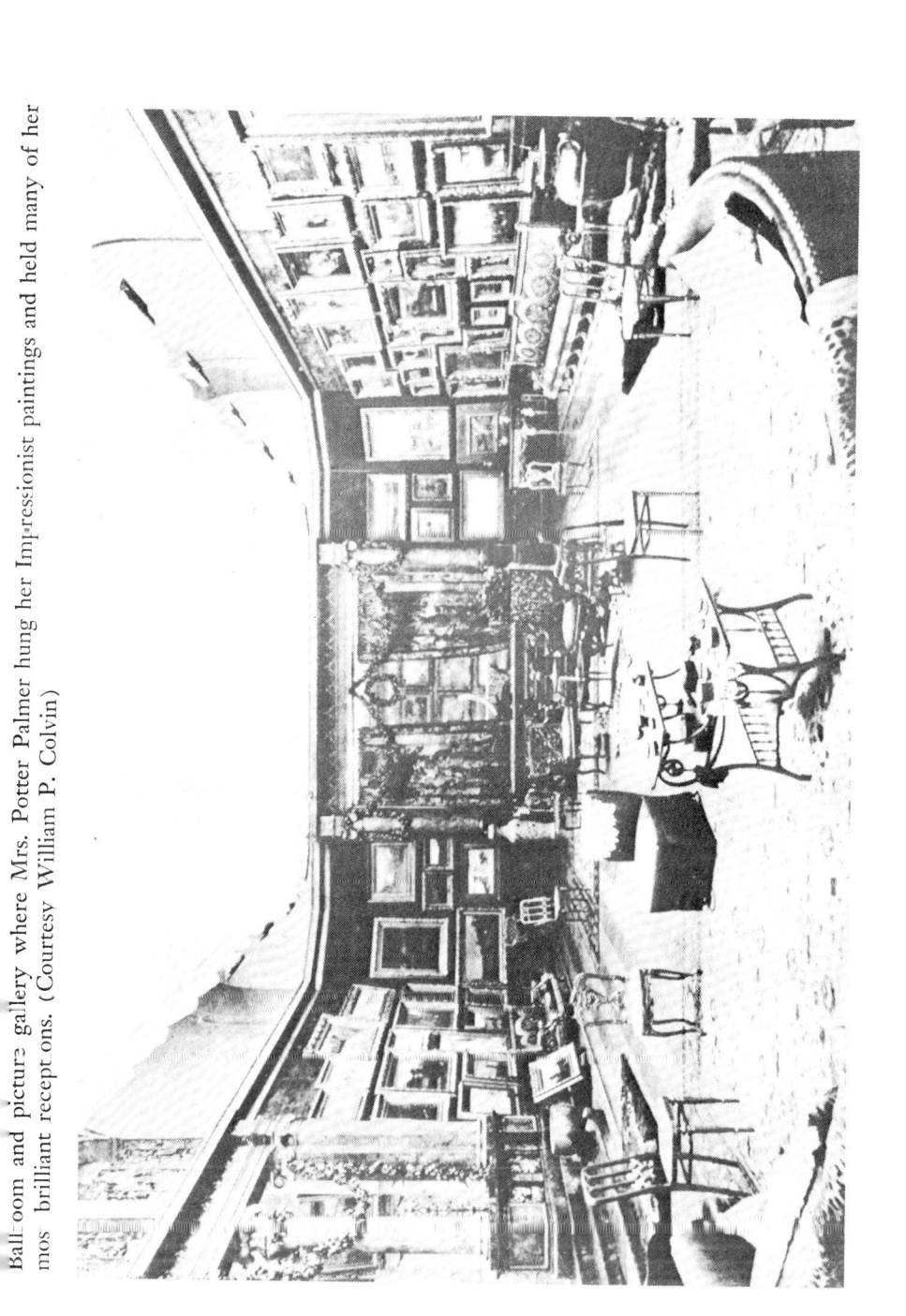

Ballroom and picture gallery where Mrs. Potter Palmer hung her Impressionist paintings and held many of her most brilliant receptions. (Courtesy William P. Colvin)

Main gallery of Potter Palmer mansion. (Courtesy Chicago Historical Society)

Library, showing carved oak decorations and Tiffany chandeliers. (Courtesy William B. Colvin)

Mrs. Potter Palmer, wearing her famous pink pearl as a pendant. (Courtesy Chicago Historical Society)

Potter Palmer. (By Steffins, courtesy Chicago Historical Society)

The Oaks—Mrs. Palmer's house at Osprey, Florida. (Courtesy Chicago Historical Society)

of heliotrope velvet with black ostrich tips and jet trimming, and her white broadcloth wrap was lined with white satin. She was now forty-four and her hair had turned prematurely gray. It was beautifully coiffed, and the effect with her dark eyes and clear skin was striking. Women from the ends of the earth gazed at her with frank admiration as she addressed them in a quiet, persuasive manner.

Her speech was largely a protest against the forced dependence and helplessness of women. She ranged the field, touching on social abuses, poor pay, inadequate education. It was neither "unfeminine nor monstrous" to compete with men in lucrative industries, said Mrs. Palmer. She deplored overdone chivalry and the tendency to put women on a pedestal. "Freedom and justice for all are infinitely more to be desired than pedestals for a few," she observed. The Exposition should benefit their sex as a whole through the interchange of thought and sympathy among the influential women of all countries, "now for the first time working together with a common purpose and an established means of communication."

She emphasized the delicacy, symmetry and strength of their building, complimenting the women who had given it its grace, and those around the world who had provided its exhibits. "Looms have wrought their most delicate fabrics; the needle has flashed in the hands of maidens under tropical suns, the lacemaker has bent over her cushion weaving her most artful web, the brush and chisel have sought to give form and reality to the visions haunting the brain of the artist—all have wrought with the thought of making our building worthy to serve its great end," said Mrs. Palmer. "We now dedicate the Woman's Building to an elevated womanhood—knowing that by so doing we shall best serve the cause of humanity."

But her colleagues were not yet uplifted enough to refrain from petty bickering among themselves. Bertha had to point out the folly of their getting excited over the fact that she had kept the Duchess of Veragua so much to herself, and had not introduced them individually to this noted guest. Some thought it pretentious of her to ride in the carriage with Spanish nobility. To make matters worse, in spite of all Mrs. Palmer's tact and good will a second visitor from Spain gave her the most deadly and talked-about snub of her entire career. None could fathom the behavior of the Infanta Eulalia of Spain to the Queen of Chicago. It was the social feud of the decade in the United States and its repercussions were heard in Europe.

The Infanta arrived in Chicago in June to represent the Queen Regent of Spain and to give prestige to the Spanish section of the Exposition. No efforts were spared to do her honor and there was much talk of the pomp the occasion demanded. The officials had been warned that their visitor would expect the utmost deference. Mayor Carter Harrison was advised to replace his slouch hat with a silk topper when he met her at the station. President Higinbotham turned up in full dress for the breakfast given in her honor by the Mayor.

Mrs. Palmer, of course, was admirably prepared to cope with every eventuality. She had already sent her personal table silver and her gold plate to the Palmer House for the Infanta's use while she stayed there. She had superintended the preparation of the royal suite. The visitor had an Egyptian parlor and a massive bed inlaid with mother-of-pearl, since the craze for Near East and Oriental décor was at its height. A private staff of waiters, chambermaids and bellboys was assigned to her. All was in order and good taste. Mrs. Palmer had invited the cream of Chicago society and all the Exposition officials and commissioners from abroad to a reception at her home in honor of the visitor from Spain.

But the Infanta was a problem from the start. She walked into the Spanish Building over a carpet strewn with pansies, showing a minimum of interest in anything around her. She declared the building officially open and attended receptions and dinners, as well as Mayor Harrison's jolly breakfast, spiked with champagne and Roman punch. An individualist till the day she died, the Infanta lit up a cigarette, to the horror of those around her. And somewhere along the way she learned that Mrs. Potter Palmer was the wife of the owner of the Palmer House.

"An innkeeper's wife!" she exclaimed scornfully. Of course, she could not go to a reception at her home. But the Spanish Ambassador talked to her in private and explained that one did not flout Mrs. Potter Palmer in Chicago.

The Infanta, who preferred that her name be pronounced "Ay-oo-lay-lya," with all its Spanish inflections, was not impressed. She finally went to Palmer Castle on the evening of June 9 but arrived in a fury. Moreover, she was an hour late because she had again jibbed at going when she found that no one had provided a scarlet carpet or canopy for her at the hotel entrance. She went back upstairs and had to be coaxed to set forth again, stepping out into a storm with only a large black umbrella to protect her white satin gown and slippers from the rain. Barbarous Chicago! The Infanta was tired, cross and hostile when she walked into Mrs. Palmer's magnificent home, where a dais had been set up in the ballroom for her use.

Her hostess suavely began a round of presentations but Eulalia neither smiled nor bowed. She glared at each friendly face that swam into view and made no acknowledgment of the introductions. Neither the gorgeous Mrs. Palmer nor the international gathering she had assembled made any impression on the sulky Princess. The arts were represented as well as the state and the Army. Among those whom she visibly cold-shouldered were Adlai E. Stevenson, Vice President of the United States; General Nelson A. Miles, Robert Todd Lincoln, Theodore Stanton, Marshall Field, George M. Pullman, Philip D. Armour, Paran Stevens, Sir Henry Wood, Leslie Carter, F. Hopkinson Smith, Julia Ward Howe, Maud Elliott Howe, Anders L. Zorn, the Governors of New York State and Kentucky, an assortment of Russian princes and distinguished representatives of countries from France to Siam. Outside, the rain came down in slanting sheets and the *Daily Inter-Ocean* reported on June 10, 1893:

Early in the evening a great crowd gathered outside on the drive to see the gay company arrive. They blocked the way until the rainstorm came, and even then those who had umbrellas stood the splashing raindrops in hopes of seeing the infanta when she arrived. From 8 o'clock until after 10 they saw the carriages roll up; they saw the dazzling flashing of the lightning bring into prominence the castellated turrets. . . . Horse drivers shouted to their prancing horses; waterproofed footmen dashed here and there, doors clanged, and orders were buffeted back and forth. A cordon of policemen drawn around the lawn kept away intruders, and the gleam of calcium lights thrown up on the building brought the sharp corners of its architectural beauties into greater prominence.

In less than an hour after her arrival the Infanta cornered her hostess and everyone noticed signs of a storm. Her manner was one of protest and Mrs. Palmer looked pale but determined. Finally the Infanta whisked up her white satin train and flounced out into the rain, ignoring everyone in sight. The guests settled down to the delectable supper that had been prepared in honor of Eulalia. They drank champagne, talked, laughed and tried to cover up the fact that they had been witnesses to an incredible gaucherie involving Mrs. Potter Palmer. However, she met the situation with Spartan detachment and gave no visible sign of embarrassment but tactfully held the gathering in tow. She had nothing whatever to say about Eulalia. But the story quickly spread that there had been a sharp exchange between the two women. It was clear to everyone present that Eulalia had been openly rude to Mrs. Palmer and had virtually turned her back on the nation's most knowing hostess and her eminent guests.

The storm soon broke in the papers, although on the morning after the reception Eulalia and Mrs. Potter Palmer shared the front pages with the collapse of Ford's Theater in Washington and the death of twenty-two persons in the ruins, as well as a violent strike in the quarries of Lemont near Chicago, with many dead and injured. But the Infanta's behavior soon was discussed from coast to coast and in European circles, where Eulalia's eccentricities were a familiar tale. There were jests at Mrs. Palmer's expense and the cartoonists lampooned the encounter. The story took on exaggerated twists. It was gleefully related that the two women had occupied separate thrones in the ballroom, but that there had not been enough room under one roof for two such regal personages. It was more than rumor that the guests had been asked to bow and curtsy twice—once to the Infanta and once to their hostess. When some forgot their ballroom manners word went down the line that they must observe this rule. It was obviously maladroit to have the Infanta scowling and Mrs. Palmer beaming at the courteous guests, who were doing their best to bend their unpracticed knees.

By this time Eulalia, slightly exhilarated in mood, was showing quite openly how much the situation bored her. She had not expected to have to meet so many people and she had no more idea what Adlai Stevenson stood for than Marshall Field, or what made Julia Ward Howe so distinctive a figure. All these vulgar presentations were not what she had come for, and she did not welcome such bonhomie, either at Mrs. Palmer's or at the Fair. When she was invited to have luncheon in the Administration Building after a tour of the German village she refused to budge from where she was and said she would much prefer not to meet the committee. The members promptly turned their backs on her and disappeared into the New York State Building, to drown their chagrin in champagne.

Hobart Chatfield-Taylor, the Ambassador to Spain and a good friend of Mrs. Palmer's, was feeling somewhat desperate by this time. He marched the Infanta incognito through the Midway and this she greatly enjoyed. But before she left Chicago the coolness of those around her, the newspaper stories, the applause for Mrs. Palmer's dignified behavior and, perhaps most of all, the counsel of her anguished advisers made the Infanta behave herself. She was charm itself at the farewell dinner she gave for those who had entertained her. In the interests of harmony Mrs. Palmer attended, although she had pointedly canceled her box seats for the concert given in Festival Hall in Eulalia's honor the day after the disastrous reception.

Potter Palmer, too, showed his good manners. Much as he must have deplored the Infanta's treatment of his Cissie, his best coach-and-four took her to the depot and flowers strewed her path from the hotel to her carriage on the day of her departure. Clad in a light cloth costume and sailor hat, her dark eyes bright with mischief, she stepped jauntily into her coach and waved to the crowd that jammed the streets. More spectators had turned out for her departure than for her arrival. They had come to stare, not merely at the Infanta Eulalia, but at the woman who had dared to snub Mrs. Potter Palmer. The Saragossa Band played the Spanish anthem. Cavalry escorted the entourage to the depot. The Infanta confided to the genial Mayor Harrison as they drove along: "I wish that I could see Chicago thirty years from now. It is a great and beautiful city now, but in thirty years more it will be the grandest place on earth."

She had scattered four hundred dollars in ten-dollar gold pieces among the staff of the Palmer House. She had also left an unforgettable picture of herself in Chicago. Few memories of Mrs. Palmer took root in the public mind as did her encounter with the Infanta Eulalia. But the city applauded its leading lady and felt that she had shown the better spirit. The two antagonists met later in Europe and became good friends. By that time Eulalia had decided that Mrs. Potter Palmer was of some account since she had been received into King Edward VII's circle in London. And Bertha, always magnanimous in her outlook, bore her no malice. She had no objection to being called the innkeeper's wife. She was quite fond of the innkeeper.

Every day while the Fair lasted he called for her with his coach-and-four at five o'clock and drove her home after her day's work. The Woman's Building was the most discussed spot at the Fair because of its lively doings, its interest for women, and the presence of Mrs. Potter Palmer in a roomy office hung with nets made by New Jersey fisherwomen. She prided herself on the fact that it was not only the most cosmopolitan building at the Fair; it was also the most democratic, with linens embroidered by the insane women in a Pennsylvania almshouse as well displayed as the Queen of Belgium's *point d'Angleterre* gown, a triumph of the lacemaker's art.

Most absorbing of all to Mrs. Palmer were the crowds themselves. They came slowly at first, but by October it was plain that a fair portion of the American population had viewed the Fair. The tabulations had passed 27,000,000. They flocked in from all parts of the country as the summer wore on—women spruce in straw bonnets, basque bodices and leg-of-mutton sleeves, men in bowlers with curled brims, and children sprinting about the grounds in sailor hats and wide-collared suits. The young and the old, the rich and the poor, the sophisticated and the rustic enjoyed the Fair, which established itself in the memory as one of the wonders of the century. It fulfilled a great many dreams, and put together an album of period interest for everyone who visited it.

The Woman's Building blended usefulness with romance. The farm women rushed to see the model kitchen with its gas range and tiled floor. The variety of handicrafts exhibited was bewildering. Women were shown as the original homemakers and tillers of the soil, as millers, weavers and tanners, as seamstresses, tailors, potters and artists. Mrs. Palmer presided over a number of receptions and gave her own distinctive touch to each. Chicago gossiped when a prelate of the Roman Catholic Church took precedence over a long waiting line and was received at once by Mrs. Palmer at a reception given in the auditorium for the Congressional Committee of the Fair. "This was the first time that social Chicago had evidence of the fact that a 'Prince of the Church' ranks everyone except a sovereign," Mrs. Addie Hibbard Gregory noted. Mrs. Potter Palmer had made it so at the Fair.

All kinds of strange duties fell to her lot during the months she spent on her novel enterprise. The East had made fun of Chicago for daring to outbid it for the Exposition, commenting on "provincial manners and customs." But it was a woman from the East, accompanying the Congressional Committee, who nursed her baby in Mrs. Palmer's library, and not a Chicago woman. This made very good sense to the hostess, who was also happy to be godmother to an Eskimo baby born on the Fair grounds. The Horticultural Department developed a perfect white petunia and named it the Mrs. Potter Palmer. Foreign girls appealed to her for work, for food and lodging. They had heard of her from as far away as Constantinople. She set up a dormitory on a lot given by Pullman and more than twelve thousand women found shelter there and were conveyed back and forth by wagonette. Others were taken into her home.

Mrs. Palmer was ubiquitous and in supreme command. She had to cope with sixty women's organizations and the suffragists were always at hand to fight for their rights, from floor space to freedom of speech. Susan B. Anthony gave sage counsel to her fellow women, watched a baseball game with Mrs. Potter Palmer and sat with her while Buffalo Bill rode up on his horse and waved his hat to both with a flourish. The temperance reformers were busy, getting millions of pledges, many of them from children. When an exhibit was not faring well it was Bertha's custom to drop around and make substantial purchases. She took home handfuls of Montana rubies, Texas opals, Colorado rhinestones and Idaho cat's-eyes at different times. She listened to many tales of woe and sent a carriage every day to take elderly or ailing visitors to and from Jackson Park. Or she paid for their folding wicker chairs at the Fair. After a few wearings she gave away her gowns to saleswomen, waitresses and seamstresses on the grounds. She gave luncheons of beefsteak, strawberries and cream in the roof garden to the errand girls and guides who flitted around the Fair.

Mrs. Charles Henrotin, a Chicago banker's wife who was already one of her close friends, was vice president of the board and a dynamic assistant. It was part of her function to smooth down the ruffled feathers of the women assembled in their own square in the rotunda, conducting their organizational affairs from behind a screen of robin's-egg blue silk curtains.

There were outbursts of temper on bad days. Mrs. Henrotin sank into a chair in Mrs. Palmer's office in some despair after a screaming match staged by the Countess di Brazza during a rehearsal for some tableaux. "She is extremely exacting and demands an amount of consideration which it seems to me her official position does not warrant," Mrs. Henrotin reported. "Moreover, she isn't even Italian. She's American."

All through July and August the board was in an uproar internally, with Mrs. Logan the chief irritant this time. She had turned her guns on Mrs. Palmer, who was ready to resign by the end of August. Mrs. Lockwood insisted that Mrs. Logan had done the board more damage than Phoebe Couzins at her worst. Moreover, she had never been near the Woman's Building since the exhibits were installed. Mrs. Logan replied that she stayed away deliberately, since she believed her presence made the troublemakers act as they did. "The cause of women has been set back a generation since the opening of the World's Fair by the action of unworthy members of our Board," Mrs.

Logan wrote to Mrs. Palmer, adding that some of the members had flattered their chairman unduly and had been willing to do anything to keep themselves in Chicago at the expense of the board.

Mrs. Logan at this time was an aging fighter who had camped with her husband during the Civil War, was a close friend of Mrs. Ulysses S. Grant and spoke up sharply on all manner of public issues. She was never afraid of an argument but she met her match in Mrs. Palmer, who thought it vulgar to fight and chose to use soft tones in reply. The men were behind the chairman of the board. "It is very hard to feel that when you have done your best, you should be attacked by your friends, or at least, made the victim of their wrath on others," Henry H. Smith, of the Treasury Department, wrote to her sympathetically. He assured her that her board was in much better shape financially than the commission and he urged her "to show her teeth" and convince the malcontents that she was in dead earnest in order to bring them to their senses.

The wrangling became so public that Eugene Field sent Mrs. Palmer a newspaper clipping about the lady managers who "splurged around splendiferously and seemed to itch for notoriety," on which he had scrawled in blue pencil: "For God's sake give us a rest. Yours muchly Eugene Field."

But Mrs. Palmer calmly rode out the storm and made it seem inconsequential in the long run against all that had been accomplished by the board of lady managers. Meanwhile, she continued to entertain most opulently at her home. Every visiting celebrity that summer and all the women who came to the Fair in an official capacity were entertained at the Palmer mansion. There were yachting parties leaving late at night from the Naval Pier while the lights still blazed and visitors reveled in the carnival spirit. The festive air was never allowed to languish in spite of all the solid work done in the daytime. The scene at night was entrancing. The splash of fountains, the rhythm of bands, the twinkling lights, impressed themselves forever on the consciousness of all who saw them.

More fleshly entertainment was to be found along the Midway, with its foreign villages, cafés and bazaars; its Turkish mosque and Algerian café; its Persian harem and Irish market town; its German village; its Chamber of Horrors and Pompeian house; its captive balloon sent over from Paris, and its panoramas. It was the jolliest, rowdiest part of the Fair, drawing the roughest element as well as children and respectable citizens looking for amusement. Visitors could sip beer to the accompaniment of Strauss waltzes in the garden of Old Vienna, ride camels in the Streets of Cairo or spin deliciously in the ferris wheel with the night lights spraying them with star-dust. There were fakirs, freaks and sideshows. Tom-toms beat out jungle rhythms, and lions were prodded to roaring fury. But the chief annoyance to Mrs. Palmer was Little Egypt, where the *Danse du Ventre* was done by hootchy-kootchy girls to the music of a Zulu band.

The Midway was close to the Woman's Building and there were constant complaints about the noise and rowdyism so near at hand. The women's organizations were shocked by the *Danse du Ventre* and Anthony Comstock made it an issue. The newspapers soon got wind of the devilment in progress. Broad-minded and worldly though she was, Mrs. Palmer sternly pushed the matter and the board ordered the dance suppressed. Ida C. Craddock, a well-known feminist and shorthand expert, promptly protested, arguing that the ban was a blow to social purity and the diffusion of scientific truth. "It is our American men and women, and not the Oriental women, who are responsible for the atmosphere of indecent suggestion surrounding the very mention of the Danse du Ventre," Miss Craddock wrote to Mrs. Palmer. "It is a religious memorial of a worship that has existed thousands of years all over the world."

She enclosed an analysis of the dance, which is now in the

official Exposition papers that the Palmer family turned over to the Chicago Historical Society. "In the interest of social purity, dear Mrs. Palmer," wrote Miss Craddock, "may I not hope that you and your associates on the Board will reconsider your attitudes toward the Danse du Ventre from the standpoint of my interpretation?" But the Comstock judgment prevailed.

The board of lady managers commissioned Anders L. Zorn, who was serving as Swedish commissioner at the Exposition, to paint their chairman while the Fair was still in progress. But before he could get under way he was thrown from his horse while cantering in Lincoln Park and his collarbone was broken. At the time he was busy with a portrait of Mrs. Charles Deering. However, he continued to work with his left hand. Mrs. Deering wrote to Mrs. Palmer that Zorn was philosophical about his accident and "places himself and his left hand at your disposal to begin your portrait when you will!"

Soon Zorn was at work on his famous painting of Mrs. Potter Palmer, doing it with his left hand. Her pose was symbolic. He gave the ivory gavel with which she presided at her board meetings the air of a scepter, a regal effect heightened by the jeweled diadem she wore. The entire conception suggested a sparkling fairy queen and Potter Palmer always preferred the Healy portrait, although the Zorn painting was considered sensationally effective when it was first viewed by her admirers. Zorn was paid three thousand dollars for his work and one of the receptions at the Woman's Building was given in his honor. He dined often at the Palmer home, both then and on his return to the United States in 1896. By that time he had many commissions for his fashionable portraits.

Late in July Ida, Fred and their children arrived in Chicago, back from Vienna. Julia was now seventeen, a tall and beautiful girl fresh from having made her debut at the Austrian court. She had much to tell her Aunt Bertha of the way the

Archduchess Maria Theresa had looked in her white satin gown, with splendid diamonds around her neck and a diadem on her heavy curls; of Lady Paget's regal air and her own mother with her soft dark beauty dancing in the immense ballroom of the Hapsburgs to Strauss waltzes conducted by the composer himself. Bertha was interested in every detail of Julia's debut, from her Drécoll gown to the way in which Ida had diverted her partners to her young daughter.

Julia had attended twenty-three balls in a few weeks' time before her departure, and she was swept at once into Chicago's social structure by her Aunt Bertha. The debutante found her aunt "radiant, with fresh skin and brilliant eyes, in the prime of her great beauty." Julia thought that she carried off her role easily, gracefully, without any sign of hurry or fatigue. Seeing her in this new light her niece found her "calm, amiable, quick and capable."

Honoré and Potter took their cousin to the Fair. All the Honorés came and went at the Woman's Building, and Mrs. Palmer's father was specially honored by Burnham at a banquet held soon after the opening. "Too much cannot be said of what he has contributed to Chicago's growth. Wherever his hand appeared there has been big broad development.... Chicago owes him a monument," said Burnham, to Mrs. Palmer's delight.

She took a proprietorial pride in the vistas of balustrades and colonnades, of lagoons reflecting towers and whipping flags, of heroic sculpture and ornate decoration superimposed on Beaux Arts classicism. The gilded dome of the Administration Building, in French Renaissance style, dominated the Fair grounds. Mrs. Palmer was responsible for Saint-Gaudens' *Diana*, of Madison Square Garden fame, being a graceful asset to the Agriculture Building. There had been some hesitancy about installing the winged goddess, on the ground of modesty, until she had said firmly: "What nonsense! We will have it on the Woman's Building." Its critics promptly relented, and it became one of the more distinctive landmarks of the Fair.

The scientific advances of the era were brilliantly illustrated in the exhibits and Mrs. Palmer drew the attention of distinguished visitors to the cash registers and adding machines, the sewing machines and typewriters. Edison's kinetoscope presaging motion pictures was on display, along with huge Krupp guns, the Yerkes telescope, the Pullman exhibit of giant locomotives, Edison's colored "Tower of Light" and Columbus' contract with Ferdinand and Isabella. She had a sharp eye for the natural wonders and novelties at the Fair, from the largest canary diamond in the United States to Venus de Milo molded in chocolate and fifty thousand roses abloom on the Wooded Island.

But the final touch at the Fair was one of disaster. Mrs. Palmer's old friend, Carter Harrison, a Kentuckian who had followed her father to Ashland Avenue in the early days of their settlement in Chicago, was shot at his own front door by Patrick Prendergast, a fanatic nursing a grudge because the Mayor had not appointed him corporation counsel. Harrison had just returned from giving his final speech at the Fair.

For two days and two nights people filed past the bier of the lusty character who had served as their Mayor. Flags flew at half-mast all through the city. He had fought the Sunday closing of the Fair and had genial ways that the people loved. Many years earlier he had battled Joseph Medill, a teetotaler, on the Sunday closing of beer gardens and saloons. He believed in personal liberty and often said: "You can't legislate morality, so leave it alone." He rode through the city by day and by night on a huge bay mare, wearing a wide-brimmed black hat on his bearded head and knee boots of the softest leather. Everywhere he went he made friends in a hearty, gregarious fashion but the town was wide-open and roistering during his regime. He was traveled and worldly, a gallant with the Continental view of the moralities. Mrs. Palmer, with a strong strain of rectitude in her make-up, had many arguments with him on social issues, but they remained good friends. He was a showman first and last, and could always be counted on to add the picturesque touch to any gathering. He had vigorous views on labor and believed that the worker had a right to strike.

His death threw a cloud over the closing of the Fair, and Mrs. Palmer was grave-faced and saddened as she carried through the final ceremony at the Woman's Building on October 31, 1893, three days after the murder of Carter Harrison. She wished things to end on a note of harmony and so in pronouncing her own benediction she deplored the "distorted stories of friction" that had appeared in the papers. "I, personally, have never had a harsh or unkind word from a member of the board, and have never uttered one," she observed in her most dulcet tones. "When our palace in the White City shall have vanished like a dream, when grass and flowers cover the beautiful spot where it now stands, its memory and influence will still remain with those who have been brought together within its walls."

6

→→→→→→→→→→→→ *The Nation's Hostess*

At the time of the Columbian Exposition Mrs. Potter Palmer described herself as the "nation's hostess and the nation's head woman servant." Beyond doubt it had made her an international figure by bringing her into touch with reigning sovereigns, statesmen and people of all classes at home and abroad.

Chicago was proud of its Exposition. Before the Fair closed it was also proud of Mrs. Palmer, its jeweled queen who had widened her realm and drawn attention to the American woman. The spotlight had played on her feuds as well as her triumphs, but she had emerged in large dimensions, the personality of the Fair. Her poise, her power to command, her deliberation, had served her well in reconciling clashing interests, in spite of some wounded feelings along the way and the general impression that she had lorded it over lesser mortals.

The ties she made at this time channeled to some extent her future course through life, and gave her a friendly audience in various European countries. Abroad, she had become the legendary hostess of the United States. Her jewels, her good looks, her style, her tact as a hostess, her castle on Lake Shore

Drive, her capacity for getting things done were discussed far afield, so that she seemed an effective public courier for her city and her times. Her parties set the pace for entertaining in the Golden Nineties aside from New York and gave Chicago an unfamiliar touch of glamour. The Middle Western city had been negligible on the social front until Mrs. Potter Palmer gave it a sophisticated flourish. With native pride and independence of spirit its people liked to see their values upheld, their millionaires in gold rather than in tinsel frames. They were among the most philanthropic and generous in the world. By this time they were giving lavish sums to education and public works. They were building up impressive art collections.

"It is a great mistake to think that we in New York possess all the elegant, rich, and ornamental outgrowth of taste, or that we know better than the West what are the luxuries and comforts of the age," Julian Ralph reported after a tour across the country in 1893 for *Harper's Magazine*. He felt that Chicago made Broadway look "desolate and solitudinous." The cable cars of the Western city outpaced the horsecars of New York. Chicago was more rapid and businesslike in all respects. He found its capitalists and storekeepers well-informed men "whose business field is the world." He liked the boulevards and avenues, the noble parks and flowers, the miles of detached villas, the mosaic, marble and onyx in private homes.

However, there still was much feeling in Chicago's polyglot population for the natural, simple and spontaneous effect, and a tendency to scoff at the pretentious. But Mrs. Palmer, through her philanthropy and hard-headed civic work, successfully bridged the gap between mere social display and her own form of pragmatism. She could show both facets in high relief as she moved from a hard day's work on behalf of factory girls to a dazzling party in her home. One great asset was the physical vitality that enabled her to function with drive and precision. Her life was highly organized, with every hour allotted to a task. It was her custom to rise early, live vigorously and eat abstemiously. Her guests might be treated to Lucullan banquets at her home but the Palmer family lived on simple fare and she watched the household bills. She had a master buyer at her side. Young Honoré often complained about this Spartan regime. "What! French lamb chops and peas again for lunch," he would protest when he came home for the holidays from St. Mark's School or Harvard.

Since wealth and civic responsibility had not yet become a popular twin conception in the United States, Mrs. Palmer seemed to many to be poised between the devil and the deep sea. Representing the last word in luxurious living she earnestly championed labor as industrial unrest crowded the set in which she moved. She was not unsympathetic to the socialistic philosophy and at times made speeches and expressed views that had her more conservative friends aghast. The Fair had changed her viewpoint on many issues. It had made her most emphatically the champion of working women everywhere. Her dealings with foreign women had opened her eyes to the worldwide picture of their status.

But she found it difficult to free herself from the fatuous legend of an empty social life. *The Woman Beautiful* commented that "people are concerned not so much about what she thinks as they are about her aloof manner, her stunning carriage, the smooth pink and white unwrinkled skin, the perfect teeth, wonderful hair, velvet gowns, her world famous furs and the sumptuous way in which she conducts her menage."

This sort of comment left Mrs. Palmer cold. It gave only one impression of her many-sided life. She preferred to have people concerned about what she thought at a time when she was aligning herself with the social reformers and temperance workers in Chicago. It was beside the point that the Palmer House bar, one of the most splendid of its kind, was crowded nearly all night long. When W. T. Stead, the British editor and reformer, visited Chicago at the close of the Fair and set out to clean up the city in a whirlwind campaign, his most imposing ally was Mrs. Potter Palmer. She found the rabid Englishman one of the most provocative guests who had ever sat at her board as he talked of the sin and corruption he found in Chicago. He seemed a merry wag as well as a zealot at the dinner table.

Stead turned loose all his powerful batteries on the Prairie City. But he did not dismay Mrs. Palmer when he shouted from the rostrum that the "idle and worthless rich were infinitely more disreputable than the lowest prostitutes." This was immediately interpreted as an attack on Chicago's social set and was telegraphed around the world. After that the appearance of Stead and Mrs. Potter Palmer on the same platform was of unique interest to the city. The Englishman held meetings at the Central Music Hall, with audiences that included preachers and saloonkeepers, gamblers, theological professors, madams and anarchists. Late at night, wet and hungry from his tours of the levee, he drank hot chocolate before an open fire in Hull House and talked to Jane Addams about her work. "It would be difficult to imagine a greater contrast between the worthless society woman who devotes her days to pleasure and her nights to more or less pleasurable dissipation, and the patient, laborious, Christlike work of Miss Jane Addams and her coadjutors in Hull House," Stead commented.

But he wholly approved of Mrs. Potter Palmer, in spite of the fact that she decked herself with jewels, and was a shining member of the class he attacked. He was not immune to the glitter of diamonds or to the benefits of financial support. For some time he had been importuning the Countess of Warwick to bring influence to bear on the Prince of Wales in matters of social reform. But the Prince merely yawned at the idea when she discussed such matters, the Countess reported.

Stead urged Mrs. Palmer to head a reform movement in

Chicago and be the Lady Nestor of the United States with the Countess of Warwick filling the same role in Britain. He would edit papers for them on both sides of the Atlantic. He wrote to her on January 30, 1894, outlining his plan and adding a touch of flattery: "In London we have the whole hierarchy, royal and aristocratic, which would in any case tower above the Countess of Warwick or anybody else. Here in Chicago there is no one who would tower above you if you were to play the part of Lady Nestor; you would not only be Lady Nestor but also queen."

In this same letter Stead gave his view of the Countess of Warwick's relationship with the Prince of Wales. "There is nothing wrong in their friendship although most people believe there is," he wrote. "He is devoted to her, and she is the best friend he has in the world, that is all."

Although Mrs. Palmer did not become Lady Nestor in the journalistic sense, she served as the energetic vice president of the Civic Federation which was established by the public-spirited men of Chicago in answer to the challenge Stead had flung at them. On his return to England he published *If Christ Came to Chicago!*, a lengthy philippic on sin that promptly became a best seller but that mothers hid from their children. Meanwhile, the Civic Federation took hold with a central council of a hundred, and branches in all the city wards. It had six departments—philanthropic, industrial, municipal, educational, moral and political—and it functioned fearlessly, particularly on the municipal front, where the appointment of corrupt men to city offices was opposed. It helped to push through Chicago's first civil service law. It campaigned for clean streets and went after grafting garbage collectors. It whipped up raids on gambling saloons and organized relief operations during the dark days that followed the Fair.

The Federation had its quota of public-spirited men of wealth. Much of the labor discontent was focused on the great fortunes built up by such men as Marshall Field, Potter

Palmer, William B. Ogden, George M. Pullman, Joseph Medill, Philip D. Armour, John D. Caton, John Wentworth and Charles T. Yerkes. Some of these men may have felt the bite of conscience as they watched the bitter misery around them —the strikes, the unrest, the yearnings of the working man for better things. The Palmers had been energetic in good works from the earliest days of their success. Marshall Field came to life as a philanthropist with the establishment of the Civic Federation. Pullman had gone in for feudal paternalism that was now coldly rejected by his employees.

Mrs. Palmer gave more than nominal service to the newly created body. She was first vice president and chummed amiably with J. J. McGrath, the union labor official who was second vice president. Her work brought her into close touch with Hull House and soon she was a familiar sight at the settlement, swathed in furs and feathers, attending meetings or organizing crusades. Jane Addams stirred up a good many women of wealth to civic action, although she always maintained that she would neither be subsidized by millionaires nor bullied by working men. This quiet Quakeress whose father was a friend of Lincoln, and whose own desire to help the poor sprang from her explorations of the London slums, eventually kept four buildings in operation, with clubs, classes, folk dances, native arts and a visiting nurse service. Fifty thousand immigrants a year were reaching Chicago, many of them unable to speak a word of English.

In spite of her interest in Stead Mrs. Palmer was not disposed to be enthusiastic about visionary schemes for social betterment. Her thoroughgoing nature demanded a practical approach to every problem that arose. She did not scorn the thundering evangelism of the era, however, believing that the passive public could stand a hard jolt. One fire-and-brimstone preacher shouted that if Chicago had a church for every two thousand inhabitants it also had a saloon for every two hundred. At this time Dwight L. Moody was addressing multitudes in the North Side Tabernacle, moving many to tears and to conversion. His hymnbooks were in nearly every home. His greeting to the man in the street was: "Are you a Christian?"

This was heady evangelism but Mrs. Palmer favored action and had a keen eye for public response. In spite of her aloof way of living she had an earthy understanding of man's needs and aspirations, and was always ready to welcome an enthusiast in her home if his cause seemed just. Her views on social questions were applauded by John P. Altgeld, the radical Governor of Illinois who refused to wear legal robes and had strong socialistic leanings. He fought the trusts, advocated the eight-hour day for the worker and pardoned three of the anarchist leaders of the Haymarket riot who had been sent to prison for life.

The rich men of Chicago did not love Governor Altgeld, but he felt he had a friend in Mrs. Potter Palmer. He was struck by a speech she made that illustrated her independence of spirit. He wrote to her praising its "clearness—its literary excellence—its wonderful force—its deep insight, and great courage in questioning doctrines which had been considered sacred, and that in high places."

He had admired her work at the Fair. When it was over he wrote to her from Springfield that the cause of women's independence had been advanced a century through the Columbian Exposition, and posterity would label the "delicate hand that directed this work 'the hand of genius.'" He had tried to see her when the Fair ended but "they guarded you jealously and spared you the affliction," the Governor wrote. He wished to call on her "not in relation to any particular business but as an expression of my admiration."

Another of her legal admirers was Judge Henry M. Shepard of the Superior Court of Cook County, whose letters were flavored with a touch of gallantry. Sending her a note with some flowers he wrote:

I except you from royalty whose invitations pass as commands, and I only do so on the ground that I like to feel myself so near the throne of your favor as to dare to presume. Don't deny me this foolish sense of privilege. You have indulged me in it till I have become presumptuous, perhaps, but it is only against your generosity. . . . I hope you will find a place to wear one of these flowers tomorrow.

Mrs. Palmer was flooded with letters of all kinds after the Fair and many requests for help. She autographed thousands of cards and photographs. She had de luxe bound copies of her speeches sent to rulers and friends around the world. The winter that followed the Fair was a grim one. A financial collapse a few weeks after it opened brought on a deep depression. More than five thousand banks failed and railroads went into receivership. Factories were shut down, stores went bankrupt, wages in general were cut in half and three million persons were out of work. The streets were filled with beggars, many of them derelicts left over from the Fair. Breadlines stretched along the streets. Soup kitchens were opened and sixty thousand a day were fed free by the saloons and relief societies. Many of the homeless slept in hallways and on stone steps.

The growing unrest that had permeated the industrial world for years exploded full strength in 1894 when Coxey's Army marched on the national capital and the Pullman riots focused the attention of the nation on Chicago. Eugene V. Debs engineered a boycott on Pullman cars, affecting the twenty-two railroad lines coming into the city. Rioting followed and transportation was halted. Cars were overturned. Capsized locomotives were used to barricade tracks. Boxcars were burned. There was violence all over town. Pullman stubbornly refused to meet the workers and negotiate, in spite of pressure from all quarters.

Finally President Cleveland sent in federal troops to quell the riots. Governor Altgeld protested that it was a state matter, and fomented a movement to strip Pullman of all power over the lives of his workers. Jane Addams called the railroad magnate a modern King Lear. Lyman Gage and Mrs. Palmer, on behalf of the Civic Federation, besought Pullman to compromise. Calm and determined, Bertha reasoned with him, but in the end was outraged by the inflexibility of the friend who had sat so often at her dinner table and discussed the brotherhood of man. She had always been interested in Pullman Town, which its inhabitants now regarded as medieval and paternalistic. Theoretically it was an idyllic setting for the workers—a model hill town close to Chicago with Dutch design cottages, Venetian arcades, retail markets and stores, a hotel, a school and churches, a bandstand and an artificial lake. But the workers disliked the ban on beer gardens and saloons. And Debs protested that the labor unions were frozen out. Finally, with the outbreak of the railroad strike, a concentrated attack was made on this particular form of philanthropy.

Pullman was a friend of Potter Palmer's. He, too, had come from New York State, working first as a cabinetmaker, then raising Chicago on stilts, and ultimately getting backing from Marshall Field for his palace car operations. Bertha had watched him grow with the city. She often rode in his private cars. He was an important exhibitor at the Exposition and she was quite familiar with his philanthropies. Of all the rich men she knew he was perhaps the most dogmatic. He lived on Prairie Avenue close to Marshall Field and Philip D. Armour. He drove around in a huge victoria, a pompous figure with clenched mouth, chin whiskers of a reddish hue, and a silk hat always worn with his Prince Albert coat. He deferred to Mrs. Palmer as a worthy antagonist but was deaf to her arguments, so that a chill developed between them after the strike. It was late August before the men went back to work. No concessions had been made. Debs was sent to jail after a defense by Clarence Darrow. The workers were frozen out of the city of Pullman's creation. The railroad man was dead within three years and was memorialized as the poor man's friend.

But before the strike was over the Palmers were on their

way to Europe. Potter had been ailing ever since the Fair. They spent Christmas, 1894, at the Grand Hotel in Paris and from there went to Egypt to pass a month on the Nile. But they cut short their tour because of Palmer's health and took a cottage at Bar Harbor for the summer of 1895, as they had done the year before. He was suffering from rheumatism and was extremely frail by this time. His hair and beard were now snow-white. He could no longer even pretend to keep up the social pace set by his wife. The difference in their ages was quite apparent now, with Bertha approaching fifty but looking no more than thirty-five. Her dark hair had been gray for years, but the effect was glamorous rather than aging. It was silvery and shining and her carefully arranged pompadour became her regular features, and emphasized the beauty of her large dark eyes.

Both of the Potter Palmers enjoyed the festivities for the young. Julia Grant had joined them for the summer and she shared in the companionship of Honoré and Potter, who had done well in school and college. Both were bright young men who responded amiably to friendly stimulus although they took the social picture much less seriously than their mother. They had sharp memories of too many large hotels, too much dressing up, too many servants at their heels, too much spit and polish that the "roughing it" periods had not quite offset. They were quiet boys, with interests of their own, and some of their father's homely sense of reality. His dry comments were a leavening influence in their lives. Julia found her Uncle Potter keen-witted and terse in his comments, and considered his judgment of men "admirable and always to be trusted."

He was an inveterate shopper and preferred to do his own marketing at Bar Harbor although they had a staff of servants always at hand. When he was not tinkering with repairs, pruning bushes, or peering over the chef's shoulder, he liked to shop. Cissie could not curb his constant interest in the small practical details of everyday living, however efficient her butlers and gardeners. But her bills for this period show how simply they lived that summer at Bar Harbor. Twenty dinners at the Kebo Valley Club cost eighty dollars. Lindall's Orchestra played at one of their parties for forty-three dollars. Roses cost three dollars and fifty cents a bunch and the Palmer menage was supplied with three melons for ninety cents, five pounds of coffee for a dollar ninety, one pound of tea for ninety cents, three pints of ice cream for a dollar fifty and a pound of butter for fifty cents. Huyler's bill for marshmallows, mixed chocolates, Italian peppermints, vanilla bonbons, chocolate caramels and cream almonds came to twenty-two dollars.

Life at Bar Harbor was uncomplicated in comparison with Newport. Most of the social activity centered on the Kebo Valley Club, which had been in operation since 1887. It had a little theater, golf, tennis, croquet and a baseball field. Most of the young people's parties were held at the club and Mrs. Palmer found familiar Chicago faces all around her. The Eastern elite scarcely noticed her but Jane Addams tramped about in rubbers on the sunniest day, sneezing madly with hay fever as she raised money for her settlement. Mrs. Joseph T. Bowen, an old Michigan Avenue neighbor, had been a Bar Harbor visitor for years. S. Weir Mitchell, the author and an old friend of Mrs. Ulysses S. Grant, was deeply committed to the foggy coast, and a scattering of well-known bishops summered at Mount Desert. Everyone was conscious of the pervasive presence of Joseph Pulitzer, running the New York *World* from his Tower of Silence at Bar Harbor.

It was simple living for Mrs. Palmer and healthful for her husband. She took long walks and inhaled the sea air and the fog and charged her batteries for another season. The coastline was awesome when storms roared in. The trails over Mount Desert were a never-ending source of interest to the young, who went tramping, canoeing, sketching, rocking, fishing and dancing. Mrs. Palmer had all the latest books on hand, and the *Century Magazine*, *Harper's*, *Scribner's*, the *North American Review* and the *Arena*, as well as the Chicago and New York newspapers, lay about on wicker tables.

She already had her eye on Newport when she returned to Chicago for the busy social season of 1895–96. She resumed her Federation work and made plans for the annual Charity Ball to be held after Christmas. Mrs. Palmer had brought this event to a new state of magnificence and had popularized it as a charity event for her own and other communities. It was regarded as a civic function of real significance and it received front-page attention in the Chicago papers, even though Ward McAllister considered this institution an abomination. Mrs. Palmer's name would always be associated with the Charity Ball. For weeks beforehand she dragooned the prominent men of the city into service. She wrote to them in simple, imperative terms, pointing out their civic duty. None dared deny her their support. The proceeds went to several different institutions.

"The committee is enlarging the opening march of the Charity Ball and wishes to have four columns instead of the usual two," she wrote to her friend and co-worker Franklin MacVeagh in December, 1895. "Gen. Merritt, Mr. Robt. Lincoln and perhaps Mr. Palmer will rally (or march) at the head of three columns and we hope you will take the fourth place. I trust that you will find it both convenient and agreeable to do so and that you will render this service to the cause of charity."

She invited Charles L. Hutchinson, president of the Art Institute of Chicago, to the Union League Club for luncheon to discuss methods of whipping up interest in the ball. She insisted that Judge Lambert Tree join in the opening march, in order to make it thoroughly representative. She urged other well-known citizens to round up those who could best afford to pay for boxes. When all the carriages unloaded their owners at the Auditorium the assembled wealth was overwhelming, since the Chicago fortunes were formidable, from packers to bankers. Mrs. Palmer always led one column herself with great dash, her best jewels and latest Paris gown on display, and the man of the hour on her arm. The West Division, representing her old Ashland Avenue district, had its own imperial column, and the South Division was invariably headed by an impressive pair.

As time went on and Mrs. Palmer spent more of her time abroad Mrs. Marshall Field cut in to some degree on the Charity Ball, but Bertha always came whipping home in time to take over. She viewed it seriously as a charity that must not be neglected, aside from the fact that her name was inevitably associated with it. Society as such was a mere excrescence on the human fabric, of no philosophic status whatever, she observed once in giving a talk before a women's club. "If life is human intercourse, why not take it at its freest and broadest and see what humanity does with its largest opportunities?"

Yet she herself was the very symbol of apartness. After the Fair she lived with the aloofness and style of a ruler, screened from the world by a staff of twenty-seven. Any attempts to reach her in her private citadel had to be channeled through this corps of social secretaries and servants. It was not yet the day of easy telephoning, and even her most intimate friends had to write for appointments. Her life was clear of small obstructions. She was buffered by servants, possessions, a devoted family. She had an impenetrable armor when she did not wish to be bothered, but a big issue caught her attention at once. Many thought her cold and distant because of the guarded life she led as time went on. Indeed, she seemed to be passing beyond the common ken. But those who reached her found her easy and tolerant. She had a mild sense of humor and she brushed off flattery as easily as she did criticism. Self-control and a cool weighing of values were habitual to her, and she was not particularly gullible. She preferred people who were interesting and amusing and she had respect for achievement in any field.

But Mrs. Palmer was not patient with the lazy, the shirkers, the shiftless. Nor did she waste time on fools, bores or sycophants. Many flatterers crossed her path. If she was not immediately alert to the siren song her down-to-earth husband was sure to put his finger on their insincerity. She grew more decisive and authoritative as the years went on, although her voice was still low-pitched and her manner serene. Even those closest to her found it a little hard at times to live up to her rigorous standards, but they also remember a disposition of sweetness and charm. By the close of the century she had survived a number of battles, but she did not like to fight. It was vulgar. It was tedious and fruitless. She preferred the art of compromise and she learned to sway small groups of men and women as she became more sure of herself in public. It was noted that Mrs. Palmer never seemed to push for what she wanted. She simply got it by exhibiting the most common sense, using a touch of diplomacy, and being so overpowering in personality that she checkmated opposition, insidious or out in the open.

She managed to juggle the humanitarian and purely social areas of her life without conflict. In the end she was credited with running her own Four Hundred in Chicago. Invitations to her New Year's Day receptions were the hallmark of social acceptance. Those who were invited were in the swim for the rest of the year. Every two years she revised her lists and people were "in" or "out" as surely as in the case of the Social Register. "Her favor could make the social success of almost anyone, but she did not abuse her great power," commented the friendly Mrs. Carter H. Harrison.

There were others in Chicago, however, who considered Mrs. Arthur J. Caton (later the second Mrs. Marshall Field) the true aristocrat and Mrs. Palmer the ambitious interloper who had used the Exposition to move up in the world. The Field and Palmer interests had stemmed from the same root and although the two families drifted apart as the years went on, inevitably there was strong mutual interest. Field's admiration for the discriminating and artistic Delia Caton was a matter of common knowledge. However, Mrs. Palmer was the hostess who loomed large in the public eye. Her methods were dashing, her prestige overpowering. She preferred to have things all her own way and indeed would insist on a free hand.

On one occasion when asked to lend her support to a charity event at the Auditorium she said she would, but only if no one else interfered. She directed the performance from start to finish, ordered the flowers, the music, the decorations, and made it a one-woman show. Things were run with such taste and skill that not a murmur was heard. It had the Mrs. Potter Palmer touch. She could not tolerate the confusion, argument and overlapping that occurred when too many well-intentioned amateurs got into the act. There was always a *right* way to do things and she could show them how.

Such was the aura of grandeur exuded by Mrs. Palmer that few ever suspected she had moments of loneliness. Other hostesses were so intimidated that they never thought of inviting her to one of their more informal gatherings. Mrs. Henry M. Shepard, one of her closest friends, was astounded when Bertha confessed that there were times when she felt positively left out of things. "Of course," she said, "I can entertain all the time, but I also like to go to other people's houses." The feeling prevailed that nothing less than a wedding, a debut or a function in honor of a visiting celebrity would bring Mrs. Palmer out of her ivory tower. The ordinary give-and-take of social life was not enough. But when she did show up for a commonplace luncheon or an informal evening everyone commented on her "delightful, cordial presence," Mrs. Addie Hibbard Gregory, a family friend, recalled.

One important man whom she could never be sure of having at her functions was her own husband. Another was Abraham Lincoln's son, Robert Todd Lincoln, who was devoted to her but was in poor health and could not always live up to Mrs. Palmer's demands. Potter had never cared for large-scale entertaining and he became both bored and restless when seated next to the dowagers his wife chose to honor. He liked to talk about horses, art, politics or business, and he did not care for dancing. His range was not narrow but he seemed tongue-tied beside his brilliant wife, who could move quite nimbly from social chitchat to John Stuart Mill. Basically he disliked small talk and was happier in the company of his business or racing cronies. He often entertained his family with his cynical observations about social pretension, although at times he was all but smothered in it. But one person who never bored him for an instant was Cissie.

Ernest Poole, the writer, who used to go to the young people's parties at the Palmer house, made a number of firsthand observations on Potter Palmer's bearing toward his wife. When he came home tired from the hotel he often went straight to a dressing room in the south side of the house which he particularly liked. It was sunny in the daytime and remote at night from the party clatter. He would appear for dinner if Cissie insisted and he liked to watch her across the ballroom as she presided at a dance or reception. Poole analyzed his expression on these occasions as being nothing short of adoration. He wrote of the "gleam in his wife-set eyes" and found that he could always start Palmer talking by asking questions about his wife. He was visibly pleased to see her enjoying herself in the ways that she preferred and he took the utmost pride in what she did, what she wore and how she looked.

"There she stands with two hundred thousand dollars' worth of jewels on her," he said to Poole on one occasion.

Another time the writer found him slumped on a sofa while a ball was in progress. He asked Palmer if he were tired.

"No, but my feet hurt," said his host plaintively.

On the occasions when he did show up at his wife's parties he usually disappeared before the evening was over. Some said that Cissie kept her unpretentious husband in the background and was even unkind to him, but the truth was that Potter Palmer chose to keep himself out of sight and could scarcely be lured into public view by his wife. He had no wish to share the limelight with Bertha or to get too deeply involved in her social enterprises, although he was always ready to act as her escort if she needed him when they were away from home. But he still worked hard at his manifold interests and found it difficult to let go the strings of business.

There were times when Cissie showed impatience over his disinclination to exert himself for a function. She looked upon the social setup as a business, however much of an "excrescence," and considered it the duty of every man and woman to find a place for himself in it. But Potter's standing in the community was so solid that he had no pressing need to engage in the scramble and he never felt particularly at home at the fashionable Chicago Club, where Pullman, Armour, Field and others of his peers liked to gather. He was essentially a retiring and rather inarticulate man who attended to his business. But since his business brought him into touch with many world celebrities, and he had traveled widely, and had known the whims of Chicago's smartest matrons right back to the early days of his store, he was not at a loss when Cissie chose to bring him into view.

By the 1890's he was even a little blasé. Fast horses, a dog-cart or coach-and-four, a celebrity or new gadget at the Palmer House, a ravishing necklace for Cissie, good marks for his sons at college, a park improvement for Chicago set him at peace with the world. His friends knew him as keen, shrewd and open-handed, and he never failed to keep his word. "He's a square shooter," said one of his colleagues about his business dealings. "Good old Potter Palmer," went the chorus when his name came up.

The guests seen most frequently at his home were the Arthur J. Catons, the Marshall Fields, the Cyrus McCormicks, the Joseph Medills, the Franklin MacVeaghs, the W. W.

Kimballs, the Augustus Eddys and N. K. Fairbanks. In the younger set Moses Wentworth, John Crerar, Huntington Jackson, Wayne Chatfield, Wirt Dexter and Charles Schwartz turned up regularly at Mrs. Palmer's parties for her sons and Julia Grant.

None knew how many of the civic measures they backed were Cissie's idea and how many were his, but together they made a strong working team and he had shown plenty of enterprise before he ever met Miss Honoré. Mrs. Palmer still insisted that she had absorbed all her business wisdom from him. However, everyone knew that a good way to Potter Palmer's pocketbook was to engage his wife's interest in a project, and he liked to spread his gifts through her. The Potter Palmer philanthropy silenced to some extent the criticism of such great expenditure for social display. Cissie in turn never failed to give him credit for what he did, and was most punctilious about bringing in her husband's name when flatterers chose to hang all the laurels on her.

Both were thoughtful of their friends and made many small personal gifts aside from their large philanthropy. Joseph Medill thanked Potter Palmer for an "elegant cane to lean on in my advancing years" and Mrs. Palmer for the "handsome umbrella to ward off the heat and shed the rain." Judge Shepard sent eggs to Mrs. Palmer from his hennery when Potter was ailing, and she did many kind things for him, in addition to liking him sincerely. She was popular with judges and lawyers, who admired her reasoning powers and her clear-headed approach to problems, but she distrusted bankers and told them little of her affairs. Mrs. Palmer could be the soul of discretion in business matters and she kept her own counsel with great pertinacity. One who knew her well observed that she was never driven into saying anything she had not planned to say. She studied a subject before she ventured an opinion on it, then weighed her words carefully, and usually refrained from hasty comments. The result was that she rarely got into hot water on public issues, although the Chicago press turned to her as a natural target for comment.

A competitive social spirit had developed in Chicago by the turn of the century. The city was losing some of its sturdy Western ways. More and more of its women went abroad as their husbands amassed great fortunes. Like Mrs. Palmer they now had chefs, butlers and footmen. They went in for cockaded English coachmen instead of Negro or Scandinavian drivers. They shopped in London, Paris, Vienna and Rome. They were becoming cosmopolitan and intermarriage with titled Europeans had deepened this alienation from their native roots. Ethel Field married Arthur M. Tree and went off to live in England. After bearing him three children she divorced him and married David Beatty, who later became Admiral Beatty, commander of the British Fleet. The three beautiful Leiter daughters found British husbands. Mary married Lord Curzon in 1895, Daisy later married the Earl of Suffolk and Nancy became the wife of Major Colin Campbell, so that the Leiter links with Britain were strong.

Although she bought most of her gowns in Paris Mrs. Palmer still liked to shop at Marshall Field & Company. Its buyers roamed the world rounding up the latest luxuries. The traveled women of Chicago had become more demanding about their linens, their china and crystal. Field had established agencies in Europe and the Orient. By this time his neat mustache had turned white and his blue-gray eyes glinted like frost as he greeted Mrs. Palmer. His rigid, courteous manner had been familiar to her for many years. He was now a much richer man than her husband but he did not like to let his affluence show. He drove to the store at nine each morning but always got out a block away and walked the final stretch, so as not to seem pretentious.

Like Potter Palmer he still preferred to rule alone. Harlow N. Higinbotham had joined the firm in 1879, Harry Gordon Selfridge in 1890 and John G. Shedd in 1893 but none was accepted into full partnership. The store by this time had thousands of employees and covered all but one corner of the State Street block. Its white columns, wide galleries and artistically arranged counters bore little resemblance to the original Potter Palmer store. It had a restaurant that seated two thousand and women used it as a club where they could rest, write letters and meet friends as well as exchange notes on their bargains.

The Field house on Prairie Avenue was designed by Richard Morris Hunt. In no way did it resemble the Palmer castle on Lake Shore Drive. It was a three-story mansion of red brick, trimmed with stone. An iron grille surrounded its lawns and its conservatory was immense. Field had insisted on a simple exterior after studying the ornate effect of Pullman's house a block away. Indoors the ivory and gold drawing room was always pleasing to Mrs. Palmer and a circular staircase of carved wood gave magnificence to the hall. But the total effect was austere, like Field himself, who drank little, ate abstemiously, rarely smoked, and moved through the business of the day with quiet aloofness. He had as little taste for social gatherings as Potter Palmer but he was a suaver type. His wife Nannie, however, worried considerably about the growing prestige of Mrs. Potter Palmer, in spite of their friendly relations. Her Mikado ball for young Marshall was the most discussed party of the 1880's in Chicago. But after the Fair Mrs. Palmer outdistanced all other hostesses and Mrs. Field was forced to take second place. Every time that Bertha came back from Europe she was struck by the rapid changes that her favorite city was undergoing. She could see the effect of the Fair in many of the new buildings going up. A fire soon after the closing had burned the Administration and Manufacturers Buildings and other parts of the Fair. But Marshall Field had given a million dollars and assembled many of the better exhibits in the Columbian Museum, which later became the Field Museum of Natural History. Now the same architects who had designed the Fair buildings were changing the face of Chicago. Italian Renaissance effects prevailed, with a scattering of French Renaissance, Georgian and Colonial houses for those who could afford them. Cupolas, cornices and the external embellishments of the brewers' castles in Milwaukee were now considered lacking in taste. But friezes and frescoes, painted cherubs and allegorical paintings were in high esteem and Hunt went in for palm courts and Byzantine rooms. The new office buildings, however, were models of solid simplicity and dignified structure.

The Cyrus McCormick home, often visited by the Potter Palmers, had tapestries on its dining room walls and a hall with frescoes copied from one of the castles of King Henry IV in France. Several of the homes well known to them had Gabriel Ferrier murals, and bit by bit private art galleries were developing from small collections of pictures. Yerkes had Dutch masters. Samuel M. Nickerson, president of the First National Bank, had works by Doré, Inness and Corot, and Hutchinson was putting together a good art collection of his own. The Palmers themselves by this time had the most dazzling collection of modern paintings to be found in the United States.

Jackson Park was now given over to boulevards, to landscaping and bathing beaches. Washington Park had playfields, bathing and pony phaetons. Lincoln Park, with its magnificent sweep along the lake front, had imposing statues and fine landscaping. Sight-seers still viewed the city from the Auditorium Tower and the Masonic Temple, the tallest building of its day. "The Fair awoke the American sense of beauty," commented Julian Street. "Chicago is stupefying. . . . It stands apart from all the cities in the world . . . a prodigious paradox in which youth and maturity, brute strength and soaring spirit, are harmoniously fused."

When Mrs. Palmer looked around her she felt that the Fair had indeed made a difference to Chicago—and to her. But early in 1896 she was hankering for other worlds. During her travels she had observed the interesting lives of the diplomats abroad, so that she was not blind to the chance to get some solid recognition for her husband and perhaps some prestige for herself when Adlai E. Stevenson, the Vice President, proposed that Potter be appointed successor to Theodore Runyon as United States Ambassador in Berlin. The Stevensons were old friends of the Palmers. Mrs. Stevenson, the former Letitia Green, was a Kentuckian, like Bertha.

Judges, lawyers, bankers, businessmen, members of the Chamber of Commerce, politicians, prominent women, all took a hand in the matter and Mrs. Palmer functioned quite openly in support of the nomination. Several of Palmer's most important supporters, in pleading the case, pointed out what an asset his wife would be on the ambassadorial front. But Bertha was realistic about the appointment.

She wrote to Senator William Lindsay on January 28, 1896, suggesting that she hoped for a strong showing, even though there was little chance of the appointment coming to a Westerner. She cited her husband's long and honorable business career, his intelligence, sagacity and probity, together with his services to Chicago along broad and farsighted lines. She reminded the Senator that her husband had constantly served his party, in days of adversity as well as prosperity, and had never asked for anything in return, adding: "I think Mr. Palmer would greatly appreciate the honor and compliment, and as for myself, I should welcome anything that would take him away from the routine of fixed business habits of a lifetime—which would allow a tapering off, as it were, without too sudden a break."

Mrs. Palmer conducted her campaign in grim earnest. She whipped up interest among old Kentucky friends to draw in outside support for her husband. She sought backing in New England and the Far West, and appealed to colleagues who had worked with her at the Columbian Exposition. Newspaper owners in Chicago, Washington and Chattanooga beat the drums for Potter Palmer. She felt sure of Chief Justice Melville W. Fuller but not of her fellow Kentuckian, Justice John Marshall Harlan. She had doubts about Daniel S. Lamont, Secretary of War.

President Cleveland, who knew Mrs. Palmer well, found the assault coming at him from all quarters. Adlai Stevenson made a personal plea and Philip D. Armour wrote to him that the country's interests "and especially the interests of the Northwest could not be better served than by his appointment." United States Attorney John C. Black, of Chicago, assured him that the appointment of Potter Palmer would be only half the ensuing benefit. There would also be *Mrs.* Potter Palmer, a woman "in every way admirably capacitated and adapted to aid her husband." Senator Daniel W. Voorhees volunteered the opinion that "Palmer and his admirable lady would give distinction to such a position abroad."

It was a strong political gesture by Mrs. Palmer but it failed. The President thought it unwise to assign a stranger to State Department matters left unfinished by Runyon. Edwin F. Uhl, his assistant, was appointed to fill the post. Joseph Medill, much disappointed, assured Bertha that her friends had done all that was possible under the circumstances. But she had to find out who had supported her husband and who had opposed him. James H. Eckels, of the Treasury Department, who had clear recollections of Mrs. Palmer's expert financial dealings with him at the time of the Fair, humored her in this although it was contrary to custom.

For once in her life she was a loser but she accepted defeat philosophically and did not bear any grudges. His failure to get the diplomatic post was no great blow to her husband. It may even have been a relief. There were times when her family wished that there were greater worlds for her to conquer. Her sister Ida believed that with all her femininity she had the makings of a statesman, a diplomat or a captain of industry. She viewed Bertha as a type whose "law was justice rather than sentiment, whose strength was stability rather than passion."

But life always moved on briskly for Mrs. Palmer. There was no time for regrets. She had no sooner learned of the Uhl appointment than she and Potter sailed for Russia to attend the coronation of Czar Nicholas II. She traveled on the diplomatic basis in any event, for all the courtesies accorded to ambassadors were extended to the Palmers, and the Russians who had been at the Exposition as commissioners paid them great attention. Bertha was much impressed with the crown jewels and the court pomp. She met the Queen of Greece as well as the Czarina. She had no idea then that her niece Julia would soon be a popular figure at the Russian court. They returned with a number of Russian treasures including a rare icon, a copy of the Kazan madonna in rhinestones, a silver medal of Peter the Great, a choice chalice in dark blue enamel.

They were back in Chicago in time to attend the Democratic presidential convention and Bertha, who never missed these quadrennial events, listened with genuine excitement to William Jennings Bryan deliver his Cross of Gold speech. She and her old friend Mrs. Henrotin attended every session and it was noted in the papers that never before had Chicago women of prominence shown such public interest in a political convention. The curious wished to know if Mrs. Palmer actually advocated free silver. She certainly occupied a platform seat, gave a big reception at her home for the delegates, and hobnobbed with the Bryans, but she had nothing to say on the subject.

She found the Coliseum an improvement over the old Wigwam, where Lincoln was nominated. Bertha had known both. She was always a staunch Democrat, even in the days of the Grants, and some of her women friends thought her overly interested in politics. She could hold her own in debate with any man in the field and dinner conversation at the Palmer home during this period was strongly political. It was a year of mass meetings, rallies and parades, and Mrs. Palmer enjoyed every minute of the political excitement. Bryan was ubiquitous, while William McKinley sat on his shaded porch in Canton and waited for the lightning to strike.

It was evident to her friends at this time that Mrs. Palmer was restless for larger things. Though her plans for her husband had fallen through she had a new goal in mind—political office for her oldest son Honoré when he graduated from Harvard. Philanthropy no longer satisfied her urge for public service. She was moving into an area where the Palmer family might aim at taking a more positive part in civic government.

7

>>>>>>>>>>>>> *Conquest of Newport*

Mrs. Potter Palmer stormed Newport so convincingly in the eyes of her fellow citizens in the late 1890's that the reigning dowagers had to pause and give the Middle West a nod. She had quietly staked out her ground while they asked one another who this rich intruder might be. Her name suggested the Palmer House, the World's Fair, some freakish art, a monstrous castle where everyone from abroad was entertained. Surely she was not a serious contender for the holy of holies.

London knew her. Paris knew her. She had a nimbus of public endeavor and a dusting of fame. She had called herself the nation's hostess at the time of the Fair but Newport, immune to invasion, sniffed at such pretension. However, where waves of contenders had tried and failed Mrs. Palmer took the hurdles with a flourish. "No aspirant for social recognition ever won a Newport campaign so quickly," *Munsey's Magazine* reported in October, 1900. She made her first strong impression in the summer of 1896 with the coming-out dance she gave at Arleigh for her niece, Julia Grant. Two seasons later she fortified her position by becoming the favored hostess of the Prince of Flanders, destined to be King Albert of Belgium, and Victor Emmanuel, Prince of Turin.

Chicago was a distant and alien city to the blue bloods of the East. To them it reeked of meat packing and strikes. But its people stood firm in their just self-esteem and a few days after Julia's debut a large bulletin hung in the front window of one of its newspaper offices, while passers-by stopped to read: "MRS. PALMER A QUEEN." This was no great surprise to those who had already crowned her.

"Newport seems nearer to Chicago since last Tuesday night when Mr. and Mrs. Potter Palmer gave their beautiful ball at Arleigh," commented *Elite* on September 5, 1896. But this same publication deplored the fulsome accounts of the party appearing in the Chicago papers. Taking another view of the event, the editorial continued:

Mrs. Palmer's *triumph*, Mrs. Palmer's *success*, Mrs. Palmer's *victory*, indeed! . . . If any such heroic words are descriptive of the event they should be applied to the "other party." Not Mrs. Palmer, but Newport *won* that right. For it was emphasized on that occasion that the social colony there had attracted and added to its circle a beautiful and brilliant member, qualified to receive and reciprocate its politest and most distinguished hospitalities.

Newport had given Mrs. Palmer the cold shoulder at first and no one had even noticed her at Bar Harbor, but the Midwesterners knew that if anyone could open the golden gates it would be their own Mrs. Palmer, however false the gods within. Those who concerned themselves with such matters were happy to see the granddaughter of General Ulysses S. Grant—who would certainly not have cared—make a splash under Mrs. Potter Palmer's wing. The soft September night was one that Julia long remembered. Her aunt shimmered like Diana, wearing a tiara and her collar of pearls and diamonds with a white satin gown threaded with silver. Honoré and Potter were with her and two hundred guests danced the night away in a ballroom decked with pink and white roses.

Garlands festooned the balustrades and Roman floral wreaths hung by rose silk ribbons. Live rosebushes bloomed indoors and the girls carried shepherdesses' crooks trimmed with lilies made from the plumage of birds, as they moved in a glow of tinted electric lights strung through vines.

The pick of the social crop was present, including Mrs. William Astor, and this was a triumph for Mrs. Potter Palmer. Newport was the summer stronghold of the first families of the East. Like other self-respecting residents of Chicago Bertha had never genuflected to New York. She was too sophisticated not to realize that only the hardiest tackled Newport, but she was used to the top classification wherever she settled, and expected it as her right. Chicago definitely considered her "in," even if her name has been somewhat obscured in the annals of Newport society.

Ward McAllister died shortly before her arrival but his dictum that "Newport was the place above all others to take social root in" still prevailed. However, he had considered it essential for the aspirant "to sit on the stool of probation for at least four seasons." He had warned them not to outshine the established cottagers with their jewels, clothes and parties. And Harry Lehr had urged those who had any doubts about their eligibility to be wise and stay away. Poised, intelligent, of good lineage and substantial wealth, the commanding Mrs. Palmer had no qualms about her acceptance. She had merely to be herself to make an impression. But she moved carefully on the Newport scene and her parties were modest compared with the costume balls, the great outdoor fetes and aquatic picnics, the imported theatrical casts for an evening's entertainment, the ten-course dinners stretching over three boring hours, and such freak events as a gathering of a hundred dogs in silly ruffles barking their way through a "Dogs' Dinner."

Like Mrs. Stuyvesant Fish, who considered herself far from rich because she had only a few millions, the Palmers, with eight millions tightly invested in real estate, were mere paupers compared with the Vanderbilts, Astors, Belmonts and some of the other cottagers. But wealth was not the answer, although it helped to tip the scales. Newport had its own particular quality, a chilling hauteur that money could not thaw nor good intentions melt. Fame, philanthropy, talent played around the edges of family prestige but the solid core was ice.

However, Mrs. Palmer moved with ease and assurance through the marble palaces, the turreted châteaux and architectural extravagances on the rocky coast of Rhode Island. She was well aware that on the international front her own castle on Lake Shore Drive was the most widely advertised of them all. She rented Arleigh, Friedheim and Beaulieu in turn, and settled smoothly into the milieu of powdered footmen and gold plate. She had stayed in some of the stateliest homes of Victorian England and in French châteaux, where she was particularly welcome. She was quite at home in the coaching parade. When it came to blooded horses and elaborate equipages the Potter Palmers could hold their own. Her maroon-liveried coachmen took their place in the flowing line of barouches, phaetons and landaus, demi-Daumonts and tandems that moved along Bellevue Avenue.

But the walls of Jericho did not crumble overnight. There were plenty of important parties to which Mrs. Potter Palmer was not invited. Great yachts that she never boarded rocked in the harbor. Chilly glances shot from passing carriages as she smiled and bowed in all the right directions. Her jewels were impressive—perhaps *too* impressive—but Mrs. Elbridge T. Gerry's diamonds quite outshone the gems on Mrs. Palmer's cuirass bodice at a naval ball. Three bands drowned out her velvety voice as she chatted with Mrs. Astor and found herself talking into space. Her husband was by no means drawn into the inner coterie of men at the Casino.

But the spray, the drift, the wholesome smell of the sea were pervasive at Newport and there was always ground for optimism. Lawns, shrubs and foliage stayed green and fresh in the misted air. Flowers bloomed in vivid patches in the Casino grounds, and the polo field at the Country Club was a flawless stretch of closely cropped sward. Yachting parties and desultory bathing in muffling togs linked the cottagers with the sea. From time to time great storms roared in, crashing on the rocks and reminding the summer colony in its buffered paradise of the violent forces of nature.

Mrs. Palmer enjoyed the storms, as she did the purple sunsets and changing moods of sea and sky. She was always alert to the wonders of nature and found nothing at Newport to dash her buoyant spirits. She had friends in court from the beginning. August Belmont admired her, and the Stuyvesant Fish family had old associations with the Grants. She was not dismayed by Mamie Fish's tart comments and witchlike proddings, but recognized her as a kindred spirit who kept her household affairs in order and knew what was going on in the kitchen of her porticoed villa high over Spouting Rock Beach. The Fishes for the time being were in mourning for their son and did not entertain, but Mrs. Fish, Mrs. Hermann Oelrichs and Mrs. O. H. P. Belmont were challenging Mrs. Astor's invincibility when Mrs. Palmer came on the scene. Bertha quietly took stock of the feuds, ambitions and inherited self-assurance that surrounded her. Since she was not in the inner circle she could view the field with cool appraisal.

Three of the reigning duchesses in Britain—Roxburgh, Marlborough and Manchester—had inhaled the choice Newport air as they summered along Cliff Walk in their early years. Bertha was already quite familiar with Mrs. Paran Stevens, who had found her own niche at Newport in spite of the fact that she, too, was an innkeeper's wife. Long before her daughter became Mrs. Arthur Paget and a favorite of King Edward VII "Auntie Paran" had rocketed across the social scene with her particular brand of individualism, giving musicales and speaking her mind to all who would listen.

If the Middle West had only a small representation at Newport, Mrs. Palmer found familiar faces among its visitors, ranging from such different types as her old friend Julia Ward Howe to Oliver Wendell Holmes and Henry James. Writers, artists and savants, as well as historic families, had found their way to Newport in the days since the Civil War, an understandable union of interests to the cosmopolitan Mrs. Palmer. Edith Wharton (Pussy Jones) had written her first novel at Pencraig and John Singer Sargent, who viewed the Impressionists with a friendly eye, was deeply committed to the rugged coast and an admirer of its lichened rocks and the hardy growth of eglantine and wild roses that thrived on the sea winds.

As she surveyed the mansions of Newport Mrs. Palmer was well aware that the more spectacular could be credited to Richard Morris Hunt, her old ally at the World's Fair who had put his stamp on American architecture. He had designed the Marble House for the O. H. P. Belmonts and The Breakers for Cornelius Vanderbilt, a mansion destined eventually to become the headquarters of the Newport Preservation Society when the old guard abandoned its stronghold. He had helped to transform the coast resort from the comparative rusticity of its Knickerbocker days into a phalanstery of marble that fifty years later would crumble and decay, giving ghostly echoes to a festival of jazz.

But at the turn of the century Newport was at its full magnificence, in the last carefree days of a dying era. There were no premonitory signs that things were about to be different. Children bearing famous names in American social history drove about with their English governesses in little basket carts with striped awnings, or spaded sand, or rode their ponies, all part of the daily ritual of the resort. Some were headed for disaster; others for solid citizenship.

Mrs. Palmer found her bearings quickly. Potter Palmer, more than his wife, felt the chill of Newport. His health was poor at the time and he stayed well in the background. He had none of the picturesque attributes that might have made him a character, like some other men of achievement who enlivened the scene at the Rhode Island resort. He was never disposed to draw attention to himself and his wife so overshadowed him on all occasions that few realized how freely he exercised his dry wit during their five seasons at Newport. He was not unduly impressed with Mrs. Astor or Mrs. Astor's horse. He had seen the world flow by at his hotel for a good many years, and he had none of his wife's reverence for social effect. He stubbornly went his own way and not even Cissie could shake him in his convictions. The impression prevailed at Newport that somehow he had lagged along the way while she had made a rapid climb to prominence. But Mrs. Palmer now had the conventional desire to see her sons and niece marry well, and she had enough social drive for two.

There was no awkwardness in her and she had perfect self-control. She brushed off small social snubs as she might troublesome mosquitoes. She was smooth, almost cold in her manner at Newport, except with her family and intimates. Unlike some other imposing matrons at that resort her diction was impeccable. She did not garble her words like Mrs. Leiter of Chicago or lace her conversation with cheerful insults, like Mrs. Fish. She was not biting, and rarely witty, so that no one could cite her bons mots. But clever men were thankful to sit beside her at dinner because she was well informed, direct in manner, and always practical in her point of view. Only a few found her intimidating. She discussed business or politics with equal authority and was not egotistical in her conversation. Years earlier she had learned to play smoothly to her audience. Wives might look scathingly at her sunbursts and the width of her dog collars but it was hard to beat down the combination of Mrs. Palmer's knowledge and Mrs. Palmer's charm where their husbands were concerned. On the distaff side she was less convincing. She did not waste her time on gossip and her dark eyes were coldly disapproving when scandal was brought up over the teacups. Although never a conformist she stood for social suavity. Good manners were fundamental to her code.

In any event the deep freeze that was Newport's prescription for the socially pushing who had somehow found their way to its rocky ramparts failed to work with Mrs. Potter Palmer. After she had roped in the European princes invitations came to her thick and fast. But Newporters watched attentively when the Queen of the West and the Queen of the East faced each other in a ballroom. It was a piquant social situation that ended in a draw.

A race was on to catch the royal visitors, but Mrs. Palmer had already established such warm relations with the House of Flanders and Queen Margherita of Italy that the princes of both houses had been primed to pay special attention to the chairman of the board of lady managers of the Exposition. It was not mere chance that Bertha walked off with the lion's share as hostess. This was an era when a foreign prince was considered a catch. Titles were in high esteem at Newport. She had a head start since she already knew Prince Albert and had promised him in Belgium that she would assemble the most attractive girls in America for his benefit, when he jestingly told her that one day he would visit the United States in search of a rich and beautiful wife.

He was the first of the princes to arrive. Albert was tall, fair and quiet, the Viking type, and he was much more interested in the small navy ships of a new design then in the harbor than he was in ballroom dancing. Wearing overalls he crawled around in the ships and examined the engines, so that the Palmers could scarcely get him away from the docks. They had rented Friedheim, which belonged to the Havemeyer family and was one of the more beautiful homes of Newport. The Prince stayed there for several days and all the social events centered around the Palmer villa for the time being. A

group of attractive young people were on hand to entertain him but he showed a serious streak that surprised them.
Eighty guests attended the dinner that Mrs. Palmer gave in his honor. A musicale and reception followed. All was done in quiet good taste. She was well aware that her critics thought her ostentatious. There were no freak divertissements for visiting royalties. The favors were expensive but plain. Tiffany designed the menus. She had invited Cardinal Gibbons to come from Baltimore for the dinner she gave for the Prince. In his reply he mentioned "a most pleasant recollection of your hospitality while I was in Chicago" and regretted that he could not go to Newport. Mrs. Palmer next gave a luncheon for the Prince in the grillroom of the Casino and he left Newport with great good will all round, although he had seemed stiff and joyless to the younger set.

But the Prince of Turin was a different type—worldly and gallant and he loved to dance. He was Queen Margherita's nephew and twice removed from the Italian throne. He stayed part of the time with Mrs. John Thompson Spencer of Philadelphia at her colonial-style house high on Ruggles Avenue. She had known him in Europe. But the dinner given by Mrs. Palmer in his honor was conceded to be the major event of his stay. It was held on a hot night in July and again Mrs. William Astor, the mightiest of them all, was a gracious guest at Mrs. Palmer's board. She, too, entertained him in majestic fashion. He stayed two weeks in all and enjoyed the informality of the resort as well as the more pompous parties. He was enthusiastic about a clambake at the Sqantum Club, and had a merry time aboard the Gerry yacht with seventy-five other guests, including Mrs. Potter Palmer breezing along in trim yachting rig with a floating cloud of heavy white veiling. He was toasted by Chauncey Depew at a formal luncheon and he golfed every day with Julia Grant and other attractive girls. The Casino dances were lively while he was there and the Italian anthem was heard repeatedly. Before he left he was rated a regular prince and the New York *World* observed that he seemed to have the social spirit more strongly developed in him than the Prince of Flanders.

Some of Mrs. Palmer's critics now came out in the open and called her the snob of snobs, snaring foreign princes, crashing a sacred fortress with Midwestern impudence, trying to marry off Julia to a prince and indulging in crass ostentation. But the more seasoned dowagers were inclined to go her way. They no longer resisted Mrs. Potter Palmer after she had proved herself so effective and talented a hostess. In addition, some liked her direct and generous manner, and none could deny that her sons were quiet, good fellows, her brothers were attractive, and her niece was an asset to any party.

Mrs. Palmer was regarded among the more leisurely and well-padded matrons as being uncomfortably energetic. She spurned feathered negligees and breakfast in bed. It was her custom to be up and about before eight o'clock. She liked to walk, and breathe the ozone, and enjoy the trail along the rocky coast where wild roses bloomed by the wayside and tall irises cast purple shadows on the heath. Hollyhocks and blue hydrangeas were more symbolic of Ocean Drive, where she was observed one day indulging in an act of mercy that seemed to astonish observers. Driving along in her landau she caught up with an old woman who was stumbling in the dust, obviously quite ill and helpless, as equipages swept past her for the afternoon drive. Bertha helped the woman into her own carriage, and ordered her driven home to a remote part of Newport, while she continued on foot. The New York *Herald* reported this as an awesome piece of good Samaritanism along the wayside by Mrs. Potter Palmer of Chicago but she viewed it more sensibly as an everyday piece of business. However, the reporters were right in concluding that she was not one of the herd but an individualist. The Eastern papers began to notice her doings at Newport.

Any girl who wished to make her way in society, Ward

McAllister had said, "should have a pair of ponies, a pretty trap, with a well-gotten up groom, and Worth to dress her." Julia Grant had all of these, thanks to her aunt, and the young people enjoyed themselves in their own way. They rode and picnicked, went crabbing and catboating, danced and dined, played golf and tennis, as the spirit moved them. Every little suburb was laying out golf links in 1896, and Mrs. Palmer had taken up the game with her usual proficiency. Bicyclists began to whiz about but her family preferred their horses. She was a keen sportswoman at this time, but was too energetic to enjoy giving up a whole afternoon to watching a tennis tournament, although always quite willing to play, or to stride across the golf course. It was her nature to be more of a participant than a spectator. She was expert at bridge and cribbage. She even learned to drive a car, an interest that Honoré, fresh from Harvard, took up with enthusiasm. O. H. P. Belmont and Harry Payne Whitney touched off the craze and soon the "bubbles," as they were called, were crowding the carriages at Newport. These daredevil objects had skittish names like Blue Butterfly and Red Devil, and women whose yachting, golfing and bicycling attire was already the cartoonist's delight, now added dusters and goggles, and swathed their cartwheel hats in foolproof veils. Automobiles became the great new rage. It was chic to race and clever to whiz past one's neighbor on the road with a mad honking of horns.

Life took on a more serious note, however, with the outbreak of the Spanish-American War. The women assembled at the Casino in the mornings to sew for the soldiers, under Mrs. Astor's direction. Fred Grant and Algernon Sartoris, son of the man who had married Nellie Grant, both were in service. Ida was summoned to join Fred in Puerto Rico, where he was serving as military governor and Mrs. Palmer decided to take Julia abroad with her that winter. Her husband's health had been wretched all summer and he was in no condition to face the Chicago cold.

Passing through New York Bertha lost a diamond and emerald bracelet in a box at the Metropolitan Opera and did not miss it until an usher turned it in to the police. It was the second most valuable piece of jewelry ever found at the opera. She was inclined to be offhand with her jewels and they were a matter of great concern to her secretaries and personal maids. Her staff were always glad when Mr. Palmer took charge of them, as he frequently did. He chose to carry her jewel case when they traveled, and he frequently slept with valuable pieces under his pillow.

Laura Hayes, one of her secretaries, once sat up all night in an armchair in a European hotel with the jewels hidden behind her in an evening cloak. The rustle of a curtain, the slightest sound, made her jump with fright, for Mrs. Palmer had flung a fortune into her hands at the last minute as she left for a ball. She had been undecided what jewels to wear that evening. She had her emeralds, pearls and diamonds brought to her suite from the hotel safe. At the last moment she chose a magnificent combination of emeralds and left her pearls and diamonds in Miss Hayes' keeping, telling her to take care of them until she returned from the ball. Mrs. Palmer never worried at all about the safety of her collection, which had now reached imposing proportions.

Most of the pieces had been bought by Potter Palmer in the Paris branch of Tiffany's. The jewel salesmen of Paris liked to do business with this knowing merchant, aside from the large sums he paid for his wife's adornment. They always felt that he knew what he was doing, and rare pieces were brought to his attention. He would survey the field, make his selections, have special designs drawn up, then have them submitted to Cissie for her approval. She trusted implicitly in his taste in such matters.

She concentrated largely on diamonds and pearls. Her pearls gave luminosity to her fine skin and she wore them quite effectively. Her most commented-on piece was a seven-strand collar which had 2,268 pearls and seven diamonds. She was also particularly fond of a pink pearl as large as a hazelnut which she wore as a pendant. Her star sapphire and canary diamond rings were famous. She had tiaras and stomachers and a necklace of diamond stars that she wore frequently with black velvet. One pearl and diamond corsage brooch was a veritable sunburst. By the turn of the century her jewel collection was rated one of the most unusual in the world. It was certainly one of the best displayed, and it was sometimes compared with that of Queen Margherita, whose gems were famous. On several occasions Mrs. Palmer and the Queen discussed their jewels and once at tea the Queen observed: "Oh, so you have a star sapphire, too."

Bertha drew off her ring. The Queen examined it closely and sent for hers. Comparisons were made and Margherita seemed to feel that hers was the choicer sapphire. Mrs. Palmer was not so sure she was right. But no one questioned the fact that she wore her jewels with real distinction. It was the fashion of the day to mass tiaras, collar necklaces, earrings, stomachers, brooches, rings and bracelets into one grand array, and at times the effect was overpowering. In 1904 when she was crossing on the *Kaiser Wilhelm* she walked in late to the ship's concert, wearing a Worth gown and her most spectacular jewels. Alois Burgstaller, of the Metropolitan, was in the middle of an aria. He stopped dead as everyone in the saloon turned to gaze at Mrs. Potter Palmer of Chicago. The dazzle of her jewels in the half-light was positively blinding.

It was noted in the papers on both sides of the Atlantic that the diamonds in her tiara on this occasion were the size of Tokay grapes, and that she wore a sunburst of diamonds nearly ten inches in diameter, as well as her pearl collar and a flashing stomacher. But she had plenty of competition at this time. George W. Vanderbilt had given his bride a ruby necklace valued at $100,000. Mrs. William Astor's jewels were reported to be worth $340,000, including a dog collar that rivaled Mrs.

Potter Palmer's. Mrs. O. H. P. Belmont had a Marie Antoinette string of pearls valued at $100,000 and Mrs. Bradley Martin outdid them all, with a necklace of pearls worth $140,000, rubies valued at $200,000 and other choice pieces.

Mrs. Palmer's Chicago friends always observed her new jewels when she returned from one of her trips to Paris. Her husband never disclosed that he was the purchaser but he invariably drew attention to the ornament. "Cis has a new pendant she is wearing tonight," he would say. Ernest Poole thought that he "loaded her with jewels" but, looking at his hostess, he felt the money well spent, and wrote:

For Mrs. Palmer could hold her own—no matter how many jewels she wore. She was the kind of woman who could look quite at home, in marvelous clothes, during a long course dinner with many wines, served by six men, on damask and plate under sparkling crystal in her house. And not only handsome but quick and smart. At big public meetings she could preside with Robert's Rules of Order right at the tips of her glittering fingers.

Her old friend Mrs. Carter H. Harrison wrote that she had never known a woman to handle a heavy load of jewelry as gracefully as Mrs. Palmer, and a bedazzled grandson remembered a vision at the top of the staircase on party nights—"a slim and handsome woman sparkling with jewels and glowing with the hospitality she loved to dispense."

The Palmers spent several months abroad in 1899. They planned a serious sight-seeing tour for their sons and Julia before Honoré and Potter settled down to business. They had a stormy crossing but found London smug and luxurious on the eve of the Boer War. While the men went off to shop on Savile Row and Albion Street Bertha pulled strings to meet Lord Cromer, since they were heading for Cairo and he was the British statesman most closely associated with Egypt at that time. Henry White, American diplomat and close friend of John Hay, did his best for her but Lord Cromer had left for Khartoum and he was also in deep gloom over the death of his wife. White warned her that he would not be in the mood for social interchanges. But in general Mrs. Palmer was the diplomat's delight, an effective courier for her country.

They hurried through Paris to get Potter into the sun and soon Bertha was leading her handsome niece, who towered many inches above her, into the terrace restaurant of Shepheard's Hotel. Kitchener had just taken Khartoum and there was much excitement in Cairo. British officers in assorted uniforms swarmed on the terrace and beauties in billowing lawns and muslins sat over cool drinks or hot tea while orchestras and military bands played Viennese waltzes and Sousa two-steps. The Palmers wandered through the markets observing the veiled women, the Bedouins, the French nurses, the camels, donkeys and general confusion.

Honoré had letters of introduction to a native newspaperman and an Egyptian sheik. The sheik invited them all to his daughter's wedding reception and they drove in a landau through narrow streets to the old part of the city, then went on foot into a courtyard where canopies were stretched over poles and native musicians played atonal music. Men in Oriental uniforms and flowing robes mingled with frock-coated figures wearing fezzes. Soon Mrs. Palmer was seated at a low table in a huge room hung with blue brocade while a solemn coterie of Egyptian men studied her with appraising eyes.

She who had arranged so many banquets was baffled for a moment when a whole lamb was brought in, with servings of rice and corn but no knives or forks. The Egyptians dived in with their fingers but after some delay forks and plates were rounded up for the American guests. They were observed with close attention as they ate and some attempt was made to follow their example but without success. Mrs. Palmer went calmly on with her lamb and whipped out a pocket handkerchief to use as a napkin. Egyptian women were not present at this feast since the occupants of the host's harem could not appear.

Mrs. Palmer had said that she wished to see a real harem from the inside. This was not an idle fancy, but part of her serious study of the status of the Oriental woman. So she and Julia soon were led to a staircase. A door opened ahead of them and they were in the harem of the sheik. They were introduced to his oldest and first wife, one of a number of women of different age and stature who lounged about on cushions. All had big brown eyes and they gazed with blank concentration at their two American visitors. They wore Paris gowns without stays, smoked cigarettes and nibbled at Turkish delight. Since there were no interpreters Bertha could only gaze at them with bright attention but it was a scene she never forgot.

The Palmers sailed up the Nile to the First Cataract in the steam yacht *Nitocris* loaned them by the Khedive. They viewed ruins and haunted bazaars. They watched magnificent sunsets and visited native villages. They rode on donkeys and the young people enjoyed themselves, but Potter's health grew steadily worse. At last Mrs. Palmer decided that they must turn back and head straight for Rome, where he could have medical treatment. They took a steamer to Brindisi, then hurried north while the invalid grew weaker. A villa was rented in Rome and Potter was ordered to bed for a long rest. For once Mrs. Palmer slowed her pace so that she could spend nearly all her time with him. She encouraged Julia, Honoré and young Potter to go sight-seeing, and to visit friends, but she stayed at the villa, reading American papers and books to her husband, and attending to his comfort. Only occasionally did she go out for special events.

The carnival season was at its height, and soon the old habit of hospitality prevailed, with guests flocking to the villa. Inevitably Bertha became a hostess again in this new setting. Americans, Britons and Russians were quartered in palaces and villas and many of them gave fiestas. The Queen Mother, a "beautiful graceful woman with delightful manners," according to Julia, invited them to tea. There were luncheons, dinners, soirees and picnics. Mrs. Palmer chaperoned Julia at a court ball held at the Quirinal. They had tickets for a mass in the Sistine Chapel and soon Potter was well enough to face a private audience with Pope Leo XIII. Bertha found the head of the Catholic Church full of life and energy, although he was then touching ninety. He expressed great interest in the United States and Mrs. Palmer at once spoke of the Vatican exhibit at the Exposition. He asked many questions about the school system across the sea, addressing himself chiefly to her, since he did not speak English and she spoke perfect French. Afterward they toured the Vatican Gardens and were shepherded around by Merry Del Val, who was already well known to Mrs. Palmer. He had been on friendly terms with Fred and Ida in Vienna.

These were enchanted days for Julia as she rode over the Campagna with Dr. Robert J. Nevin, pastor of the American Church in Rome, whom her parents had known since childhood. He had been a young soldier with General Grant and had later joined the church. He lived in a simple rectory but all manner of worldly people called on him just to hear him talk. He was one of the six best shots in the world, and had hunted and explored in Asia, Africa and America. He was handsome, a good horseman and he knew Rome extraordinarily well, having lived there for thirty years. He gave Julia lessons in its art and history, and reports soon spread that she would marry him.

She and Mrs. Palmer dined with him at the Grand Hotel, one of the first really de luxe hotels in Europe, and all around them were women of great chic and reputation, such as Lady Randolph Churchill and the Duchess Grazioli, known for her elegance. But Mrs. Palmer stood out among them all and it was characteristic of her that a man of the cloth should be her dinner companion in this worldly paradise. But Julia had many beaux and although traveling Americans whispered that her aunt was trying to promote a good international marriage for her Julia later said of Mrs. Palmer: "I found in her a true friend whose advice was easy to follow as it coincided with my own ideas of what was right. I was grateful that in spite of our small means I was not pushed into a 'brilliant match.' "

But it seemed a brilliant match to the public, at least from the worldly point of view, when Julia married Prince Michel Cantacuzène. He happened to be in Rome recuperating from a horse-show accident while she was there with her aunt. The young diplomats often accompanied Julia and her cousins on picnics and this was how they met. After that, he was her escort at various balls and parties, and he fell deeply in love with her. Mrs. Palmer raised no objections. He came from an old Rumanian line and was well established at the Russian court. He was young, handsome and liberal-minded. Although not particularly well off, he could scarcely be accused of fortune hunting, since Julia's father had little more than his army pay.

By this time Potter was feeling better and his physicians advised him to move on to the Riviera for the sea air. A week after they got to Cannes Julia was passing through the hotel lobby, her arms filled with bundles, when Prince Cantacuzène confronted her. Although they had made plans to keep in touch she was so surprised that she dropped her parcels. She had understood he was going to Paris but a telegram from the Grand Duke Kyril had brought him to Cannes.

Two days later they were formally engaged. Mrs. Palmer telegraphed to Julia's parents. The Prince communicated with his family in Russia. Everyone was agreeable and Bertha at once began making plans for the wedding. She announced the engagement from Paris and delightedly began to order a trousseau for her niece, who seemed like her daughter. In June they sailed for the United States and the Prince went to Russia for a brief visit. Mrs. Palmer took the Astor villa, Beaulieu, at Newport and decided that this would be a suitable setting for Julia's wedding. Its gardens overhung Cliff Walk. The younger generation had gathered there for many fetes in the past.

Letters of condemnation poured in about General Grant's granddaughter marrying a foreigner and Mrs. Grant was reported to deplore a second international wedding in the family. Her daughter Nellie's marriage to Algernon Sartoris had foundered in England and by this time she and her children were back in Washington, living with Mrs. Grant.

Fantastic stories appeared about Julia's trousseau and the Cantacuzène family jewels and estates, but the truth was something simpler than the public believed. However, Mrs. Palmer saw that nothing was lacking at the wedding. She was in her element making the arrangements. This was the first marriage in her immediate family since Ida's a quarter of a century earlier. She began to explore her own lineage. She visited Hockley, the ancestral Honoré estate in Maryland, and found the house still standing. By this time Mrs. Palmer felt completely at home in Newport.

The wedding was held late in September, 1899. There were two ceremonies, Episcopal and Russian Orthodox. A special dispensation had been obtained so that the Russian service could be conducted in a private home. An altar was installed in the drawing room, which was otherwise stripped to look like a church. Pictures of saints were hung on the walls. No one was invited to the Russian service but members of the family, the ushers, Bishop Henry Codman Potter and Dr. Nevin, who had come from Rome to assist in the Episcopal service.

Honoré Palmer held a jeweled crown copied after the imperial crowns of Russia over Julia's head. Mrs. Palmer held another crown over the Prince's head, while the priest intoned in Slavonic and the choir chanted. Both bride and groom held lighted tapers and exchanged gold and silver rings three times, until the gold ring remained with the bride and the silver ring with the groom. Icons and incense were in use and the ceremonies lasted until nearly midnight.

The following day the Episcopal service was held in Trinity Episcopal Church, with Bishop Potter and Dr. Nevin officiating. The church was decorated with autumn flowers and a screen of feathery greens framed the altar. Since her father was in four battles during the week in which Julia was married, her brother, Ulysses S. Grant, III, then at West Point, gave her away. Their mother seemed tiny beside her two tall children.

Julia's gown was a simple one of white satin. Her tulle veil was severely plain and since jewels were forbidden for the Russian service she abode by this edict for both ceremonies. Prince Cantacuzène wore his regimental uniform of white cloth with red and silver trimmings, high black boots and gilded helmet tipped with the imperial eagle of Russia in silver. Luncheon was served under a great marquee at Beaulieu and the guests scattered over the lawns, salons and balconies. Henry H. Honoré, Mrs. Palmer's father, had come on from Chicago and Mrs. Ulysses S. Grant from Washington. Both wandered happily around the grounds, arm in arm, talking of the wedding of Ida and Fred in Chicago a quarter of a century earlier. Neither could see very well by this time. Mr. Honoré had cataracts and Mrs. Grant's vision was greatly impaired but they beamed happily at the bride and groom. By this time Mrs. Grant had decided that Julia was marrying well.

The young pair left for Russia, where Julia was presented at court and embarked on a full life of her own. This season was the climax of Mrs. Palmer's social career in the United States although she continued to entertain on a lavish scale wherever she was. The city officials of Chicago called on her regularly for assistance when distinguished guests arrived. They knew that she would open the doors of her home and receive them in royal style. When President Cleveland and President McKinley visited Chicago, she was always asked by the city fathers to lend her knowing touch to the occasion. When Prince Sadanaru Fushimi came to the United States as representative of the Emperor of Japan Honoré Palmer was his host at a memorable dinner at the Chicago Club. Again the Potter Palmers were hosts to the Comte de La Fayette and the Duc de la Rochefoucauld. Only once was Mrs. Palmer missing from one of these official receptions. When Prince Henry of Prussia arrived she had one of her rare illnesses, but Honoré, Potter and her brother Adrian functioned on her behalf.

She always adapted her menu, decorations and entertainment to the occasion when receiving guests in her own home. It might be Zorn or Elihu Root, Cardinal Gibbons or W. T. Stead, William Jennings Bryan or Chauncey Depew, a diplomat or a suffragist, but she juggled them all with great dexterity and things were never dull, nor did her parties fall too heavily into the conventional social pattern. When entertaining Baron and Baroness Hengelmuller of Austria-Hungary she had all her gold plate out for a formal dinner. Later in the evening she gave a reception in the French drawing room and a musicale in the art gallery. Both classical and popular music was provided—Gounod, Schumann and Archie Crawford. The tempo changed at suppertime, when wooden tables were brought in with beer steins and bologna. The guests sang choruses and all through supper they had a vaudeville performance with banjos playing, sleight of hand and skirt dancing. Mrs. Palmer wore a gown of crimson and yellow satin that night, trimmed with layers of orange and black chiffon to suggest an evolving nasturtium. The Baroness, black-haired with deep blue eyes, smoked cigars and sparkled with diamonds. This was remembered as one of Mrs. Palmer's more original parties and it helped to soothe the Baron, who had stamped out in high dudgeon when a hostess at Bar Harbor failed to seat him at her right. He had viewed this as an insult to his Emperor.

But no one could be more formal than Mrs. Palmer when the occasion demanded it. On party nights her turreted castle blazed with light from its towers to the porte-cochere. Japanese lanterns threw tinted beams on arriving guests and swayed among the palm, banana, ginger and other tropical trees in the conservatory. The sound of mandolins and guitars drifted out to Lake Shore Drive and things seemed secure along the Gold Coast when Mrs. Potter Palmer was giving one of her parties. Her mother attended many, her dark hair now turned white, her distinguished face reflecting the pride she felt in her daughters. Bertha and Ida Honoré of Louisville had indeed made their way in the world. Now Julia had picked up the tradition and would spread it farther afield.

8

➤➤➤➤➤➤➤➤➤➤➤➤ *Art Collector*

If all else about Mrs. Potter Palmer were forgotten she would still be remembered as the person who introduced Impressionist art to the United States in a convincing way. From the 1880's on she was a bold collector who displayed her paintings with pride and dared the traditionalists to spurn them. A tour of the gallery that her husband added to their mansion became one of the more esoteric rites of Chicago's social life at the turn of the century.

Her collection covered three periods—the Romantics, the Barbizon school and the Impressionists. But she stopped short of the Cubists and Abstractionists and never owned a Cézanne, Gauguin, Matisse or Picasso. By the time they flourished her husband was dead and she was overstocked with pictures. She had moved on to medieval furnishings and Oriental porcelains and jade. But she had definitely affected the prevailing taste in art.

Daniel Catton Rich, director in turn of the Art Institute of Chicago and of the Worcester Art Museum, views her as a true pace setter in American art. He believes that if she had rounded up old masters, like Sir Joseph Duveen, she would have drawn her own following in that field. But Mrs. Palmer found it adventurous and chic to back the Impressionists. They made fashionable interior decoration as well as being experimental art.

"In collecting you always have to have a leader and she was prescient enough to realize that they would catch on," Mr. Rich comments. "She made the Impressionists a style and helped the independents to move ahead. She was definitely creative and never a copyist in any field. She had an open mind and an alert eye for new trends and her interest in art was genuine. In collecting Impressionist, Chinese and Renaissance art she was a great eclectic in policy. She made few mistakes in her selections, from her Millets, Corots and Daubignys of the Barbizon school, to a Romantic like Delacroix, and on to her Impressionists."

Only a few of her friends could accept at first her frieze of Monets but today the Art Institute of Chicago glories in her paintings by Sisley, Pissarro, Delacroix, Corot, Degas, Renoir and Monet that they acquired in 1922 through the terms of Mrs. Palmer's will.

In 1893 she lent the French section of the Fine Arts Palace at the World's Columbian Exposition some of her best Barbizon and Impressionist paintings, thereby giving national stimulus to modern art. But it took some weathering for the critics and the public to accept the artists whose work seemed freakish and mad to them when Paul Durand-Ruel in 1886 brought over an exhibition of three hundred paintings valued at eighty thousand dollars. The critics condemned them, using the masters as yardsticks. So little was known about the individual artists that Monet and Manet were confused in the catalogue. Even Parisians had threatened to punch holes in the canvases with their umbrellas at an earlier showing by Durand-Ruel. But at least the Impressionists caused talk and their carefree, flowing art and intense use of light had insidious appeal.

When Mrs. Palmer gave her approval to the new school of

art her friends took a second look. Most of them viewed its blurred pitch with suspicion. She was well aware that she was breaking ground and could spot their skepticism at a glance when she led them into her gallery and they stood face to face with the unfamiliar. However, when Mrs. Palmer backed some new development she was apt to command support, or at least to engage the attention of those around her.

She made her finds sound provocative as she described the artists, their ways of living and their varied techniques. On her trips abroad she had come to know a number of them. She and her husband had driven out to Barbizon to see the painters at work. She had climbed to their garrets in Montmartre and Rome. They had joined her for tea at the Grand Hotel. She had chatted with Georges Clemenceau, Edmond de Goncourt and the Comte de Montesquieu at Raffaelli's studio in Paris. She had visited Monet at Giverny and had seen for herself his golden haystacks and silvery poplars, the crimson and lemon lilies floating in his pond, the misty lilac light streaming through weeping willows, the bright marigold borders in his dreamlike garden, all of which contributed to the shimmer of his work. She accepted Monet's judgment that "Impressionism is only direct sensation" and agreed with his friend Clemenceau that he was a "lyrical poet in paint."

Cazin was well known to Mrs. Palmer and she had met Degas and Pissarro. What the Impressionists thought of their American patron is not recorded, but Whistler, on his only visit to Rome, recalled "a bit of an old ruin alongside of a railway station where I saw Mrs. Potter Palmer." In time she came to know the major figures in the art world. Antoine Proust, Minister of the Beaux Arts in France, never forgot Mrs. Palmer after his dealings with her at the time of the Exposition. She left sharp memories, although he had not succumbed to modern art.

The appearance of the Palmers at the salons in Paris or at Sotheby's in London always caused a stirring of interest.

Bertha became as familiar a figure at Durand-Ruel's in Paris as at Tiffany's and Worth's. She followed the trail of modern art wherever it led her and was an astute bargainer at home and abroad. It was noted by those who dealt with her that she always knew what she wanted. Men liked to deal with her. She was decisive and judicial to the point of coldness in her thinking, yet warmly feminine in her presence.

When she called on Benjamin K. Smith, her favorite art dealer in Chicago, in a victoria drawn by handsome bays, and stepped out, trim, small-waisted and beautifully gowned, he prepared himself for a brisk exchange. Her softly cadenced voice and firm manner presaged the outcome. If the silver vegetable dishes were fifteen hundred dollars she would offer a thousand and stick to her bid. But her sense of humor came into play when she was bargaining. She would leave everyone in good spirits when she strolled out, unfurling her parasol as she stepped back into her carriage.

Ida, who had perhaps the most intimate knowledge of her from childhood, believed that her sister's art collection was a true expression of her nature, and that she bought a picture, not to get the work of some particular artist or school, but because of its personal appeal for her. However, her choices suggest considerable concentration of interest and approach. After her early initiation she relied chiefly on her own and her husband's judgment. He was more of a factor in her art purchases than anyone outside of the immediate family ever knew, since he always wanted Cissie to get full credit for everything. But he was the inveterate buyer, with the same knowing approach to pictures as to other material possessions. However, his wife's taste prevailed.

She was influenced in the beginning by Mary Cassatt, who was pushing the Impressionists for all she was worth and already had Mrs. H. O. Havemeyer in tow as an interested buyer. Miss Cassatt was a godsend to Durand-Ruel, and so was Sara T. Hallowell, another American who acted as agent and go-between in the art world. Mrs. Palmer's first purchase of modern art was *On the Stage* by Degas, Mary Cassatt's particular protégé. This was a much admired twenty-two-inch pastel which she bought in 1889 for five hundred dollars. Three years later she picked up another Degas, *Dancers Preparing for the Ballet*, and added two more in 1896. She was particularly fond of Degas's work.

Although the Palmers had been buying art in a desultory way before 1890 their interest was greatly intensified when they went abroad immediately after Mrs. Palmer became chairman of the board of lady managers. With the Fair in mind they concentrated on the subject and a whole new world of art opened up before their eyes—the world of the Impressionists. They acquired the bulk of their collection in 1891 and 1892. It was guaranteed to cause a sensation. All through life Mrs. Palmer sought the unique or superlative, and she never hesitated to make the plunge when she saw what she wanted.

Her association with Miss Hallowell flowered at this time. Sara had charge of the art loans from France for the Fair, but the Palmers were already quite familiar with her capacities. They had used her as their personal agent and scout in making their own art purchases. Although Mrs. Palmer liked to encourage new talent, she always wanted to be sure that it really was talent before she embraced it, and here Miss Hallowell was of inestimable help. She was as knowing as anyone in the business and Bertha could always rely on her expert professional advice. Sara circulated among the Impressionists. She looked them up in their studios and visited them in their forest retreats. She staked them at times, appraised their work, cheered them in dark moments, established American links and worked smoothly with Durand-Ruel, who had pushed them with more faith than success. Mary Cassatt was the inspiration. Sara was the work horse.

She scurried around Paris when she knew the Potter Palmers

were arriving, seeing what the dealers had to offer, haunting the studios. She kept in touch with Mrs. Palmer by letter, too, and in 1892, when she was scouting for their private collection as well as for the Fair, she wrote of running into Erwin Davis's apartment to look at his collection. He had already parted with a Degas that Mrs. Palmer admired but Sara was not going to let another elude her. Davis was seriously ill at the time but she had carte blanche to visit his apartment and look around. His housekeeper showed her some Chinese embroideries that had interested Mrs. Palmer.

She soon found that it was easier to influence Mr. Palmer than his wife, and she could usually persuade him to do what she wished. Both were fair and considerate in their art dealings, in Miss Hallowell's estimation. Once persuaded of the quality and distinction of a painting there was no trouble about price, but so obscure were the Impressionists when the Palmers did their early buying that they picked up paintings for next to nothing that today are worth fortunes. They paid much higher prices for their Millets and Daubignys than they did for the pictures of men who were still too controversial to draw big prices on the market.

Palmer liked to prowl in the art shops when he did not go to the races, and he listened quietly and without expression to the bohemians who buttonholed him in the studios or at Bertha's teas. As the rich American in quest of pictures he was not underestimated but Madame Palmer was always the star performer. She conversed easily and fluently with the artists in their own language, and gave sympathetic attention to their whims and aspirations. It piqued her interest when Sara took her for a foray into Montmartre, its most characteristic self at the turn of the century, with its cabarets, clowns and equestrians, its Moulin Rouge and at night the warm yellow light streaming from round gas globes.

In Rome she hunted up H. C. Andersen, an unknown sculptor, and soon had Americans calling on him to buy his work. She climbed up to his bare studio and bought a Florentine bust. Henry James followed suit, purchasing the terracotta Bevilacqua bust. Andersen was a friend of John Elliott, the son-in-law of Julia Ward Howe, who also lived in Rome at this time and welcomed Mrs. Palmer to his quarters. Elliott was already known to her. He had painted the *Story of the Vintage* in his Via Flaminia studio for her dining room ceiling on Lake Shore Drive. He also did an ivory miniature of Mrs. Palmer, which she liked.

Elliott was in Chicago at the time of the Exposition and "some of the merchant princes made us welcome to the city they loved as men only love the things they create," he commented. He was impressed by the fact that eight of these men, including Potter Palmer, had agreed "to put their hands in their pockets and pay down one million dollars each, to insure the success of the World's Fair and to ask nothing in return."

In the winter of 1892 Miss Hallowell was rounding up animal pictures in Paris for Mrs. Palmer and was on the trail of two by Delacroix. Durand-Ruel was asking $25,000 for his *Tiger Hunt*. Another of a single tiger that she coveted was owned by the American Art Association at that time. "I know of nothing here which is fine enough for you to place in your great collection excepting the two works by Delacroix of which I speak," Sara wrote. Albert Spencer had a Monet that she wished Mrs. Palmer owned. It was "the very incarnation of refined color and poetic expression, not to be bought." Although her work for the Exposition went slowly, "I will not disappoint you or Mr. Palmer in showing you the finest collection of the works of this century ever brought together."

Miss Hallowell finally got across the Atlantic with her paintings in March, 1893, but she had many troubles en route. Her responsibility was great, since she had entire charge of the loan collection for the Fair. Cholera broke out on the *Aurania* and when she reached the Grand Hotel in New York she dashed off a note to Potter Palmer, assuring him that

Sisley's *Street at Moret* was so carefully packed in the hold that it did not have to be fumigated. But she feared the Corots would be late reaching Chicago. She urged Mr. Palmer to have them sent direct in bond to the Exposition. She also asked him to use his good offices with his wife to persuade her to lend some of her best paintings to the Exposition. Sara wrote:

> Unless Mrs. Palmer rebels altogether at my persistence, I think our great loan collection must count upon you for (besides the Corots) your beautiful Puvis de Chavannes, Cazin's *Judith* and *Elsinore*, Raffaelli's *Absinthe Drinkers* and two smaller ones (a living artist is allowed but three examples and I find no Raffaellis equal to yours), and one of your works by Delacroix, unless in requesting the last, you find us altogether unreasonable. It *is* cruel to ask you, but I am lost to all sense of consideration at this time. Moreover you have the most fascinating collection in the country and it is a matter of such pride to me to have this fact recognized even by the showing of a *few* of your pictures. If you think you are going to consent—and you know Mrs. Palmer whom I adore in *all else* has begged me not to ask—I want your values for each separately, for the insurance bureau is now adjusting its matters for the loan collection. I can never sufficiently express the gratitude I feel for all of your generous thoughtful kindness shown me personally. . . .

Both of the Palmers consented and some of their choicest pictures graced the Fair. The official French art show had only one Impressionist picture, but the loan exhibition included pictures by Degas, Manet, Monet, Pissarro, Renoir, Sisley, Cazin, Corot, Raffaelli and Puvis de Chavannes. The donors were A. J. Cassatt, James S. Inglis, Potter Palmer, Albert Spencer and Frank Thompson. This exhibit turned out to be the sensation of the art showing at the Fair. It was much discussed and the story of the crazy pictures seen in Chicago was carried back to the farms, the small towns, villages and other cities. Nothing like them had been seen by so large a body of Americans up to that time.

After the Fair Mrs. Palmer hung her paintings in her private gallery, grouping them according to schools. She gave much time and thought to their arrangement. They were displayed in three tiers against a rose-red velvet background. Cazin's *Judith* was the largest picture in her gallery. Corot's *Orpheus* hung between two tall medieval pillars supported by urns. She was the most effective of all guides in drawing her guests' attention to the best points of her collection. When she led a parade of spectators through her well-stocked gallery she was consciously fostering a movement. As an eloquent advocate of the Impressionists she took time to justify her liking for certain paintings when she felt the frost was thick around her. She read closely on the subject, since Mrs. Palmer went in for specifics in her conversation.

Her guests always lingered over Renoir's *Dans le Cirque,* the two little circus girls who never ceased to delight her. This was perhaps her favorite painting in the entire collection. She admired the luminous color and the vivacious attitude of the two poised figures and for a time this painting hung in her bedroom. She paid $1,750 for it when she bought it in 1892 and it has since been valued at $200,000. She acquired eleven Renoirs altogether in that same year. They were quite generally admired, even by the traditionalists, and Martin A. Ryerson was of the opinion that Renoir's smooth faced girls went well with old masters. *The Wave* and *Rowers' Luncheon* caused talk in Chicago.

Mrs. Palmer greatly loved her Monets and they made a brilliant but bewildering show for the uninitiated. His *Argenteuil-sur-Seine*, which she bought for fifteen hundred dollars, was rated one of the gems of her collection. She bought seven Monets in 1891, twenty-two in 1892, one in 1903, one in 1904 and another as late as 1910, making thirty-two in all. Monet was in Paris early in 1892 for a Renoir exhibition and met his American patron then.

Mrs. Palmer also bought four Sisleys and six Pissarros in

1892, her big buying year. Miss Hallowell was a Delacroix enthusiast and his painting *Combat Between the Giaour and the Pasha*, which was added to the Palmer collection, is rated one of his finest works. Her Millets, which included *The Woodchopper* and *The Little Shepherdess*, were a choice group assembled while the Barbizon school was in high fashion, and the Impressionists were little more than a disturbing whisper on the breeze, so far as the art market was concerned. But Mrs. Palmer moved into the experimental field without hesitation.

Her art treasures ranged historically from Tanagra terra cottas to Monet's last study of a London dawn, which she called "the finest singing of this singularly lyric art." They were drawn from different epochs and nations but she had no old masters. The porcelains and ivories which she collected in her later years filled four cabinets in the large drawing room of her Lake Shore home. Her Chinese porcelains were of the rarest sort and she was among the first Americans to collect Tang figurines. She had particularly fine examples of the gray pottery horses of the Sung dynasty. Her jade was famous, but she soon saw that visitors did not linger over her Oriental collection. They preferred to spend time on her paintings, so that after her husband's death she had them removed to her house in Paris where they were more appreciated.

Like all collectors, Mrs. Palmer on several occasions blundered into fakes. She thought she had an original Corot in *Girl with the Lute*, but after her death it was found to be a copy and was withdrawn from a projected sale. Another of her Corots that came into question was the *Woman with Water Jar*, later bought by the Phillips Memorial Gallery in Washington. An identical painting, also attributed to Corot, was *Gypsy Girl at the Fountain*, in the George W. Elkins collection, Philadelphia. Both were subjected to technical study by infrared photography at the Fogg Museum. Shortly before her death in 1918 Mrs. Palmer's Corots were appraised variously at thirty, forty and fifty thousand dollars and their value today is proportionate. Although the early paintings of Corot, the great dissembler who could imitate the style of any painter, ancient or modern, have declined in value, some of his later figure pieces and his finest landscapes have weathered this depreciation.

Mrs. Palmer's only investment in what she believed to be an old master turned out to be a copy. This was the Veronese she had stored in London at the outbreak of the First World War. After her death experts noted several small discrepancies in her listings. One of her favorite paintings was a rare figure piece by Corot which she called *Reverie*. Later it developed that Robaut, the leading Corot expert, had it listed as *La Lecture Interrompue* or *Interrupted Reading*, the title it bears today. Pissarro's *Place du Havre* in Paris was incorrectly identified as the *Place de la République* in Rouen.

Mrs. Palmer did not limit herself to European art. She collected American paintings, too, and her husband was bidding for a George Inness in New York as far back as 1889. She had paintings by Mary Cassatt and Whistler, by F. Hopkinson Smith and Eastman Johnson, by George Hitchcock, George Fuller and Inness. Zorn's painting of her hung in her gallery after the Exposition, and she had some Gari Melchers portraits, including paintings of Honoré and Potter.

There were times when Mrs. Palmer's enthusiasm for art purchases brought mild protests from her husband. Young Potter, hearing one of these discussions, feared his parents were short of money. "If you need cash, I could sell my English bicycle," he said. The Palmers reassured their sensitive son.

Mrs. Palmer made a habit of lending her prestige to openings and was a closely observed figure at art exhibitions. Her presence was regarded as an event in itself. Now and again she gave talks at the Institute. On these occasions she was a well-informed and sometimes even a piquant speaker. The newspapers seized gleefully on one of her chance remarks: "You women know how it is. The more you put on, sometimes, the worse you look, and the more you take off, the better you look."

When Mrs. Palmer was caught in a malapropism—which she rarely was—she made good newspaper copy. Not that a merry quip in the press at her expense bothered her greatly. She was too sure of herself and her standing for that. But her stately façade invited pinpricks. She always preferred that her husband's name alone should appear on their art contributions to the Institute. The Palmer name is indissolubly associated with the Italian Reinaissance building, which combines schools, libraries and a museum and now houses a considerable part of the Palmer collection. Bertha's children and grandchildren have been identified with it in one way or another and her second son Potter and his wife Pauline became zealous collectors on their own account. The younger Potter served as president of the Institute from 1925 to 1943.

When her sons came of age Mrs. Palmer wrote quite frankly to Charles L. Hutchinson, saying she would like them to become members of the Institute and to show an interest in its development. "If you could put them on any of your committees, I should be very glad to have either of them be of service to you," she suggested.

Later she again wrote to Hutchinson with a more specific request, urging that Honoré be made a member of the board. In this letter she was quite explicit:

> I mention this to you quite frankly, for I feel sure that so old and valued a friend as you are, would help to realise my wish in case it becomes possible. We have always taken great interest in the Institute and would like to give evidence of it.
>
> Honoré is very fond of art and would be very sympathetic with all of the aims and purposes of the Art Institute and you would, I am sure, find him a congenial and useful co-worker. Please give this a thought at a suitable moment.

Mrs. Palmer had many professional interchanges with Hutchinson, a banker who had inherited a fortune from his wheat-trading father and was a brisk promoter. He and Ryerson, a studious and traveled man who cultivated the arts in Chicago and was deeply committed to the Impressionists, worked with unity of purpose in building up the Institute. They frequently consulted the Palmers and relied on their judgment when they were abroad to do art scouting for them. They had loan exhibitions every autumn and Mrs. Palmer was always ready to round up material for these events. This went beyond paintings. She helped to build up the medieval textile collection of the Institute, among other things. When the Frederic Spitzer collection of antiques and medieval and Renaissance furnishings went on the market Mrs. Palmer was in Paris and Hutchinson wrote asking her to survey the situation for him. She replied at once that she would assemble information on prices and values. At that moment she was about to meet Sir Philip Owen and this led her to comment: "The South Kensington Museum has of course been of inestimable advantage to the artistic development of England and I trust our own Museum may one day be well enough equipped to play a similar role in our part of the world."

Actually, her family's taste for art was of long cultivation. It did not spring into being with her discovery of the Impressionists. Her husband was one of the small group of men who worked both before and after the fire to foster interest in an art school and exhibitions of paintings. He was drawn into active participation when the Chicago Academy of Design was reorganized after the fire from a small art school which had worked with plaster casts. Palmer was appointed to the board in 1877 and after another reorganization the Institute itself was established in 1883. From the Romanesque building it occupied in the beginning it took possession in 1893 of the Italian Renaissance edifice of today.

Both of the Palmers showed keen interest in all these developments and Potter was behind an exposition of the industries and art of the Middle West long before the Columbian Exposition was held. Chicago, enterprising and alert to all the current movements, was not slow to foster the arts. Hutchinson and Ryerson had a much discussed showing of old masters in 1890. By that time Ryerson, Charles T. Yerkes, James Ellsworth, Marshall Field, Potter Palmer, W. W. Kimball, Arthur Jerome Eddy, Frederick Clay Bartlett and Kate Buckingham were building up imposing collections. By degrees some moved gingerly toward modern art. The Henry Field collection included forty-one Barbizon masters and a few paintings by artists of the Paris Salon who were considered *avant-garde*. W. W. Kimball, whose wife was one of Bertha's closest friends, also was a convert. But Mrs. Palmer, Ryerson and Hutchinson were consistently independent and far-seeing connoisseurs, much ahead of their time.

An extraordinary range of people viewed Mrs. Palmer's private art gallery, from factory girls to princes. Her paintings received a good many puzzled glances as well as polite comment. The most articulate on the subject were the writers, artists and stage stars, who had no hesitation about expressing their views. The arts were usually represented in one way or another at her gatherings, invariably from the upper strata, and all the Palmers took a lively interest in music, books, the theater and the press. The bohemian set then beginning to flower in Chicago viewed the Impressionists as kin. They thought it amusing that the sacrosanct Mrs. Potter Palmer should be the leader in this movement. Art had become one avenue of approach to her aloof presence although her staff still intervened while she spread bounty from a distant cloud.

The 1890's added a sparkling chapter to Chicago's history. Seventy new periodicals were established. George Ade was contributing his *Fables in Slang* to the Chicago *Record*. Hamlin Garland was just getting under way as a writer. Finley Peter Dunne was on the editorial staff of the *Times-Herald* and he had brought Mr. Dooley to life. Eugene Field, who occasionally gibed at Mrs. Palmer, died in 1895. Robert Herrick and William V. Moody both were teaching at the University of Chicago and were turning out books. Henry B. Fuller had written *The Cliff-Dwellers* and the story spread that Cecilia Ingles was none other than Mrs. Potter Palmer.

Visiting authors and artists from Europe turned up regularly at the Palmer House, as well as stage and opera stars. Bertha could look back on a long procession in the half-century since she had moved from Louisville to Chicago. She had watched two generations of stars come and go, both European and American. She invariably took boxes for opera, the best concerts and plays, and her particular devotion after art was to music. She had heard Melba, Nordica, the De Reszke brothers, Paderewski, De Pachmann, Patti, Nilsson, Calvé, Ole Bull, Josef Hofmann and many others play or sing in the Central Music Hall. From 1879 to 1889 this hall was Chicago's musical and cultural center. Singers from the Metropolitan Opera traveled west and in 1884 Walter Damrosch headed his father's company and added Wagner's *Tannhäuser* and *Lohengrin* to his repertoire. The Boston Symphony Orchestra was heard in 1887, and Strauss thrilled Chicago three years later with his Vienna Orchestra.

Mrs. Palmer was always a good friend to Theodore Thomas and helped to support his orchestra. After the fire he came to play each year and during the Exposition he was a stand-by for the Woman's Building. He dined often at her home, a strong and fiery maestro who thought nothing of hurling a slipper or his wig at a wavering player. He encouraged American artists like Edward A. MacDowell and introduced works that had not yet been heard in New York. Mrs. Palmer liked his enterprise and spirit. "Chicago is the only city on the continent, next to New York, where there is sufficient musical culture to enable me to give a series of fifty consecutive concerts," he commented on one occasion.

Bertha and Ida, who still played the harp and piano, were among his most attentive listeners and the glitter of diamonds in the Palmer box was always a reassuring sight on concert nights. In the late 1880's Mrs. Palmer was seen often at the theater, attentively watching Edward H. Sothern, Robert Mantell, Richard Mansfield and other stars of the period. Henry Irving and Ellen Terry visited Chicago repeatedly after 1884. Helen Modjeska played in *Camille*, Sarah Bernhardt in *Adrienne Lecouvreur* and Lillian Russell in *La Tzigane*. Bertha watched Lily Langtry act with Maurice Barrymore and Mrs. James Brown Potter with Kyrle Bellew. Minnie Maddern, later Mrs. Fiske, was one of the enchantments of the summer of 1882, and Ada Rehan, John Drew and Otis Skinner were appearing at the same time. Mrs. Patrick Campbell said that stage stars were received with warmth and enthusiasm in Chicago. It was a good theater town.

Bertha's memory went back even further to the days of Crosby's and McVicker's, where *Aida* was sung in 1874, the year of Honoré's birth and Ida's marriage, and where Albani gave Chicago its earliest *Lohengrin*. Hooley's Theater opened in 1872 for plays, operettas and classical works and there were variety shows at the Adelphi after 1874. In these earlier days Chicago welcomed Charlotte Cushman, Edwin Booth, Lawrence Barrett and John McCullough. Although it would have been unthinkable to invite an actress to her home in the 1870's, by the 1890's Mrs. Palmer spiced up her most exclusive parties with a dash of the stage.

Toward the turn of the century she was seeing the best of theater and opera on both sides of the Atlantic and was as well known at Covent Garden and the Paris Opera as she was in Chicago or at the Metropolitan. She was never strongly identified with New York, except for brief visits as she passed through on her way to Europe. Chicago was unmistakably her home. But she was always observed when she did arrive and she had friends everywhere. She went to the opera, the theater, the horse show, art exhibitions and the shops. Invitations pursued her wherever she settled. In the early days she stayed at the Fifth Avenue Hotel, then at the old Waldorf, the Manhattan Hotel and ultimately at the St. Regis Hotel. She invariably visited Ida and Fred in New York and Mrs. Grant in Washington until the death of the General's widow in 1902. But by the turn of the century she had become a citizen of the world.

9

>>>>>>>>>>>>>> *The Paris Exposition*

In 1900 Paris was in its most enchanted mood. The Exposition was in progress and visitors came from all parts of the world to view it. Mrs. Potter Palmer, appointed by President McKinley the only woman member of the National Commission representing the United States, arrived to find the city sparkling with life. She and her husband immediately took a large house on the Rue Brignole near the Trocadéro, staffed it with servants and began to entertain on an elaborate scale.

The American colony was at full strength but Mrs. Palmer could reach beyond it to the Faubourg Saint Germain because of her French ancestry and her perfect knowledge of the language. She moved with ease in both worlds and found the cosmopolitan touch much to her liking. The Prince of Wales came over to Paris for visits. The King of Greece was at the Bristol Hotel. J. P. Morgan, now assembling his great art collection, drove about looking aloof and morose. An endless stream of carriages flowed along the Avenue des Acacias through the violet haze of late afternoon but the automobiles were increasing in number. There were morning drives in the

Bois, afternoon gatherings at the Petit Trianon. The fashionables assembled for afternoon tea in their favorite haunts near the Rue Royale and the Boulevard Haussmann, or in the leafy resorts on the Bois. Many drove to the Pavillon Bleu of Saint-Cloud. They dined at Paillard's, the Ritz, the Pavillon d'Armenonville or the reopened Cubat's near the Rond Pont.

Meanwhile, great dinners and balls were given by the American and British hostesses who had taken quarters in Paris for the Exposition. As the one woman commissioner and a noted hostess in her own right Mrs. Palmer fulfilled her role with her customary magnificence and efficiency. But she could not function with quite the freedom she had enjoyed in Chicago, where her word was law and she had hordes of willing workers. She did not have the office organization she had built up at that time and much of her work was done in the salons by persuasion and suggestion. The French officials were won by her eloquence and charm, although in the first instance they had protested the appointment of a woman commissioner. They had been nurtured on pictures of American Bloomerism and reedy spinsters in red shawls serving on committees and battling for women's rights. Here was a woman of the utmost elegance, one of Worth's choicest products, telling them in impeccable French what must and should be done. Mrs. Palmer kept the feminine angle well to the fore all summer and did it with style. Her specific task was to look after the interests of her fellow countrywomen in Paris and she made people realize, both on and off the Exposition grounds, that American women were present.

She scored point after point in a quiet way. She got Jane Addams appointed to an important post over the opposition of the French directors. She staged a strategic campaign to get women on the award juries, an issue she had battled out in Chicago at the time of the Columbian Exposition. And she functioned on a regal scale as hostess. But she had not counted on subversion in her own ranks. Old feuds and enmities arose to plague her. Two of her compatriots staged a powerful rebellion against her. Mrs. John A. Logan, who had once been her friend and now was her enemy, tried to block her appointment in the first instance and, when that failed, she fired a gun point-blank into the Commission headquarters, charging that Mrs. Palmer had snubbed her and that she catered to the French at the expense of the American colony.

More damaging to Mrs. Palmer was the wide-open campaign conducted by Mrs. Ferdinand W. Peck to curb her power. Mrs. Peck announced publicly that she would not let Bertha, an honorary commissioner, precede her at social functions connected with the Exposition. Peck, an old colleague from the days of the Chicago Fair, was official head of the American Commission and he felt that his wife should have precedence at public functions. But it was clear to everyone that Mrs. Palmer was running away with the honors. The Pecks, too, had taken a fine house and were giving dinners for a semi-official coterie. But they could not match the assemblage of world celebrities that Bertha gathered in.

Peck was a zealous promoter of the arts in Chicago and he and Mrs. Palmer had many mutual interests, although they did not always see eye to eye. He was the son of a pioneer who had founded Chicago's fire department and was one of the builders of the city, like her own father and husband. Music was Peck's special interest and he was responsible for the Auditorium, which was planned originally to house opera and promote the arts. He maintained that there was no place in Chicago for a privileged class and he kept the number of boxes in the large hall to a minimum. He scorned the Metropolitan in New York as a building sacrificed almost entirely to boxes. He preferred to have the Chicago Auditorium represent "the future and not the corrupted past."

Echoes of old debates divided the Pecks and Mrs. Palmer as the Paris Exposition opened. How had she maneuvered the appointment, her critics asked. Had she pulled strings through the White House? Was she up to her old tricks of playing the field with a lone hand? Mrs. Logan and several other women who had worked with her at the Columbian Exposition were now her most vocal critics. They felt that too much of the credit had gone to her, and that she had been high-handed in her dealings with her colleagues. They sought to curb her power at the Paris Exposition from the outset and keep her from running away with the show. They saw at once that her French inheritance paved the way for her in Paris and she made the most of this sympathetic response.

Since the turn of the century native comment on Mrs. Palmer had become less reverential in tone. She had come under the blight in Middle Western eyes of foreign entanglements and pretension. There was not the old, warm applause for every move she made, nor the proprietary feeling that she was theirs alone. The Easterners viewed her coldly, too. The New York Senators had opposed her appointment to the Commission. Why a woman—and in particular a woman from Chicago? Rivalry between New York and Chicago entered into this attitude, however.

Her critics thought her ambitious and scheming in her plans and the opposition to her was both veiled and out in the open. But the organizing touch was quite irresistible to Mrs. Palmer. She had everything on her side—strategic skill, capacity, money, position, contacts the world around and considerable suavity in her approach, as well as a will of iron which she could impose on others in beautifully couched language. Mrs. Logan's efforts to block her career that summer as she sailed along, the brightest star in the French heavens, came to nothing. On her official trip to Paris in 1891 she had entrenched herself firmly, leaving a strong impression of her own personality and competence.

The papers and magazines in Paris and London played up the fact that she was of French ancestry, that she was rich, well dressed and was known as the Queen of Chicago. Claire de

Pratz, writing in *La Fronde* on May 10, 1900, found her a combination of "French elegance and much allure." This writer was also impressed by her practical approach to the Exposition and her frank concern that Frenchwomen—"so marvelously dressed, so clever at their work, so well balanced" —should not have a larger part in the administration of the Exposition and share in the awards. She favored more women's congresses, and executive power for the brainy women of France. At this time Mrs. Palmer was fifty-one and Mlle. de Pratz found her looking remarkably young with her effective "aureole of gray hair." She likened her eyes to black velvet.

A correspondent for *Society*, a London publication, reported that she was a handsome woman, "still very young looking, and has had the high compliment paid to her of being told by a Royal personage that she was the best dressed woman in Paris, and that during Exhibition year." It was noted that she got in and out of her carriage with supple grace and moved most flexibly in ballrooms in spite of the iron corseting and heavy brocades of the period. All through life Mrs. Palmer managed to look regal, although she was below average height. But she was graceful rather than stiff in her bearing, and was apt to capture the attention of everyone present when she entered a room. Not only was she serene and poised, but her intelligence was never dormant.

Another journalist collided with Mrs. Palmer on her way to attend the preview on the Place Vendôme of the fashions to be worn at the Exposition. Both had to fight their way through the assemblage of automobiles with dust-colored satin linings jammed close together at the entrance. Everyone knew who Mrs. Palmer was when she took a front-row seat in the scented salon and watched the parade go by. She was well known at such showings as a shrewd judge and lavish buyer. At this time she went for her own clothes to Worth, Paquin, Callot Soeurs and Doeuillet.

It was a period of great picture hats loaded with artificial fruit and flowers, accompanying lacy gowns; of neat little toques worn with linen or tweed bolero costumes; of swirling skirts over a froufrou of lacy petticoats; of gossamer tulles sparkling with arabesques of *diamanté;* of wide elastic belts studded with rhinestones and tucked parasols with lace insertion. Everything sparkled and glittered.

Mrs. Palmer made her own selections swiftly, notably a yellow velvet mantle with a gray sheen and chinchilla collar that her friends considered one of the most becoming garments with her gray hair that she ever owned. She saw much of Jean Worth while the Exposition was running. His father Charles, who had dressed her for years, had died in 1895. The younger Worth was unhappy at the start about the space allotted him. There were more exhibitors than there was room and he had one of the dark corners of the exhibition hall. But he installed a Louis XVI drawing room and made it the stage setting for a composite picture of British life, from court costume to maid's uniform. This show became a sensational success and was one of the chief drawing cards for women at the Exposition.

Worth had his favorites among the women he dressed and Mrs. Potter Palmer was one of them. He liked those who showed off his gowns to good advantage and circulated widely. He considered Queen Alexandra "something of a dowd" and had made only one dress for her. The fact was that she preferred to buy in Britain. One of his great favorites was Lady de Grey, later the Marchioness of Ripon, who was more than six feet tall and remarkably graceful. Queen Margherita of Italy, Princess Orloff and Madame de Metternich, all good friends of Mrs. Palmer's, were among his customers at this time. The Metternichs had a splendid house in Paris near the Rue de la Varenne. Lily Langtry, whom Bertha did not count among her friends, launched fashions for Worth by reason of her fame and magnificent figure. He introduced his first jersey costume, a blue pleated skirt with tight-fitting bodice and red sash, through Mrs. Langtry, whose green eyes and alabaster skin always aroused comment when she arrived for a fitting.

Paris was the showcase of the world at the moment. Its Exposition had all the dash and spirit of its Gallic setting. Great crowds poured into the Champs de Mars and *joie de vivre* was rampant. Mrs. Palmer went back and forth every day attending to official business, studying the crowds with interest, showing up at the social functions and giving elaborate entertainments of her own. Old friends from other countries who had been at the Columbian Exposition were again in view in Paris. Horace Porter, who had been a military aide to General Grant and was devoted to Fred and Ida, was at the Embassy at this time. He gave general receptions for visiting Americans once a week and smaller dinners and receptions for a limited circle. The Palmers were essential guests at these gatherings. Most of the members of the original American colony in Paris had apartments or hotels near the Arc de Triomphe and they engaged in a round of dances, dinners and soirees while the Exposition was on. The Thaws, who had been at Newport when Mrs. Palmer was there, had come from Pittsburgh and were entertaining lavishly. Mr. and Mrs. C. Oliver Iselin had arrived from New York. Mrs. John W. Mackay, who had won her way years earlier by sheer personality and warmth of heart, was still one of the most beloved hostesses on the scene. Mrs. Pierre Lorillard had a château near Versailles.

The Baroness de Seillière, stepdaughter of the New York banker, John O'Brien, was a close friend of Mrs. Palmer's. She was the former Mrs. Livermore, now white-haired and stately, and she had a handsome hotel where she entertained Bertha and Mrs. William Astor together in the summer of 1900. They were an interesting study in contrasts—Mrs. Palmer with her silvery coif, Mrs. Astor with her dense black pompadour, Mrs. Palmer dulcet-voiced and tactful, Mrs. Astor forceful and opinionative. They were on affable terms by this time. Nothing had occurred at Newport to upset the *status quo*. Each recognized the quality and influence of the other, although Mrs. Astor chose to be blandly unconscious of the Middle West. Her orbit was strictly social and she observed the political drive and ambition of such women as Mrs. Palmer with detachment. She did not covet her role as lady commissioner to the Fair. Mrs. Astor might wield the scepter in Newport and New York but at the Paris Exposition Mrs. Palmer was welcome to the title of queen.

Bertha had no difficulties with the international alliances. She was schooled in Debrett and many of the titled women she met were Americans already well known to her. The Duchesse de la Rochefoucauld was Mattie Mitchell, daughter of Senator John H. Mitchell. The Duchesse de Dino was Adele Sampson, who was first the wife of Frederic William Stevens, then after a sensational divorce married the Marquis de Talleyrand-Périgord, who, in turn, became the Duc de Dino. The Marquise de Choiseul came from a New York family. Madame Clemenceau was American. The Baroness de Brin was from New Orleans. The Countess de Pourtales and the Countess de Rohan Chabot both were American. The Baroness de la Grange was from Carrollton and the Baroness de Blanc was another compatriot. All visiting Americans discussed the fetes and cotillions given by Anna Gould, who had married Count Boni de Castellane and already had cause to regret it.

Mrs. Palmer steered her way tactfully through the social shoals of the international set while Mrs. Logan laid traps for her. There was much gossip among the visiting Americans about this Chicago feud, but Bertha took no notice of petty attacks, never answered criticism, and did her work with her usual drive. Her days were tiring for she had many official duties. At times she and Potter sought relaxation at the art showings and they often went to Auteuil and Longchamps. Potter also appeared at the races by himself. His health had improved but his doctors had ordered him to retire early and get considerable rest. He could not move about Paris with the indefatigability of his wife, who kept up a killing pace.

When Queen Marie Henriette of Belgium invited them to visit her at Spa he hesitated about going with Cissie, but he rarely left her in the lurch on a really important occasion. The Queen, who was Austrian by birth, had promised Mrs. Palmer that she would attend the opening of the Austrian section of the Exposition. They had met before at Lacken and on the Channel Islands.

The details of this visit, which throw as much light on Mrs. Palmer as on the Queen, are set forth in two of Bertha's letters to her mother from Belgium. "Dear Ma," she began, "I think you may like to hear from me when I am visiting Queens." She then proceeded to give Mrs. Honoré, who had an ancestral interest in social matters, an hour-by-hour account of their stay at Spa. Here and there Bertha tossed in light shafts of humor, showing that she had a lively eye for the absurdities of pomp, although an able practitioner herself in this field.

When they arrived from Brussels the Queen's gentleman-in-waiting met them. They drove to the royal villa and were ushered into the salon where the Queen and her daughter Princess Clémentine were waiting to receive them. The Queen kissed Mrs. Palmer on both cheeks and "this time I had the presence of mind to get my veil up & not have her kiss the chenille wiry dots as she did the last time." She settled Potter in an armchair and led Bertha to the sofa to sit at her right hand. She was "full of kind phrases" about their having honored her by coming so far. She ordered tea for Mrs. Palmer and wine and whiskey for her husband.

Bertha, calling him Mr. Palmer even in her letters to her mother, said that she gave them their choice of driving around Spa or of going to their rooms to rest "for Mr. Palmer's sake." They chose to rest and were escorted to a pleasant suite, simply furnished like the rest of the villa. But a footman in scarlet and gold preceded them every step of the way and opened doors for them.

At dinner that night the conversation was mostly in English, the Queen discussing American literature, scenery and trees. Bertha, used to lengthy banquets on such occasions, was surprised to find that dinner consisted of four courses only. They finished in half an hour and went on to a concert at the Casino, where Mrs. Palmer sat to the right of the Queen and Princess Clémentine to her left. Potter had retired early. "You cannot fancy anything more simple & intimate & cordial than the reception she is giving me," wrote Bertha.

Her next letter to her mother picked up the story. "We have returned to real life once more having come back from Spa this morning on the Queen's train," she began, then went on to give all the details of the rest of her stay at the villa. The morning after the Casino concert Bertha, up early as always, was standing in the courtyard when the Queen appeared bareheaded and asked her to wait until she got a hat, then they would go for a walk together. She soon returned with a jacket, a black hat and a veil. Her three poodles were at her heels and they set off for a brisk walk together "in the most democratic manner." She stopped in a little shop and bought them souvenirs of their visit to Spa. Bertha's was a wooden picture frame with a view of Spa, and Mr. Palmer's was a little tray with flowers painted on it.

You would have been amused by the way to see how much pleased Mr. Palmer was to go to visit the Queen. I accepted for him in fear & trembling thinking he might decline—but no—he was very pleased to go and enjoyed everything greatly tho he was feeling particularly weak and languid.

They walked down the village street looking in shop windows while the dogs ran in all directions. They stopped at the spring for a drink. After an hour's walk they returned for twelve o'clock breakfast. Spa was recommended for rheumatism, and Bertha told the Queen that since her husband suffered from it he should return for the cure.

"Oh, come," said the Queen. "I should enjoy so much having you and we would have such merry days together."

After *déjeuner*, which was longer and had more courses than dinner, the Queen took them to the grounds of the village to show them her horses. They went without hats and a groom brought carrots and brown bread. As they walked along the Queen called out the names of the horses and "each put his head out of his box stall and answered her." She had thirteen in all, both saddle and driving horses. She fed them and the groom brought out a new one and he stood on a tub for her. She trained them herself and was quite a sport and expert horsewoman, commented Mrs. Palmer. She seemed to be very proud of her accomplishments and particularly of the power she had over her horses. Then they drove away in phaetons, Mr. Palmer going with the Queen and Mrs. Palmer with Clémentine. For three hours they ambled over hills and valleys, through forests, past villages with distant views of the mountains. The landscape reminded Mrs. Palmer of the White Mountains, except that the hills were not so high. Describing the Queen for her mother's benefit she wrote:

The Queen is tall & commanding though thin & much aged. Yet her back is as straight & erect as a grenadier & she never leans back. She was gotten up in a sporty way for driving with black Alpine hat & trim black jacket & looked quite distinguished & fine. As her daughter did also. They are both devoted to trees & flowers and to simple country life and are cordial & kind beyond measure to every one, tho' you never lose sight of the fact that the forms of etiquette are preserved and that beyond a certain point it would be dangerous to venture. Nevertheless the etiquette was very simple and really amounted to nothing.

Everyone stood up and curtsied when the Queen entered a room and went through the same routine again when she made her exit. That was about all the formality required. No one waited for her to lead the conversation and she had her say on any subject introduced. Bertha assured her mother that it was all as intimate and cordial and friendly as with one's best friends, although she was careful about the details of getting in and out of the carriage and where she seated herself in relation to the Queen.

Bertha thought her better dressed on this occasion than when she had taken her driving in Sark two years earlier. But she cared nothing about such matters:

Mss. Worth and Paquin would not acknowledge her gowns and as for her bonnets & hair dressing—well. She combs her hair straight back flat on her head & it is thin & she is thin, and does it up in a little knot behind & has a cap on top of her head when she hasn't a bonnet & yet her carriage is such that she is a queenly distinguished looking woman—& would be remarked anywhere.

Bertha observed that her maid made her bonnets and caps but she did her own hair. They wore high gowns in the evening and after dinner a singer brought from Brussels for the occasion gave a concert. Mrs. Palmer asked the Queen to play on the harp, which she willingly did. "She did not play very well but she was evidently frightened & the harp is a bad instrument for a nervous person, as I have found."

When she learned that Bertha also played the harp she urged her to practice regularly and promised that next time they would play duets. Her own routine was quite exacting. She rose at five in the morning, attended church at seven, and visited the little hospital back of the villa almost every day. She read a great deal and astonished Bertha with her knowledge of American literature and political affairs. She attended conscientiously to affairs of state and for recreation rode and drove. Usually she got to bed by half-past nine.

The Queen and Mrs. Palmer had a great deal to talk about, for Bertha had the friendliest relations with Austria through Ida, Fred and her niece Julia. On the Palmers' last morning at Spa she took Bertha across the courtyard to her own quarters to show her her paintings. The courtyard reminded Mrs. Palmer of the Whitelaw Reid mansion on Madison Avenue in New York, built around a quadrangle fronted with a high iron railing. On their departure from Spa Mrs. Palmer suddenly found herself walking over a crimson carpet at the Queen's side, in advance of the bowing officials. Marie Henriette seemed "most superb in her presence & walk," followed at about five paces by her daughter and after that by the ladies and gentlemen in waiting. "And then," Bertha finished with a dash of humor, "I realized how grand we had been when lifted up for a few minutes to that altitude. It had all seemed so natural and easy that we had not appreciated what we were going thro' till we trundled back to our places."

These letters were typical of Mrs. Palmer's correspondence with her mother, although she did not always walk with queens. Mrs. Honoré enjoyed all the social details and Bertha asked her to show the letters around to the other relatives, as she did not have time to write to each member of her family.

Her visit to Spa and her success with the Queen of the Belgians was another feather in her cap at the Exposition. Although charges of ostentation were made by her enemies none could criticize her work for the Fair. She made an authentic impression and by the time it closed her name was well known all over Europe. "The splendor and originality of her entertainments have made a stir in Paris," *Munsey's Magazine* reported in October, 1900. "Other women have won high social position, some have gained business success, and a few have won honors in politics. They have felt that they have accomplished much by achieving their ambition in one line of endeavor. Mrs. Palmer has distinguished herself in all three."

On closing night silent crowds tramped along the muddy walks under a blaze of colored lights to get one last glimpse of the Château d'Eau, the magical electric fountain. A gun boomed from the Eiffel Tower at eleven o'clock. The figures 1900, defined in starlike lights on top of the arch, faded slowly.

Suddenly the fountain was dark and still. "*On ferme!*" cried the guards. The Exposition was over. An era had ended, too.

Mrs. Palmer went back to the United States on the U.S.S.S. *St. Paul* and en route wrote to Mrs. Mackay, telling her of her visit to Spa and other chitchat about their mutual friends.

Mrs. Mackay had asked her to serve on a New York committee on her return but Bertha was doubtful that she could do so, since she would not be available at any time except during December. "You know how little service I can be on the committee and I hate to be mere deadwood," she replied characteristically. Mr. Palmer was "infinitely better," she added and they were heading for Newport.

In the following April the Legion of Honor was bestowed on Mrs. Palmer for her work at the Exposition. Up to that time only two other women had received this decoration—Rosa Bonheur and Florence Nightingale. The distinction again roused a storm among her critics. An American banker's wife in Paris gave the New York *Sunday World* correspondent an interview that spotlighted the envy and animosity directed at Mrs. Palmer and made clear the strong social rivalry between the women of the East and this powerful figure from Chicago. She described Bertha as the most ambitious woman in America and expressed the opinion that her "neatly-gloved hand of steel may amalgamate and control the high life of our continent," just as Armour, Carnegie, Gates and other great combiners from the West held the industrial reins.

Western contenders for social eminence had been held off by the New York dowagers, this observer conceded, but Chicago, St. Louis and the Pacific coast had added some impressive figures to the new aristocracy and Mrs. Palmer was the one best qualified to effect a "great vitalizing social combine." Moreover, she was quite conscious of being far in the lead, said the banker's wife:

I have long realized that since she tasted the sweets of real social prominence . . . she would never be content till she had reached the top notch of eminence. I doubt if even such unchallenged position as that enjoyed today by Mrs. Astor would satisfy Mrs. Palmer. Her dream is to be known as the final arbiter of all that is select on the American continent. She believes she is equipped for leadership by wealth, breeding and tact. . . . Some irreconcilable elements will have to be forced and others brought into line by cajolery or sheer bullying. She is ready to do a good deal of all that.

But Mrs. Palmer was concerned with other matters. The social scramble was only one facet of her life. She had work to do. A thousand duties lay ahead of her. Julia L. Cole wanted an article for the Marshall Field sewing school in Chicago. "I desire your interest in forty dear, sweet-faced girls, who assemble in these rooms two nights a week for study after working at tasks, and behind counters all day. I need the aid of all good women in this work," she wrote.

William Gardner Hale reminded Mrs. Palmer that two years earlier, when he went to Rome as director of the American School of Classical Studies, he had asked her to become a member of the managing committee and she had not given him a definite answer. He now wished to visit her in Newport and to enlist her support. "If the interests of the school do not seem to you important, I can hardly hope that they will to others in Chicago," Hale wrote. "And without the cooperation of Chicago, I do not see how the school can succeed."

Mrs. Palmer was always receptive to schemes involving education or the arts, but she was averse to lending her name to committees on an empty basis. She believed that a patron should work for a cause. Thus, although she was besieged by requests to sponsor movements of all kinds, she made her final choices with care. Her interest now was focused on a new goal. She had come back from Paris determined that Honoré should enter the political field and she undertook the management of his political campaign when he ran for alderman of the Twenty-first Ward. Her oldest son at this time was twenty-seven. He had attended St. Mark's School and Harvard and had spent his summers abroad with his parents. He was a serious youth in spite of his mania for racing cars and speed, but in later years he never made any secret of the fact that he would not have thought of entering politics but for the prompting of his mother. She had always taught her sons that wealth meant social responsibility of the most practical kind and if her husband could not serve abroad in the diplomatic service her son might help to clean up the civic mess in Chicago.

None of his friends was convinced that Honoré wished to be a politician, but he had a sincere, thoroughgoing nature like his father and he entered into the campaign with spirit. He was unaffected and candid by temperament. There was none of the show-off about Honoré and he performed his part with unerring zeal. When his political opponent, Fletcher Dobyns, circulated the report as a joke that Honoré had joined the waiters' union, he dashed down to the Palmer House to make the story come true. He donned a white uniform belonging to a member of his father's staff and was photographed carrying a tray. Then he announced that he was proud to wear the uniform of so honorable a profession. Dobyns' little joke had boomeranged. The Democrats of Chicago applauded Honoré's enterprise.

His headquarters were on Clark Street and his mother called on all her old friends to help him. She sent a typical note to Judge Lambert Tree, who had figured so often on her Charity Ball lists: "You are such a favorite in the party and your presence would be such an encouragement and compliment that I sincerely trust that you can gratify Honoré, and his parents, by being with him at his little informal house warming."

Knowing his mother well, Honoré was not at all disconcerted by what went on at the Palmer mansion during the campaign. The most discussed function was a sumptuous reception she gave for the ward workers who were supporting him. Wives, mothers and sweethearts romped happily through

Palmer Castle, looking with equal curiosity at Mrs. Palmer's Monets and Mrs. Palmer's diamonds. Some of the zealous voters who joined this parade were more familiar with the saloons and lodging houses of the Twenty-first Ward than they were with Renoirs or Coromandel screens, but Mrs. Palmer wore her smartest Paris gown, her favorite jewels and roamed among them shaking hands, making apt comments and thanking them personally for what they had done for Honoré. The house was banked with flowers. A concert was given with hearty songs in which all could join. The guests partook of the kind of refreshments that she served to visiting princes and diplomats. All left in a happy glow, to talk for some time to come of their visit to Palmer Castle. Of all the assorted gatherings in her home, none equaled this one for novelty and enthusiasm.

"We read of the social life of our hostess in Paris, London and in the other great European cities, where she is surrounded with luxury in palaces," commented Alderman Minwegen, who headed the Tuscarora Club, a power on the North Side. "But I think right here in Chicago she has a tolerable kind of a home herself."

Between them, Mrs. Palmer and Honoré proved to be good vote-getters. Honoré went through the round of speechmaking and hand shaking with unwavering spirit. His mother often appeared at his meetings and wives asked their husbands when they returned home at night if Mrs. Potter Palmer had been there, and if she had worn her diamonds. Honoré danced at Turner Hall parties and gave interviews about the state of Chicago, if not the state of the nation. Like his mother, he spoke French well, and he had studied enough German at Harvard to enable him to speak to the German voters in their own language. He made a hasty study of Italian so as to be able to say a few sentences to the Italians in their native tongue. All thought him a regular fellow, no more given to high-hatting the underdog than his famous mother.

He was up at four o'clock on election morning and by six

the entire Palmer family were breakfasting together in the carved oak dining room. He canvassed the ward on foot, hurrying from one booth to another and greeting the voters heartily. The family awaited the day's result in their home and for once Mrs. Palmer showed agitation as the returns came in by messenger and telephone. Honoré won by a majority of 1,308 votes. He served two terms and showed a touch of the parental reforming spirit. One of his first acts as alderman was to push through an ordinance requiring numbers on all automobiles. His brother Potter was promptly picked up for violating the new rule. The regulation was highly offensive to the members of the Chicago Automobile Club. Honoré happened to be its president. He was going back on his own class, his fellow motorists insisted, as they kicked him out of office. Honoré argued that the new ordinance was essential for the common good, with so many automobiles on the roadways.

But he did not cease to be a speed demon on his own account. His ardor for racing was considerable. With his first car, a French model bought abroad for eight thousand dollars, he set out on a trail-blazing run from Chicago to Boston in June, 1902, taking with him Paul Pickard, whose car was known on Lake Shore Drive as "The Yellow Devil."

All through his two terms of office Honoré backed progressive measures for the public welfare. Like his mother, he never expressed himself until he had studied a question carefully; then he stuck to his convictions against any odds. He brought a certain freshness and objectivity to the Council Chamber where so many cynical politicians had sat as Chicago roared its way into big-city politics from the comparative simplicity that his parents both could remember.

But the pioneer of 1852 was failing badly now and Bertha was deeply worried about her husband's health. He no longer wished to go anywhere, or even to leave the house. Sadly she told Mrs. Carter Harrison one day: "Mr. Palmer has decided that California, Florida, Cuba, in fact no spot in the world seems as comfortable and warm as a dressing room on the sunny side of our house. He has been ensconced there for the past month and none of us, singly or combined, has been able to persuade him to move. He declares he will spend the winter there, and, of course, I shan't leave him."

Mrs. Harrison expressed the view that the disparity in the ages of the Palmers never affected their home life and that while Bertha was "pre-eminently his greatest admiration" she in turn never faltered in her devotion to him. It was always understood that she might appear at any time at a function without her husband and now that his health was so precarious no one expected him to show up for entertainments of any sort. But he kept up his civic interest to the end and in 1899, three years before his death, he was pushing a measure which resembled his early determination to widen State Street. His aim was to have Lake Shore Drive extended a hundred feet toward the lake, in order to enlarge the park. The effect of the water breaking over the sea wall where it then stood was serious during heavy storms, he pointed out.

But his own days were numbered. He died unexpectedly from edema of the lungs in the late afternoon of May 4, 1902, at his home on the Drive. He had been ill with grippe but his condition was not considered alarming until three hours before the end. His wife and two sons were at his bedside when he died. He lay in state in the gallery where so many great parties had been held. The public streamed past as though he had been mayor or a public official. Among hundreds of business and social friends were many Negroes, old and young, who had worked for Potter Palmer. Tears streamed down the faces of some and they all agreed that he had treated them well. The Palmers had always been liked by their servants and had attended their weddings and funerals. Bridget (Bridey) Mullarkey Lynn, among others, liked to recall that when she was married in Holy Name Cathedral she had Mrs. Potter Palmer, Mrs. Ulysses S. Grant and Mrs. Fred Grant as guests. She had been second maid to Mrs. Palmer and was a favorite of the household.

Mr. Palmer left all of his fortune to his wife without any strings. She and her brother Adrian were made trustees of the eight-million-dollar estate, which consisted largely of real estate. It was divided into two parts. The first, which was to be administered by the trustees, was designed to give Honoré and Potter such funds from time to time as Mrs. Palmer deemed advisable. In short, she was to have control of their pocketbooks.

In drawing up this will the lawyer pointed out that Mrs. Palmer might marry again.

"If she does, he'll need the money," Potter commented realistically.

When Marshall Field heard that his old colleague had left everything to his wife, he frigidly delivered one of his more memorable phrases: "A million dollars is enough for any woman."

Potter Palmer was seventy-six when he died. Bertha was then fifty-three. Onlookers noticed how pale and beautiful she looked in her widow's weeds as she drove away from the cemetery. But the death of her husband was one of the crucial points of her life and for a time she was uncertain about the course she should follow. Mrs. Ulysses S. Grant died in Washington just before Christmas that year. Old links were going. Her mother was failing but Mr. Honoré was as brisk and energetic as ever. Ida and Fred, who was on leave from the Philippines, had recently gone to Russia to visit Julia and had met the Cantacuzène family at Bouromka for the first time.

There were great fetes at the Czar's court to which she was invited but Julia was not so tied to her new environment that she could not join her aunt in the summer of 1903. Mrs. Palmer had gone abroad for the wedding of Honoré and Grace Greenway Brown, a match that she thoroughly approved. The bride belonged to a prominent Baltimore family and she fitted smoothly into the Palmer orbit. She was talented, rich in her own right, and good-looking. She and Honoré met at the Fete of All Nations ball held in Chicago while she was visiting her sisters, Mrs. Walter Keith and Mrs. Stanley Field. They were married in England that September with Mrs. Palmer in half-mourning at the wedding. Julia, who had come on for the occasion, now set off on a motor tour with her aunt through the south of France and northern Italy. Bertha's hobbies, if she might be said to have had any, were motoring, collecting antiques and the study of history. She always felt at home in France and Honoré recalled in later years that his mother's favorite and most consistent reading was the *Mémoires* of Saint-Simon. In the summer before Potter Palmer's death the Cantacuzènes had toured Normandy and Belgium with the Palmers, and the Prince and Potter Palmer had come to know and like each other. But on the 1903 tour Julia was dismayed when her aunt came down with typhoid fever on her return to Paris. All the members of her family were astonished to hear that she was ill, since her radiant health was accepted as a matter of course. Julia stayed on with her until Christmas and as she got better Honoré and his wife returned to Chicago and went into residence at the Palmer house on Lake Shore Drive until their new home at 187 Lincoln Park Boulevard was completed.

Bertha, who disliked invalidism intensely, accepted her fate with philosophical calm and received many visitors as she convalesced. She avoided the spas as much as possible. The soft, relaxing atmosphere and the congregation of people concentrating on their physical ills did not appeal to her. She preferred the seashore, a high healthy wind and wide-open spaces. But she visited Carlsbad and Marienbad upon occasion. Honoré was an outdoor enthusiast, who liked to hunt and fish and race his cars and horses. His bride was a horse lover and they soon set up racing stables near Paris.

Mrs. Palmer was still in the French capital and Honoré was

back in Chicago when word reached her of the Iroquois Theater fire in which nearly six hundred lives were lost, or nearly twice as many as in the Great Fire of 1870. Eddie Foy was playing in *Mr. Bluebeard* when the flimsy scenery was touched off by a spark from the footlights. "For God's sake don't stop—play on," he begged the orchestra as he stood on the stage urging the audience to leave in an orderly manner. But someone had opened a door at the back. The flames shot out over the orchestra pit and chaos followed. Iron bars blocked the stairways. Most of the doors were locked. Soon the dead lay in heaps in the demolished theater. It was Christmas week and all Chicago sorrowed as identifications were made in morgues and hospitals.

This disaster had worldwide repercussions and focused attention once again on Chicago. It was depressing to Mrs. Palmer, and it brought up many memories of the Great Fire she had gone through as a bride. She did not go home that winter. There would be no Charity Ball or anything but mourning in the city. Soon afterward more stringent fire laws were passed, in Chicago and in many other communities.

Mrs. Palmer lived very quietly at this time, but gradually the period of official mourning ended and she was drawn back into the social current. She changed from black to lavender and gray, and finally emerged altogether from mourning. She resumed her trips back and forth across the Atlantic, although she spent more time in Europe and less in the United States as the years went on. Claridge's was her stopping place in London until she took Hampden House, the property of the Duke of Abercorn. She stayed at the Bristol in Paris until she found an ideal background for herself at 6 Rue Fabert. It was in a different key from any other house she had owned. The décor was essentially French and bore small resemblance to the curious melange of the mansion on Lake Shore Drive. Turkish and Moorish effects, mother-of-pearl inlay and Oriental touches were on their way out. The Victorian influence was waning, too. Queen Victoria was dead and the Prince of Wales, who was crowned in 1902, was already changing the tempo of life in Britain.

Mrs. Palmer abandoned all lugubrious effects and created a sunny, airy setting for herself with Louis XVI furniture and a Beauvais set that became quite famous among her friends. Gobelin tapestries hung in the main salon and behind it were two charming rooms opening on a garden. She brought her favorite paintings from the United States and decided that the Impressionists looked particularly well against her white and gold background. She hung them so that they caught the light and sunshine, and visitors were struck by the artistic flower arrangements on low eighteenth-century tables that greeted them as they walked in. Her little circus girls hung in her bedroom. Raffaelli's misty Parisian effects, Cazin's Norman landscapes, the brilliance of a Diaz scene and Corot's haystack infused with sun were much admired by guests who were beginning to accept modern art. Cazin and Raffaelli were among her visitors, too. Her house became a show place and a haunt for cosmopolitan society.

The habit of collecting continued although she ceased to buy pictures after her husband's death. She concentrated for the time being on faïence, statuary and medieval wood carvings and was in and out of Raoul Heilbronner's in Paris along with Mrs. Jack Gardner of Boston, John Wanamaker, Baron Henri de Rothschild, W. K. Vanderbilt, Clarence H. Mackay, Pierre Lebaudy and Stanford White, who before long would be murdered by another art collector, Harry K. Thaw.

Traditional art bound for the United States was now being bought on a Homeric scale by J. P. Morgan, Henry E. Huntington, W. K. Vanderbilt, Henry C. Frick, Harry Payne Whitney, Andrew Mellon and Joseph Duveen. But modern art was beginning to get serious consideration. Mrs. H. O. Havemeyer, helped by Mary Cassatt, was buying paintings by Renoir, Manet and Monet, as well as Goyas and El Grecos.

The Salon d'Automne, held for the first time in 1903, showed paintings by Monet, Sisley and Manet, all of whom had been turned down earlier by the Luxembourg Museum.

In London Mrs. Palmer took up Mrs. John W. Mackay's fad for collecting silver tankards. Her prize purchase was a cylindrical mug of the Charles II period, dated 1677. On the same day she picked up a rare set of old silver goblets which she used in Hampden House. She and the Duchess of Roxburgh, the former May Goelet of New York, bought Chelsea statuettes and milk glass with equal zeal. Bertha was particularly proud of a pair of Charles Morland's animal pictures which she hung in her London drawing room. She had 150 antique lanterns of one kind and another and she shared in the current craze for celadon bowls, Fabergé boxes, little jeweled clocks and trinkets mounted in enamel or ormolu.

A passer-by at the Palmer mansion in Chicago in the spring of 1905 sadly observed that it was dark, silent and closed. It had always been the custom to keep the picture gallery brightly lighted and music was so often wafted out to the Drive that there seemed to be a social gathering every night. But at the moment Mrs. Palmer was at Claridge's in London and her untenanted castle looked grim and dark. The grounds still were cared for and Adrian Honoré and young Potter Palmer lived in it intermittently, but the life seemed to have gone out of it. *Elite* commented:

The friends of Mrs. Palmer's married life are here, but quite the same may be said of them as of her family. Some of them are ill, and some have been growing old, while she has been growing young. Some have lost their fortunes and none have developed along lines sympathetic with Mrs. Palmer's tastes. Mrs. Palmer goes along on her shining way. She is absolutely unaccompanied in Chicago. Mrs. Palmer was married when very young . . . and now is having out some of the youth denied her then.

Bertha had the knack of making friends easily and of enlisting lasting devotion but she had few intimates. Among those who were closest to her in Chicago were Mrs. Franklin Mac-Veagh, Mrs. W. W. Kimball, Mrs. Henry Shepard, Mrs. Charles Henrotin, Mrs. A. L. Chetlain and Mrs. T. W. Harvey. Most of the prominent men who had threaded their way in and out of her life had disappeared from the scene. Pullman died in 1897, Philip D. Armour in 1901, her own husband in 1902, Charles T. Yerkes in 1905, and now disaster seemed to have settled on the house of Marshall Field.

His only son was killed by gunshot wound under mysterious circumstances in 1905 and some months later Field died of pneumonia. He had recently married Mrs. Arthur J. Caton, whom he had worshiped for many years. When her husband died the way was clear for this long-delayed and much-discussed union. Mrs. Cyrus H. McCormick's twelve-year-old daughter Elizabeth died from appendicitis in 1905, the year in which Mrs. Palmer's first grandchild was born to Grace and Honoré Palmer. He was baptized Potter D'Orsay and in time the papers referred to him as the ten-million-dollar baby.

Bertha was back in the United States that winter, running the Charity Ball and urging all her old friends to chip in for the benefit of indigent soldiers and sailors, who were to profit by the function that year. Caruso was making his first appearance in Chicago, singing with Madam Sembrich. Richard Mansfield was playing in *Beau Brummell.* Clyde Fitch was drawing crowds to *The Toast of the Town.* Viola Allen was appearing in Shakespearian plays. Madam Gadski was delighting the music lovers of the Middle West and Isadora Duncan had brought a fresh and pagan touch to the dance. Mrs. Palmer's old friend Theodore Thomas had died in 1905. A new philanthropist now loomed into view to take the place of some of those who had gone. By this time Julius Rosenwald was building up a vast fortune through Sears, Roebuck & Company. And the Marshall Field benefactions continued on a munificent scale through the founder's descendants.

Cable cars had disappeared from the streets of Chicago and

elevated trains ran overhead. The winds blew off the lake with their old fierceness, but tall buildings now made canyons through which they roared. At home or abroad Mrs. Palmer kept in close touch with all that went on in the Windy City. She read the local papers, met her compatriots in London and Paris, sustained a constant flow of letters with her family and friends in the Middle West, and never lost her interest in local or national politics. By this time she had become a legendary figure. The phrase "Mrs. Potter Palmer of Chicago" carried its own implications after the turn of the century. It suggested the superlative hostess, the jeweled queen, the collector of modern art, the champion of women's rights, the philanthropist, the effective campaigner who could wage a tough fight and come out of it unscarred and without a grudge. To some she seemed a pretentious snob, but all were agreed that Chicago had contributed a fabulous personality to the social scene. None followed her career with more pride than her ambitious mother, who watched Bertha's progress with the closest attention until she died in 1906, leaving a great gap in the lives of her two daughters. Mrs. Honoré had been failing for years, but her husband had yet another decade to live.

10

➤➤➤➤➤➤➤➤➤➤➤➤➤ *Edwardian England*

King Edward VII greeted Mrs. Potter Palmer as she strolled about on the lawn at Ascot on a June day in 1907. "You are coming on," he told her heartily. "I never saw so many Americans in all my life. We outdo New York surely."

The King admired American women and welcomed them at court but some of the peeresses viewed them coolly. However, Queen Alexandra bowed publicly to Mrs. Palmer on this occasion, thus informing onlookers that she was in favor. Bertha went on her way serenely, chatting with Lord Roseberry, the Duke of Richmond, Lord and Lady Churchill, August Belmont, and Miss Jean Reid, the daughter of Whitelaw Reid, who later became Lady Ward. Although Mrs. Marshall Field, II, was at Ascot with her sister-in-law, Mrs. David Beatty, who had taken a house nearby for race week, she took no part in the festivities as she was in mourning. Her son, Marshall Field, III, was attending Eton at this time.

The King and Queen had driven to Ascot in landaus drawn by four horses with postilions in scarlet coats. The Edwardian scene was at its most brilliant. The sun shone. The King was in good humor, with his horses doing well after a long period of reverses. The celebrities of the social world moved across the sward in white and pastel colors, their hats as large as cartwheels, their voluminous skirts sweeping the turf. They wore feather boas although it was June and twirled parasols of delicate hue. Mrs. Palmer's gown was buttercup yellow, with a bolero embroidered with humming birds, flowers and stars. Her jewels were emeralds and diamonds.

It was noted at once that the Duchess of Marlborough was missing from the scene. The former Consuelo Vanderbilt had disappeared from view and was passing the summer quietly at Deauville. By this time the public was aware that the Marlboroughs had parted. Lady Paget's efforts to bring them together had failed and they were in royal disfavor. The Duchess' absence from Ascot and the other events of the season pointed up the situation. For the first time since her marriage Consuelo had failed to appear at the annual Devonshire House dinner party or the Royal Ball, given that year in honor of the King and Queen of Denmark.

Mrs. Palmer and Mrs. John Jacob Astor were invited to the ball under the top classification of distinguished foreigners on a par with ambassadors, while Mrs. William Astor's name appeared on the secondary list. "It was a signal compliment to those two American women, and another evidence that they are growing in favor with King Edward, that they were on the list embracing the diplomatic corps and other foreigners of distinction," the New York *World* reported on June 16, 1907.

It was distinctly an American season in London. When Mrs. Palmer went to the International Horse Show at Olympia with young Potter early in June she found E. T. Stotesbury, Clarence H. Mackay, Alfred G. Vanderbilt, who had a string of thoroughbreds on exhibition, and other American horse lovers. Although she did not ride, Bertha had listened for so many years to her husband and sons talk horses that she had an alert eye for their points.

She attended a garden party given by the King at Windsor to wind up Ascot Week. The bands of the Grenadier Guards and Horse Guards played as eight thousand guests promenaded in the castle grounds. Mark Twain, who visited London that summer, was being lionized on all sides. He was driven back to town from the garden party by Sir Thomas Lipton. Mr. and Mrs. Whitelaw Reid gave a dinner in his honor at Dorchester House. The Bradley Martins entertained him and the editors of *Punch* brought him and George Bernard Shaw together at a banquet for wits and writers.

American dollars were flying in all directions, although the invasion was viewed with some skepticism. "American Cash Floods Europe," the New York *World* reported on June 16. It was estimated that $228,000,000 was spent that year by 300,000 tourists from the United States. Thirty thousand women spent eight million dollars on gowns and one and a half million more on hats. The picture dealers garnered in five millions, as the visiting Americans bought pictures and objects of art for their great new mansions.

A number of American debutantes and matrons were presented at court that summer, among them Anita Stewart, Marguerite Drexel, Muriel White and Mrs. David Beatty. Henry White, who had just been appointed Ambassador to France, wrote to Mrs. Palmer that his daughter Muriel would go straight back to her studies in Paris as soon as she had made her bow.

Anita Stewart, the daughter of William Rhinelander Stewart, was presented by the Dowager Duchess of Manchester, a peeress who was anything but cordial to Mrs. Palmer. Bertha was encountering opposition from some of the women closest to the King. It was not so much that they objected to her as that they resented the American invasion encouraged by the King. This was not what separated her from the Duchess of Manchester, however, since the peeress was an American herself, a vigorous personality with a Louisiana, New York and

Newport background. She was born Consuelo Iznaga del Valle and her father was a wealthy Cuban. She married Viscount Mandeville in 1876 before he interited the dukedom. Mrs. Palmer already had a number of friends among the peeresses when stories were cabled back to the United States early in 1907 that she and the Duchess of Manchester were at odds.

They first came into conflict at Biarritz. Mrs. Palmer had taken rooms with Princess Cantacuzène at the Hotel du Palais while the King was holidaying there. She had larger and better quarters than the Duchess, fronting on the sea. There was much competition for rooms with the season in full swing. The Duchess suggested that Mrs. Palmer yield some of her space to her. Bertha, with "firmness, tempered with infinite sweetness," refused to exchange her rooms and the Duchess promptly moved to a villa. Mrs. Palmer eventually followed suit.

For the next few weeks she saw a good deal of the King. She played golf with him on the nearby links and he dined with her three or four times and gave a dinner for Princess Cantacuzène. Julia discussed Russian affairs with the King. He had taken a trip up the Baltic and was in the mood to talk to her about the Czar and conditions in Russia. She found him adept at throwing the conversational ball from one to another. "He would draw from you all sorts of information which he would store away in his mind and then bring out in later conversations," she noted.

Mrs. Palmer knew that she had to be politically alert to talk to King Edward. Although he did not have much to say himself and his pronunciation was syllabic he enjoyed good conversation and listened attentively. Abstract discussion bored him but he liked factual conversations with a leavening of anecdote and gossip, if it were not malicious. He probed for outside impressions of personalities and conditions in other countries and he showed close knowledge of things American in his conversations with Mrs. Palmer.

There were never more than eight at the small dinners she

attended, which were usually arranged by Sir Ernest Cassel. The guests were carefully selected and they all sat at a round table, with their attention focused on the King. His big blue eyes bulged and suggested somnolence but he was surprisingly agile and rapid in his movements, considering his bulk.

Mrs. Palmer was well primed on his likes and dislikes before he dined with her. His intimates knew that he liked ortolans, lobster and game of all kinds. She had heard of the hearty luncheons at Sandringham, the fourteen-course dinners, the great feasts on the moors. She knew that however friendly and informal in his approach he never forgot that he was King and could snub the obtrusive in the most decisive way. He liked pomp, punctilio and decorations but at Biarritz he was incognito as the Duke of Lancaster and was friendly to all. This resort was his favorite after Sandringham and he took long drives in his Renault or Mercedes past the tamarisk-fringed rocks to visit King Alfonso at San Sebastian. He enjoyed the sweep of the sea, the bright colors, the long roll of the Atlantic breakers.

Mrs. George Keppel, London's most discussed woman in 1907, was at Biarritz and she spent much time with the King. Mrs. Palmer saw them golfing, having tea and playing bridge together. When questioned later by friends about the fascinating Mrs. Keppel she always gave the same answer: "Nobody ever saw her in any position where she could be criticized." She considered her genuinely *grande dame*, a distinguished figure with impeccable manners. She admired her stately bearing and her clothes, which were simple but perfectly adapted to her striking shape. She rarely wore jewels and never anything at all eccentric or extreme.

Bertha observed that the King did not take anything for granted where Mrs. Keppel was concerned. He would send a messenger to ask if she wished to play bridge with him, which of course she always did. For her own part she found Mrs. Keppel clever, kind and discreet. She was always well posted on news of the stock market, on the latest political move, on the choicest bit of gossip. She and her husband, the younger son of the Earl of Albemarle, were invited frequently to Sandringham and Windsor. Queen Alexandra viewed her with a tolerant eye and Mrs. Keppel made her own way in court circles with her unaffected manner and her wit, which was without sting or malice.

Mrs. Palmer enjoyed Sir Ernest Cassel's conversation at their small dinners in Biarritz. This son of a Cologne banker, ambitious, reserved and blunt, talked freely to her about his charities. He had given more than a million pounds for cancer research, hospitals and education. His chief ambition, he told her, was not to leave the world until the cure for cancer had been found. He was one of the King's closest friends, as well as being his financial adviser, and Edward had been godfather to his granddaughter, Edwina Ashley, later Lady Mountbatten. Sir Ernest liked to entertain in a princely way. He was bearded, wore rings like the King and smoked cigars constantly. He had little luck with his horses but much with his investments.

During this period Mrs. Palmer also came to know another of the King's favorites, the Marquis de Soveral, the Portuguese Minister in London and a popular figure, familiar to his intimates as "The Blue Monkey" because of the bluish cast of his skin between shaves. He was witty, diplomatic and ubiquitous. Women pursued this popular bachelor, who was known for his monocle, his Kaiser mustache and white boutonniere. His stories amused the King and he and Sir Ernest Cassel were as close to the throne as Palmerston and Beaconsfield had been in the days of Queen Victoria.

Court life had become more cosmopolitan with King Edward. He welcomed the merchants and bankers of humble origin who had built up great fortunes through their own efforts. By 1905 the House of Lords had thirty-five bankers on its rolls and businessmen of all kinds were becoming peers.

Freed at last from the Victorian restrictions that had smothered him, the King modernized the court and dispelled the somber clouds of the past. Drawing rooms were held at night instead of in the afternoon. They were called "Courts" and were moved from the throne room to the ballroom, where they were stage-managed like pageants and wound up with magnificent balls.

A period of extravagance was ushered in, a fleshly era with feasts of Georgian proportions, great balls, dinners, garden parties, country weekends and entertainments of one kind or another. Beautiful women were much to the fore. The theater was encouraged. Money flowed through all the channels that catered to high living. The picture seemed larger than life size. Much of the court life was spent outdoors, since King Edward sought the sun to clear away the cobwebs of his mother's self-imposed isolation. He went from one country house to another and had pheasant shooting and partridge driving at Sandringham. The old stiffness was gone. The King visibly enjoyed himself and spread a hearty glow in all directions. The public liked to see him at the races surrounded by pretty women and they approved his diplomatic forays on the Continent. Where Queen Victoria had used her statesmen he set out to sell the Empire by himself. Casting aside the prejudices of the Victorian era he built up a reputation for smoothing out political differences. Much of it was done through his own genial personality. However, he quarreled with his cousin the Kaiser while he courted the Czar, and Queen Alexandra was an implacable foe of the German Emperor.

Mrs. Palmer was quite at home in Edwardian England. When she moved decisively into the King's circle in 1907 she had stormed the last social citadel of that particular era in Europe. She had made her first court connections as far back as 1891 through Princess Christian but now she sailed along on the top stratum. After she took Hampden House she cast her own particular aura as an adept hostess and was reported to have spent $200,000 in a single season there.

The hotel restaurants of those days were not noted for their food, particularly in London, and most of the important British hostesses had French chefs. Scarlet-coated footmen, gold plate and champagne suppers were the accepted order. The houses had Queen Anne, Georgian and Adam decorations or else were solidly Victorian. Hampden House was pure eighteenth century, unremarkable on the outside but magnificent within. It had only two floors but its hall was imposing and the ballroom was decorated by Angelica Kauffmann. The furnishings were Louis XVI. French doors in the back opened on to a garden that ran the width of the house. Here Mrs. Palmer gave teas and garden parties. Indoors she had balls, dinners and receptions. She was well established with the official set. The American embassies in every European capital were well aware of Mrs. Potter Palmer, and she was a friend of the Whitelaw Reids, who were particular favorites of King Edward VII.

But the pace was fast, even for her. She moved vigorously with the social tide. She took a house on the Isle of Wight for Cowes. She went to Biarritz and Scotland. She was in London for its three-month season, on the Riviera in spring and in Paris whenever the spirit moved her. She attended innumerable balls, garden parties, race meets and horse shows. She put in appearances at Ascot, Henley, Lord's and Goodwood. She watched the Derby and the Oaks and drove to Ranelagh, Roehampton and Hurlingham. She followed the polo matches and went on yachting parties and country weekends. Mrs. Palmer and her jewels were often observed at Covent Garden or in theater boxes in the West End. Even the chilliest members of the peerage were forced to notice her presence among them.

The theater flourished. New life had been breathed into it

by Ibsen, Oscar Wilde and Pinero. Shaw had come along like a bombshell. Henry Irving, Sir Herbert Beerbohm Tree and George Alexander had helped to raise the status of actors in general. The Ellen Terry jubilee had been celebrated at Drury Lane in 1906 with Caruso, Tree, Duse and Tosti present. King Edward liked the theater and encouraged its stars. Here he broke away completely from the stodgy tradition of the past and heartily approved an era of growth and innovation.

Champagne was drunk in theater boxes. Stalls cost half a guinea. Clara Butt, six feet tall, was singing at Queen's Hall. Lily Elsie came tripping down a stairway at Daly's in June, 1907, and soon all London was dancing to the *Merry Widow* waltz. The Gaiety Girls were the toast of the day and chorus girls were marrying into the peerage. Gertie Miller became the Countess of Dudley. Gertrude Elliott played in *The Passing of the Third Floor Back*. Gaby Deslys had been appearing regularly in London since 1903. Operetta was the rage. Trilby's Parma violets might still be seen buried in the furs of dreamy-eyed girls. Four-wheelers, hansom cabs, victorias, barouches and four-in-hands were dwindling in number, although some lingered on among the landaulets and motorcars that now invaded the streets and hastened Londoners to their country weekends. Mrs. Palmer believed in progress. She was not a sentimentalist, and she shared Honoré's enthusiasm for motoring.

With her usual efficiency she decided that she must become a good shot before joining friends in the shooting boxes of Scotland and northern England. Honoré, a crack shot himself, was delighted to choose her guns for her and they took an expert named Bross north to Newtonstewart with them to practice on the moors. Bertha had heard guns, like horses, discussed all her life, for Fred Grant had hunted ever since his Civil War days and often took young Potter and Honoré on trips with him.

Honoré now watched his mother with great interest as she

planted her broganed feet on the heather and handled her shotgun with determination. She backed up over the first explosion but got used to the backfire and in time became a good shot. Soon she took to the butts with her British friends, in plaid skirt and feathered hat. She had learned to play golf at Newport so that she was not at a loss on the links with King Edward and his friends. But Bertha was less fond of sports as she got older. She did not greatly relish the shooting party luncheons in the damp tents or out on the open moors. However, she never gave a sign that she was not enjoying herself to the hilt, and she tramped over the moors with the agility shown by Mrs. Keppel, who was always said to walk through the streets of London with the stride of a Highland gillie.

She liked the numerous changes of costume, however. Even at shooting parties women changed four times a day and she could bring out her Paris tea gowns and most gorgeous frocks for afternoon and evening. Tweeds or town dresses were worn early in the day; then at teatime women appeared in seductive, low-cut gowns of gossamer fabrics, to eat their watercress sandwiches and crumpets with no thought of their figures. The men wore bright-colored velvet smoking suits for tea or short black jackets and black ties when the King was present. The women then made another change and appeared for dinner in full panoply, with tiaras, trains and ostrich feather fans. Here Mrs. Palmer was at her best. She traveled with mountains of luggage, from tartan rugs to diamond stomachers, and with enough attendants to look after them. But she could live on a simple scale, too, and her niece saw this side of her when they toured the Continent by car.

With Julia, Honoré and Potter Mrs. Palmer was most truly herself. When her sons used to join her in Europe during their college vacations they all traveled happily together. Honoré chose her motorcars for her. He bought his first Mercedes in Stuttgart and then drove his mother in it to Carlsbad. On other occasions he drove her from St. Moritz to Cadenabbia and through various parts of France. She liked the Mercedes and Renault cars, then switched to Rolls-Royces when they became fashionable before the First World War. But she was an indefatigable walker and exhausted them all when they toured art galleries.

Mrs. Palmer was fond of the Italian lakes and she made them all live on the native fare when they were touring there. She liked to eat the food of the country, wherever she was, and Honoré and Potter often longed for hearty Middle Western fare. When traveling in this fashion with the young people she put up at small inns and enjoyed them. The Palmers were connoisseurs in hotels. The name Potter Palmer had always been a magical one on hotel registers and Bertha did not suffer from lack of service wherever she went. But when touring she never made any fuss about the quarters she got and she and Julia usually shared a bedroom on these expeditions.

Her niece would never forget wakening up in the night on different occasions, to find her aunt sitting bolt upright in bed, her coiffure in perfect order, her dark eyes bright and alert as she studied pamphlets and books, to nourish future conversations. The subject might be forestry, or ballistics, or genealogy, or woman suffrage, or ceramics, or the Tang dynasty, or the French châteaux, or British politics, but the fare would be strongly factual and historical and Bertha would corral the gist of what she read and use it to good purpose in all the proper places. Whenever she knew that she would be meeting a specialist in some field she prepared herself in this practical way and earned her reputation of being well informed on all manner of subjects. Actually, she had been reading history all her life and was an able conversationalist but she had an inquiring mind and was genuinely interested in the problems of the day behind her façade of opulence and worldliness. She read very little fiction and was flooded with pamphlets of one sort and another, because of her many interests. Her Chicago links followed her from point to point.

Julia found her a good-humored and good-natured traveling companion. They lunched happily in St. Mark's Square, Venice, ate green figs on Lake Como, or sampled bouillabaisse in little French coast towns. They wandered along cobbled streets and poked in antique shops wherever they went. Mrs. Palmer never seemed to be in a rush, although she was alert and decisive. She gave the young people plenty of leeway in their operations and had great serenity of manner with them, rarely showing impatience. In retrospect Julia, to whom she seemed like a second mother, wrote of her:

> She had a talent of comradeship both in silence and in talk, which made her presence an ideal one. I never saw her cross, selfish, or hard, yet she inspired one to do right, through suggestion more felt than heard, and her own mind was so quick, brilliant, and unpretentious with it all, that unconsciously one flashed the light back and was at one's best. I felt a deep devotion for her, and always found her ready sympathy and understanding a great comfort.

When mutiny broke out in the Russian Army and Navy in 1906 and a general strike was called Julia telegraphed to her aunt that she was bringing Prince Michel and Baby Bertha to London to be sent back to her mother in the United States. Her husband was deeply involved in the political situation and there was turmoil all around. It was not safe for the children to remain where they were.

Bertha was delighted to have her grandchildren stay with her in London. She bought toys for them at Morrell's and took them down to Southampton personally while Julia caught the Dover-Ostend boat, heading back to Russia and her husband. When the Princess reached home she found that the first Duma had been set up. Her husband was appointed to serve on the staff of the Grand Duke Nicholas. They bought a cottage at the military camp of Krasnoe Selo, within an hour's drive of St. Petersburg, and turned it into a garden spot. Until the First World War broke out the Cantacuzènes lived in this flowery acreage, with an old-fashioned summerhouse from which they could see the gilded domes and spires of St. Petersburg, a distant line of forest and the blue Gulf of Finland. Prince Orloff's palace was a political center and he and his wife were intimate friends of the Cantacuzènes. By this time Julia had borne a third child, named Ida, and her Aunt Bertha followed her fortunes with the closest interest.

Mrs. Palmer was more cosmopolitan in her friendships than most of the British peeresses. Her links with Russia and Austria and her work for the Exposition had brought her into touch with people of different races, and when friends arrived from Central Europe or other parts of the world she entertained them in the way she thought suitable. She was cordial to all religions and to all races and was on extra-good terms with the diplomats, and particularly with Sir Charles and Lady Hardinge, who had known the Cantacuzènes well while they were at the British Embassy in St. Petersburg. Lady Hardinge was now one of Queen Alexandra's ladies-in-waiting and the King chose Sir Charles as Minister Plenipotentiary while visiting sovereigns abroad. They made an effective combination on diplomatic missions. The King paved the way by creating a favorable impression, and Hardinge followed up with conversations on detailed points, as they went from one country to another.

Crete was seeking union with Greece at this time and the roots of imperialism were being shaken in different parts of the world. The Boer War was still a hotly debated issue at home and Olive Schreiner was being widely read. But the Triple Entente spread a warm glow for the time being and everyone who moved in Mrs. Palmer's sphere was convinced that the King had done a brilliant job. As an American of vigorous outlook she could be quite independent in some of her findings and she did not always applaud the imperialist theme. She was well informed on politics and watched the forward sweep of events in both Europe and the United States. In 1907, in the midst of all the splendor and lavish spending there was agitation among railway employees in Britain for better wages, shorter hours and recognition of their unions. It was the Pullman story all over again. The fall of the Conservative Government in 1905 had brought the Liberals into power. New and assertive voices were being heard. R. B. Haldane headed the War Office and Herbert H. Asquith was Chancellor of the Exchequer in 1907.

Although the Countess of Warwick had faded from the social scene Mrs. Palmer was still greatly interested in her, because of her novel work, her philanthropy and the old stories told her by Stead. The Countess now filled Warwick Castle with radicals of every stripe. The lessons Robert Blatchford had taught her in the 1890's were irreversible and she plunged deeper into schemes upsetting to conservative thinkers.

The suffragettes by this time were the talk of London and Bertha watched their operations with interest. Although she never failed to champion the advancement of women in public life her old convictions about the methods used were strengthened as she observed the militant tactics of Mrs. Emmeline Pankhurst and her followers. They seemed to her to be going too far when they threw themselves under horses, chained themselves to lampposts, kicked policemen, poured acid into letter boxes, and went on hunger strikes in jail. Asquith was their pet aversion. They held a great parade in London in 1907, their dresses trailing in the mud, their banners flying, as they demanded votes for women. Mrs. Palmer was deeply interested in this demonstration. She believed in the dual arts of diplomacy and compromise, which she practiced herself upon occasion. But she was not blind to the fervor and devotion of the women who followed Mrs. Pankhurst. Some had banked on her as an ally, but she did not declare herself in public.

In London, as in Paris, Mrs. Palmer was surrounded by American women married to Europeans. She counted among her friends Lady Paget, whose gray-blue eyes were clear and observant under dark brows, whose speech was faintly American but who had become thoroughly English in outlook. She was the daughter of Mrs. Paran Stevens and a formidable figure at court. Another hostess whom she knew well was Lady Randolph Churchill, mother of a son named Winston. The former Jennie Jerome had King Edward's approval when she decided to marry young George Cornwallis-West after her husband's death. Petite Mrs. Cornwallis-West, with golden hair cropped short and hazel eyes, stepped politely out of the picture.

The Countess of Craven was Cornelia, the daughter of Bradley Martin of New York and her daughter Daisy later became Princess Henry of Pless. The Marchioness of Dufferin and Ava was Florence, the daughter of John H. Davis of New York. All of the American set had been well aware of Mary Leiter's devotion to Lord Curzon and his great love for her. After her death he became a member of The Souls, a group of intellectuals whom Mrs. Palmer encountered here and there on her social rounds. Both Lady Curzon and the Duchess of Marlborough, who had entertained with great style at Sunderland House, were missed in London. Now and again the tall and willowy Consuelo with her swanlike neck and melancholy hazel eyes crossed Bertha's path, but they did not know each other well. Mrs. Ronald Graham Murray was one of her most intimate friends in Britain.

Mrs. Palmer became familiar with the great ballrooms of London and the stately homes of England during this period. She was on good terms with Millicent, Duchess of Sutherland, and she enjoyed her intimate parties for clever, amusing and distinguished guests as much as she did the formal occasions when the beautiful Duchess stood at the head of the stairs in Stafford House to receive her guests. She admired the magnificent ballroom of Grosvenor House, where the Duchess of Westminster presided, and the white marble staircase of low-ceilinged Devonshire House, where the Duchess of Devonshire held sway. She observed Lady Londonderry's famous diamonds with interest but the Duchess of Manchester continued to slight her. The country house parties were particularly liked by Mrs. Potter Palmer and one of her favorite hosts was the Earl of Strafford, whom she had known first as Robert Cecil Byng. She and Potter had been friends of Sir Thomas Edward Colebrooke, who had married into this family, and they often visited Wrotham Park in Herts, the family seat. It seemed a long way from her own turreted castle on Lake Shore Drive to the medieval fortresses of Britain with their moats and ivy-covered stone walls, their velvety lawns and bosky glades where hares and deer still postured as in the ancient tapestries.

11

➤➤➤➤➤➤➤➤➤➤➤➤➤ *Chaliapin Sings for Mrs. Palmer*

When Chaliapin walked into Mrs. Palmer's drawing room in Hampden House and saw her for the first time he thought at once of Catherine the Great. She was anxious to have him try a few ballads in advance, so that she would know what his voice was like before he sang for her guests. She had assembled some experienced critics to hear him. When he sat down at the piano and sang to his own accompaniment his tones seemed to shake the walls and she hastily ordered the windows flung open to let the sound roll out.

Bertha had pursued him all over Europe by telegram to get him to sing at one of her receptions. He had not yet appeared in London and was not internationally known although he had been a sensational success in Russia and had sung in Milan and Paris. His name at the time was most closely identified with "The Song of the Volga Boatmen." She had asked Julia to find a Russian artist with a good voice, someone who was really new and not yet too well known. She was to offer him any price to sing for her in London.

Julia went to the director of the opera in St. Petersburg and he proposed Chaliapin as the perfect choice. But Chaliapin was fishing, swimming and hunting in France at the time and had no particular interest in a private offer. A deluge of telegrams reached his retreat from an "enormously wealthy American lady who wished me to come to London for one evening to sing a few ballads in her drawing-room," Chaliapin later recalled.

"The idea of going to London for a single evening was too eccentric for me," he added, "and I therefore wired in reply, asking for terms which seemed to me to be incredible that the lady could accept; but the result was not what I hoped for; she replied immediately, accepting my terms, and thus I was obliged to go to London."

He called on her at once "at a very fine house in the middle of a beautiful park." She was not exactly the type of American woman he had expected to see. "Young in face, although greyhaired, my hostess reminded me very strongly of the portraits of Catherine the Great," he noted.

Chaliapin was introduced to Lady de Grey, to an impresario from Covent Garden, to several knowing listeners. As he drank tea with his hostess and conversed with her in French he quickly got the idea that she was waiting for him to sing. "To set her mind at ease I sat down at the piano and sang to my own accompaniment," he recalled.

His great voice rolled out like thunder. Mrs. Palmer and her guests were surprised and impressed. Next day he returned to sing formally at an evening reception. He was led to a large room opening out on the garden in the back. The trees were hung with Japanese lanterns of various hues, a favorite touch of Mrs. Palmer's from her Chicago days. Malmaisons, then the preferred flower for house decoration, were artistically arranged on tables and stands. Chaliapin listened to the hum of voices as the guests moved back and forth between the salon and the garden. He was struck by the sweet trill of a bird. Ah, England and the nightingale! Chaliapin thought, although it seemed odd to him that the nightingale should be singing at night in the midst of such a babble of voices. When he expressed surprise the butler informed him that the bird was an artist with a whistle who sat in a tree in Mrs. Palmer's garden and trilled for ten pounds an evening.

The bird was silent while Chaliapin sang Russian ballads. Mrs. Palmer's guests were stirred by his noble voice and he was encored time and again. Lady de Grey, deeply impressed, urged him to sing at Covent Garden and told him that she would arrange for the Queen to hear him at Windsor. She was adviser for the concerts and music at the royal residences. It was not always easy to strike the perfect balance between the King and the Queen, as the bandmasters were well aware. King Edward liked French and Viennese light opera and Queen Alexandra preferred grand opera and particularly Wagner.

Although he did not sing for the Queen at this time because he had to hurry back to the south of France to keep an engagement, Chaliapin soon appeared for the first time at Covent Garden, the sequel to Mrs. Palmer's party. Both she and Lady de Grey pushed him into view in London. When he sang *Boris Godunov* he found that his performance "became a veritable triumph for Russian art." Sir Henry Beecham led the applause and the "cold English" gave him a memorable reception. On his next visit to London King Edward came to hear him and stood up in his box to greet Chaliapin after he had sung.

In the season of 1907–08 he appeared at the Metropolitan with Geraldine Farrar and Riccardo Martin but his American debut was a fiasco. "My artistic ideals were misunderstood, my performances were adversely criticized, and in general, it seemed that I was looked upon, artistically, as a barbarian," he wrote with some bitterness in later years. But his days of triumph at the Metropolitan lay ahead.

His friendship with Mrs. Palmer and Princess Cantacuzène

continued and he visited them in Florida. But he ran into heavy trouble when he sang in Chicago. He was in and out of the headlines there and charges of fisticuffs, envy and amours flew thick and fast around him. "As such things have happened to me only in Chicago, I am obliged to conclude that the newspapers of that city have a special psychology," he wrote of Mrs. Palmer's favorite city. But she always felt that she had played a part in introducing him to a wider audience.

Another of her professional entertainments created even more of a sensation in London and made headlines on both sides of the Atlantic. In 1907, shortly after the May court at Buckingham Palace, she brought Olive Fremstad over from Paris with her entire cast to sing *Salome* at Hampden House. This was startling, even to the most advanced Edwardians, since the Strauss-Wilde opera was under a censorship ban at the time. It had one performance in Dresden, three in Paris and was withdrawn at the Metropolitan after one showing.

Mrs. Palmer daringly introduced the opera to Londoners at a party given in honor of Mr. and Mrs. Whitelaw Reid. It was such a success that the King asked to have it repeated for him and he arrived next morning for a private showing. The Fremstad performance gave Mrs. Palmer one of her more memorable evenings. It was preceded by a dinner at which champagne was served in priceless Venetian goblets of an odd shell pattern, and her gold and silver plate was in use for the epicurean feast her French chef had prepared.

Bertha wore plain black velvet molded to her trim figure, with a dazzling necklace and stomacher but no tiara. Ropes of pearls were strung from shoulder to shoulder with dramatic effect. Mrs. Keppel, in gold brocade, sat with her after dinner and they discussed their plans for the later events of the season. Bertha announced that she intended to entertain at Cowes. Lady Paget wore stiff white silk with turquoise satin bows in her hair, and turquoise buckles on her turquoise satin shoes. Lilies edged Mrs. Ernest Cunard's bodice and two large lilies spiraled from her hair. Mrs. Reid wore magnificent sapphires with a midnight blue satin gown. Bertha used her most expert party touch on this occasion, according to the New York *World* correspondent, who wrote:

> Mrs. Palmer was tireless, standing near the door of the concert room seeing to everything herself. Every guest had a comfortable chair for the concert, and chairs and couches were placed along the corridor, where the gentlemen and the ladies, too, finished their cigarettes while enjoying the music. It is becoming the rule rather than the exception at parties for some of the women to remain with the men, after dinner, to smoke. Six ladies, including Lady Paget, did this at Mrs. Palmer's party, not going into the concert room until the musical program was half over.

Both Lily Langtry and Mrs. Patrick Campbell had already made headlines in America by smoking cigarettes in public. The craze was catching on, and Mrs. Palmer's *Salome* party gave it fashionable emphasis in London. She continued to use professional entertainers of the first rank at her major parties. Melba sang for her and she had Pavlova dance at her Paris home at a reception given for Honoré and his wife. On that occasion she entertained the entire Russian ballet, along with Pasquale Amato of the Metropolitan.

Each hostess tried to outdo the other with the artists she was able to lure into her drawing room. The stars were not by any means reluctant to lend themselves to these occasions. It spread their fame and added to their wealth. Paderewski played at a concert given in William Waldorf Astor's house at 18 Carlton House Terrace within a week of Mrs. Palmer's *Salome* party. The Reids had Jean de Reszke sing at Dorchester House. Lady de Grey gave lively and amusing parties at which the De Reszkes and Madam Melba often entertained her guests. Reynaldo Hahn conducted the *Bal de Beatrice d'Este* at the Duchess of Manchester's in the presence of the King and Queen. The Rothschild cousins, Albert and Ferdinand, drew front-rank artists to their London homes and their country seats in Buckingham. Albert had his own private orchestra which played in his Park Lane mansion, a thoroughly Victorian creation of plush, marble and gilt. Ferdinand, in Piccadilly, favored Louis XVI decorations and had a notable white ballroom.

Always original, daring and different, Bertha introduced a new custom in England that summer by inviting her women guests to delve into huge baskets of lilies, forget-me-nots and roses, and fish for their own dinner partners from slips pasted to the stems of the flowers. "I am sick of the grumbles of men and women regarding the way I pair them for dinner, and so in the future I mean not to be responsible," she announced. "I shall let the ladies draw for their partners, and I shall do likewise for my own, even if the most insignificant man in the room falls to my lot."

The year 1907 was the most brilliant socially of the Edwardian era. When the American exodus began in September the excitement still went on, with a transatlantic race by the new turbine liner *Lusitania* to surpass the record. Mrs. Palmer booked passage for the maiden voyage of the 45,000-ton liner, which had 550 first-class passengers aboard. Millionaires and their wives abounded on this crossing and she tramped the decks energetically with Cyrus H. McCormick, the Robert Goelets and other friends and acquaintances.

A hundred thousand spectators saw the new turbine liner sail from Liverpool and sang "Rule Britannia" as she moved down the Mersey. Bertha found it the most stimulating crossing she had ever had and she was now an annual transatlantic passenger. She followed each day's run with the liveliest interest and even sent back bulletins to a Chicago paper. The passage was smooth and everyone believed that the *Lusitania* would make it, until she ran into fog off the American coast and was slowed up. When they docked in New York the *Deutschland* still held the record.

Ida met her sister and was with her when the ship newsmen

swarmed into her suite and found her wearing a gray French broadcloth costume with wide stripes of a darker gray. This was topped by a huge purple hat with gray plumes, for she was still in half-mourning for her mother. She talked with reserve to the New York reporters, merely telling them that she had had an unusual and most enjoyable crossing. "The passage was smooth and the feeling that we were breaking the record was stimulating to everyone," she announced.

She took the train at once for Chicago and wound up there next day, having traveled roughly four thousand miles by sea and land in less than a week, a considerable feat at the time. She knew the Chicago reporters individually but she looked at them coldly as they gathered around her at her home on Lake Shore Drive. Their papers had been linking her name with a succession of romances in Europe and she did not approve. She had saved her powder for the home press and she meant to set them straight. One paper earlier in the summer had gone so far as to run biographies and pictures of King Peter of Serbia and the Queen of Chicago, as if marriage were in the offing.

The new generation of reporters in Chicago had grown brash. Once none would have dared to ask her specifically if King Peter had actually proposed to her, as the dispatches said, but she met the question without shock and responded huffily.

"The idea is ridiculous," she said in her most matter-of-fact tones. "I have never even contemplated a union with him and do not intend to. You cannot be too emphatic in your denial of this. . . . The newspapers make so much of me. I do not want notoriety. I really have nothing to say. If I said anything it would be commonplace and if I said nothing it would be banal."

The reporters pressed on. How about the Earl of Munster? Mrs. Palmer insisted that she did not even know him. How about the Duke of Atholl? She shook her head, although it was a fact that she had been seen with him in public, as with several other peers whose names had been linked to hers—Sir Algernon West, for instance, a widower with a large family.

Mrs. Palmer was quite convinced that most of the rumors about her romances were emanating from a newspaper office in Chicago and she pointed out that no one abroad attached any romantic importance to her appearances at the theater, races and balls with well-known men until the Chicago papers presented speculation as fact. There had been widespread reports that a newspaper owner's wife in Chicago was given to working up stories of this kind about well-known people of whom she did not wholly approve.

"It is very annoying to a woman who is traveling alone and unprotected to have such things printed," Mrs. Palmer told the reporters severely. "Coming from one's own town, too!" But King Edward had whipped up some of this speculation by saying to Sir Schomberg K. McDonnell, who had been secretary to Lord Salisbury and was the brother of the Earl of Antrim: "Why don't you marry a really rich American lady like Mrs. Potter Palmer?" The New York *American* promptly ran an eye-catching headline on March 17, 1907: "King Tries to Make Match for Mrs. Potter Palmer." The Four Hundred looked on with skepticism but her Chicago friends wondered if it might be true.

Bertha was none too pleased about this. But she had many interesting conversations with "Pom" McDonnell, as he had been known since his days at Eton. He was Secretary to the Commissioner of Works from 1902 to 1912 and when Buckingham Palace, Windsor and Balmoral were overhauled after the Queen's death, he had much to do with the removal and restoration of paintings. When working at Holyrood in preparation for a state visit to Scotland by the King and Queen he proposed hanging tapestries over the faded old portraits, imaginary in conception, of the early King of Scotland. But since these portraits had dominated the historic banquet given for Prince Charles Edward Stuart in 1745 and were part of the history of Scotland, "Pom's" plan aroused an outcry and they remained as they were.

As Mrs. Palmer was interested in anything that had to do

with art she liked to discuss his work with Sir Schomberg. Sir Lionel Cust considered him an admirable official of the "best Whitehall type." He was a conscientious public servant who sometimes was at odds with officialdom and he was not an admirer of modern art, though he was of Mrs. Potter Palmer.

She came closer to true romance in France than she did in England, however. Although aging she was still quite beautiful. She accepted gallantry as a matter of course but did not encourage it. Among those who frequently called on her in Paris and Biarritz were the Count Louis de Lasteyrie of the Lafayette family, with whom her Honoré ancestors had been so friendly, Prince Charles de la Tour d'Auvergne, and a French duke who gave her the final accolade by inviting her into his Saint Germain family home. But Bertha did not think seriously of remarrying. She valued her freedom and enjoyed being Mrs. Potter Palmer, an ambassador at large for her country, feted wherever she went, sure of having her way. Her position was well established and she was wary of fortune hunters. The tragic results of titles bartered for millions already showed around her. Of all the American women who put down roots in France she and Consuelo Vanderbilt, later Madame Jacques Balsan, best understood the French nature and loved the country. With Mrs. Palmer it was a question of inheritance.

By this time the Infanta Eulalia was back on her calling list and they met several times in Biarritz and Paris. She had decided to bury the hatchet with "this bibulous representative of a degenerate monarchy," an uncommonly sharp phrase that the tactful Mrs. Palmer was reported to have applied to the Infanta soon after the Columbian Exposition. Eulalia was still untamed and was in hot water again, this time with her nephew, King Alfonso, who had objected strenuously to a racy book on morals that she had written. It had been withdrawn from circulation and Eulalia hid out for a time.

However, on her return to Chicago after all these stories about the brilliant season of 1907 had appeared in the local papers, Mrs. Palmer was eyed with more than customary interest, even by those who had known her for many years. Some wondered if it might be true that she planned giving up her famous name.

The *Inter-Ocean*, while headlining the fact that she laughed at stories of her engagement, went on to comment:

Mrs. Potter Palmer returned home yesterday, and at once resumed her undisputed sway and sceptre as sovereign leader of Chicago society. During her absence in Europe there have been many speculations as to who would wear her regal crown this winter; each section of the city, each particular faction of society had its aspirants, its heirs-apparent, its pretenders, and its claimants to the throne. But they all faded in a flickering glimmer yesterday morning when the Pennsylvania's eighteen hour flyer rumbled into the Union Depot and Mrs. Potter Palmer was in Chicago again.

She gave one of her Monday "at homes" and all Chicago knew that she still led the field, although both Mrs. Marshall Field and Mrs. Harold F. McCormick, daughter of John D. Rockefeller, had been challengers. The *Herald-Examiner* noted that she "turned on her charm, chatted with her guests about Chicago's problems and achievements, and . . . there was no more debate about who was who."

As usual, she looked over the lists with an appraising eye. The scene was changing. Veterans were dying off. Pretenders and newly rich of whom she did not wholly approve were coming to the fore. Mrs. Palmer always sought for solid values as well as the external trappings of wealth and status. Snob or not, she had the Middle Western knack of keeping her feet firmly planted on the ground. She was quite adept at dropping or cold-shouldering the pushing, the merely rich and the dissolute.

The Charity Ball as a means of raising funds had been at

tacked by a group of Chicago ministers. They had called it a "left-handed, hypocritical, and thinly disguised effort to ease a guilty conscience." Somehow there was frost in the air and Mrs. Palmer was indignant when Higinbotham and Mrs. Bowen between them dug up old issues about the Fair. Her own horizons had widened and she felt far removed from malice and petty attack.

Although she disliked personal publicity of any kind Mrs. Palmer understood its value for public causes. She had felt its sting herself upon occasion and did not underrate it. But she was always wary in talking to reporters and she knew it was wiser to mollify than to annoy them. They had been writing about her for years in one way or another and had called on her for everything in the way of symposiums from sex to religion, from etiquette to football. She had learned all the ins and outs of publicity at the time of the Columbian Exposition and had a sound understanding of newspaper needs. She had even considered starting or backing a paper in Chicago. However, as the years went on it became ever more difficult for reporters to break through her staff to get at her for anything, unless they happened to catch her on shipboard or in a public place.

Only Charles MacArthur ever dared to ruffle her with deceit. Feeling prankish one night he made a bet with his barroom friends that he would bring Mrs. Palmer to the phone.

"Impossible!" the skeptics exclaimed.

"Wait and see," said Charlie.

As usual, all the intermediaries were on guard, until he announced himself as William Randolph Hearst. Mrs. Palmer quickly came to the telephone but it did not take her two minutes to decide that she was being fooled. When she learned the name of her tormentor she was not amused and put up her guard more firmly than ever toward the press.

Mrs. Palmer went west soon after her return from Europe in 1907 to join Honoré and his wife at a ranch they had taken in Oregon. Honoré loved the open spaces, and his mother joined heartily in their healthy life there. Julia and her children were with them and little Potter D'Orsay Palmer, aged two, was another grandchild for Mrs. Palmer to cherish. She was back in Chicago in time to run the Charity Ball. It came off with the usual success, and she led the Grand March. The Cantacuzènes returned to Russia that spring and she visited them there and saw things settling back into an uneasy armistice after the disturbances of 1906 and 1907.

She was in Europe in the summer of 1908 when word reached her from Chicago of young Potter's engagement to Pauline Kohlsaat. She hurried home at once to make friends with the serene, blue-eyed girl that her younger son had chosen for his bride. Pauline was the daughter of Herman H. Kohlsaat, whose progress Mrs. Palmer had watched for many years. His childhood was passed in Galena. He moved to Chicago at the age of fourteen, worked at various small jobs, then founded a string of stool and counter lunchrooms where a meal could be had for ten cents. From this he branched off into a large bakery business and became a wealthy man, eventually buying a half-interest in the *Inter-Ocean*, then selling that and buying the Chicago *Times-Herald* and the *Evening Post*.

Mrs. Palmer knew him as one of the pioneers of her beloved city. Pauline was a quiet, conservative girl and she had a simple wedding at her father's home. Her sister, Katherine Kohlsaat, was her only attendant and Honoré Palmer was his brother's best man. There was much talk in Chicago over this alliance but soon Mrs. Palmer was back in Europe again. The papers speculated now as to whether she might settle permanently in England or France. But when questioned about this she always insisted that she would never sever her ties with Chicago and she never did. However, she passed less time now in the Windy City. She was at Biarritz in the spring of 1908. King Edward VII was there as usual but was mourning the death of his good friend the Duke of Devonshire, who had succumbed to pneumonia at Cannes. They had been friends for forty years. Sir Ernest Cassel and Mrs. Keppel were again with the King and he was trying to get rid of the bronchial cough that had plagued him all winter. Later that summer his horses were lucky, which added to his popularity throughout Britain. "Good old Teddy," the public called him now.

Mrs. Palmer was abroad again in 1909, the year in which Blériot made the first crossing of the English Channel by airplane. Theodore Roosevelt, an old friend of Fred Grant's, was making history in the White House at this time and H. G. Wells was predicting that the wars of the future would be fought in the air. The public had found new ways of enjoying itself. Country weekends were the rage and the Sunday parade in Hyde Park was dwindling. The motorcar had made country pleasures more available to the average man. Great crowds attended the football and cricket matches. The cinematograph was in its infant stages and a restless groping for recreation was fomenting among the working classes.

The King and Queen cruised in the Mediterranean in the spring of 1909 and had a picnic party halfway up Vesuvius. Edward was ailing on his return to London for the season. He had repeated bouts of laryngeal and bronchial catarrh and he no longer seemed to be able to shake off his fatigue. Mrs. Palmer was at Cowes when the Czar joined him there in the autumn of 1909. The King had been greatly cheered by winning the Derby that year. But this was a tumultuous and troubled year for him politically, with the threat of war hanging over Europe. Late in 1908 the Austrian Emperor had annexed Bosnia and Herzegovina from Serbia, and early in 1909 Arthur Balfour drew attention to the growing threat of German shipbuilding operations.

Mrs. Palmer followed these developments with the closest interest. But meanwhile the social whirl went on and the Countess of Stafford gave a great ball in her honor in 1909.

Bertha was considered the handsomest woman present, wearing her diamond stomacher, a circle of diamond stars around her neck and a high collar of jewels, resembling Queen Alexandra's. She had won the London hostesses by easy stages. Few resisted her now and it was known to all that both the King and Queen approved of her.

Mrs. Palmer admired Queen Alexandra. At sixty she looked no more than thirty-five. She was stone-deaf, unpunctual on all occasions, but she was gentle, had a sprightly wit and was much beloved by all who knew her. The King paid her every honor in public and insisted on his friends treating her with deference, even to the point of reproving the Duchess of Marlborough when she showed up in the Queen's presence without her tiara.

The theater and literary world of London was in full flower as the Edwardian era neared its close. The giants of the Victorian age—Meredith, Hardy, Wordsworth, Swinburne, Tennyson and Browning—had given way to a new and vigorous crop of writers. Wells, Shaw, Bennett, Galsworthy, Barrie, Beerbohm, Belloc, Conan Doyle and Chesterton were turning out books and plays that everyone discussed in the drawing rooms of the day. Kipling's jingles lived on with the British Army and his short stories delighted the sons of Eton and the entire English-speaking world. E. M. Forster, Hugh Walpole and J. D. Beresford were having their early books published. Ouida, Mrs. Humphrey Ward, Marie Corelli and the Baroness Orczy drew women readers. Robert Hichens' *Garden of Allah* was a best seller. Hall Caine and Rider Haggard fed the popular taste and *King Solomon's Mines* and *She* were current favorites.

Mrs. Palmer saw little of her old journalist friend, W. T. Stead. He had had a nervous breakdown soon after the Columbian Exposition and his interest had veered to automatic writing, crystal gazing, and the promotion of movements for peace. He had made himself thoroughly unpopular during the Boer

War by attacking the war lords and he remained a stormy element at the heart of government. Although Bertha encountered the Countess of Warwick as she moved around London there was no close link between them. The Countess was still a beauty, with masses of light hair framing her pale, proud face. She was the half-sister of the Duchess of Sutherland, of whom Mrs. Palmer saw more. The Countess had long ago given up all hope of converting King Edward to her political views or of softening him on the subject of woman suffrage. Although he had signed the register at her wedding and had been an "intimate and dear friend" for years, he was chilly when she brought up the subject of socialism. Nor could he endure the feminists who were giving trouble at this time and whose pertinacity was applauded by the Countess of Warwick. "God put women into the world to be different from men and he could not understand why women did not recognize this instead of trying to copy men's pursuits," the Countess reported regretfully.

Whitelaw Reid was due to return to the United States in 1909 but he was so popular with the King that his term was prolonged and his warm relations with the court continued. He had been the American plenipotentiary at Queen Victoria's Diamond Jubilee in 1897. He had attended the coronation in 1902 and returned as Ambassador in 1905. He was just making plans for the approaching visit of Theodore Roosevelt in the spring of 1910 when the end came for King Edward. He had given a great dinner party at Buckingham Palace in March before leaving for Biarritz. He returned late in April and went to the theater that evening. Next day he talked to Asquith about the political situation. A general election was brewing and the House of Lords was under attack. He received ministers and governors from the Dominions and Colonies but had terrible spasms of coughing as he tried to talk to them. He played cards at Mrs. Keppel's but his heart was already failing.

The Queen was summoned home from Corfu. Word ran

through London that the King was dying. Nothing else was discussed in the great mansions and the humble pubs of England. It was quickly known to Mrs. Palmer as to other Londoners that in his last hours Queen Alexandra personally led Mrs. Keppel by the hand to his bedside. Soon afterward a member of the royal household went down to the railings and solemnly informed the great crowds gathered there: "The King is dead."

Next day the Empire was in mourning. Flags hung everywhere at half-mast. Children marched to school in remote villages with wide black bands on their sleeves and black streamers dangling from their hats. The newspapers appeared with deep black borders and people everywhere wore mourning. A fortnight later King Edward was buried with his ancestors at Windsor in the final pageantry of his reign. Nine rulers and many princes and nobles attended the funeral ceremonies in London and at Windsor. Theodore Roosevelt was there to represent the United States. Many wept in the hour that the King was committed to the vault in St. George's Chapel, where forty-seven years earlier he had married the King of Denmark's beautiful daughter.

London became a city of gloom. Black Ascot was held in 1910 with every one present dressed in mourning from head to foot. Black ostrich feathers and paradise plumes drooped from cartwheel hats. Long sable fringes swung from gowns as men and women moved at a funereal tempo, remembering their life-loving monarch. Mrs. Palmer rarely went to London after the death of King Edward but used her house in Paris more. Court life changed. Old groupings broke up as King George V and Queen Mary ascended the throne.

The year 1910 marked a big shift in her own way of living. As if she were starting life all over again she bought a vast acreage of wild land in Florida and found a fresh career for herself in this jungle.

12

⟩⟩⟩⟩⟩⟩⟩⟩⟩⟩⟩⟩⟩ *Back to Nature*

Mrs. Potter Palmer was sixty-one when she sought a new and simpler life for herself in an unpromising wilderness close to the small town of Sarasota, which then had a population of nine hundred inhabitants. It was cut off from the rest of the world and the people supported themselves chiefly by growing fruit and catching fish. But life had not gone stale for Mrs. Palmer. She had merely reached the point of satiety in the ceaseless round of entertaining, and turned with vigor to creative effort in the sphere where her fortune was founded—the purchase and development of land. She was fulfilling the family tradition to buy, to build, to expand, to make money and at the same time to serve the community. Both Henry H. Honoré and Potter Palmer had shown her the way.

"You must realize that the Palmer family is quite an institution," she told A. B. Edwards, Sarasota real estate dealer, after she had bought up thousands of acres of land in Florida. "The very foundation of the family is real estate. That is why we have invested so heavily in land down here."

For the last eight years of her life she devoted her best

energies to developing her acres, to farming and ranching and establishing a domain in which she moved with the authority of a ruler. It was an early experiment in community farm planning and it gave her some of the bitterest lessons of her star-dusted life as well as much satisfaction.

Perhaps at no time in her career was Mrs. Palmer more incomprehensible to her fashionable friends or more interesting to the impartial observer than during this final phase of simple associations and arduous work. She dug down to the grass roots of living in a way that satisfied something basic in her strenuous nature. There were no pretenders here, no crowned heads, no haughty duchesses, no aspirant hostesses, all of whom she had known in her time. Nor were there any further social pinnacles for her to scale. But she had abundant energy still to expend and all her business affairs and philanthropies were going well in Chicago.

At one point she conceded that the minute she settled in her home town she was deluged with requests to serve on committees, to organize events, to join in a whirl of urban doings. She may well have been tired of it all, although none who knew her personally would admit that they ever saw traces of fatigue in Mrs. Potter Palmer until the closing months of her life. But she may have felt the need to seek refreshment in fundamental things. Her life had become artificial, high-powered and demanding. In any event, few ventures in her eventful life gave her more stimulation than her final years of farming.

She became the builder, the planner, the doer. Her strong, enterprising touch was in full operation, but the cards were stacked on her side, too. Thanks to the Palmer fortune, she need spare no expense when experts were called for, when crops failed, when costs mounted. Yet the practical strain in her nature was strong. It was not enough to create a beautiful estate. She expected to make money as well as to head a sylvan community. Everyone in Chicago knew that as a business woman she was shrewd and daring. But she had not counted on floods, sour soil, balky homesteaders, inept employees and the disasters of nature when she first viewed the sparkling waters of Sarasota Bay on a February day in 1910. Her plans were utopian, her means unlimited.

Mrs. Palmer's attention was first focused on this region by J. H. Lord, a real estate man in Chicago whose father had moved south in 1889 and bought more than 100,000 acres of land at from seventy-five cents to four dollars an acre. She sent her father to see Lord when a small advertisement for the sale of a citrus grove in Sarasota appeared in the Chicago *Sunday Tribune*. Then she invited the real estate man to dinner and listened to his expansive talk on the possibilities of real estate development in Florida. She and her father decided to go south and see for themselves.

News that the famous Mrs. Potter Palmer of Chicago was coming to Sarasota shook up the small community. How could they house this elegant lady and her staff? She arrived with her father, her brother Adrian, her general manager, W. A. Sumner, and some servants. Edwards, who was commissioned by Lord to give her a royal welcome, decided that the local Belle Haven Hotel was too run-down for the widow of the man who had built the Palmer House. So Dr. Jack Halton's newly finished sanitarium at the water's edge was prepared for her use and she promptly began her explorations.

Later, when they came to know her, the men who had worried about her reception realized that none of the fuss had been necessary. They found her a good sport—"a swell girl," in the words of Albert Blackburn, who managed her ranch. She was equal to any emergency—mutiny on her ranch, cut fences, unfriendly homesteaders, flooded crops, dying cattle, broken-down trucks. She could take a joke and see the best side of calamity and those who worked with her found that she kept her temper under stress.

She was captivated by Little Sarasota Bay as she sailed along with Edwards in a cabin boat and urged him to point out everything of historical interest, or merit, or any property that was for sale. Since he had wandered barefooted through the region as a boy he was able to give her a picturesque account of its natural wonders and the history of its settlers. On the way back her comments showed that she had absorbed every fact.

When they reached Osprey, a little settlement in the woods founded by Judge John G. Webb, who ran a small guest house, Edwards told her of a curious growth, where two tall trees, a palm and an oak, intertwined. The coastline had already caught Mrs. Palmer's eye.

"I must see that property," she announced decisively.

The captain headed in to the dilapidated dock and the little group urged her not to go ashore. They feared that the priceless Mrs. Palmer might flop in the water. But she jumped nimbly ashore over rotted planks and tramped through the jungle to view the enmeshed trees and the boxlike house that stood on the property. It had belonged to Lawrence Jones, a member of the John Paul Jones whiskey family of Kentucky. She asked if the place were for sale. The owner was absent. Edwards told her it was listed at his office and the price would be eleven thousand dollars for thirteen acres.

Early next morning she hired a boatman and went back with her father and manager to see the owner. She thought she might do better by dealing direct with him but the price was the same. Although Edwards lost this transaction Lord and he had a hand in most of her subsequent land dealings. Eventually she bought close to eighty thousand acres around Sarasota and her total holdings at one time, including property at Tampa, amounted to 140,000 acres. The men who dealt with her found her a shrewd bargainer but a just woman.

"Your Aunt Bertha has bought some rocks in Florida," Princess Cantacuzène was told when she returned from Russia in the winter of 1910 for a four-month stay.

Mrs. Palmer had been captivated not only by the tropical growth at Osprey but by the huge mounds made by the Indians in the distant past from millions of individual sea shells. The strange protrusions covered ten acres of land and rose thirty-five feet above the smaller bay, creating a picturesque strip of coastline that appealed at once to her eye.

"Here is heaven at last," she told her father as she studied Sarasota Bay. "It reminds me of the Bay of Naples."

Mrs. Palmer had sampled all the best resorts in Europe. Now she had spotted a winter home in her native land where she would find warmth and sunshine. Her father was very old. The Chicago winters were severe. Here she found the Riviera effect, but without the rococo touches and the overdone sophistication that she knew so well. The sun was strong, the birds and flowers were dramatic, the land was wild and she could do with it what she willed. But above all she was fully persuaded that she was making a good investment.

The rush to Florida was only a whisper at the time but her father, who had prophesied Chicago's future, had followed Henry M. Flagler's development of the east coast with interest. Mrs. Palmer, who had been advised by her husband at the end of his life to invest her money in real estate, was ripe for this move. She would bring order out of the wilderness, cultivate citrus groves, create a model community of fruit and truck farms, build an Italian villa in the heart of the jungle and establish a colony of her own.

Lord arrived from Chicago to spur on the fulfillment of this ambition. He drove her over his lands by horse and buggy and she soon acquired half of his extensive holdings. She quickly bought up all the property surrounding the Jones place at Osprey. There were no paved roads or easy means of communication around Sarasota, Osprey or Venice at this time. But before investing she stipulated in the purchasing contract for fifty thousand acres that a railroad spur must be built from Sarasota to her property. Pressure was brought to bear on the

Seaboard Air Line Railroad to make this gesture for Mrs. Potter Palmer. It was even suggested that she would organize a railroad of her own if the plan did not go through with expedition. Within thirty days the spur was under way, running from Sarasota to Venice, and serving her property.

Mrs. Palmer went to work with her customary drive and large-scale planning. There were roads to build, irrigation ditches to be dug, crops to plant, landscaping to be done, and the house to be designed. She commissioned a Boston architect to draw up plans for her Italian villa but in the end she contented herself with remodeling and enlarging the house that stood on the property. She named her place The Oaks.

All manner of experts were summoned to Osprey for consultation. Gardeners, landscaping specialists, architects, engineers, horticulturists were called into counsel. A geologist from the West coached her on the nature of the Florida soil, the water elevations, the substrata and general irrigation problems. Mrs. Palmer studied books and pamphlets on likely crops. She experimented and became as knowing about Florida land and as technical in her talk as she had been about her Impressionist paintings, factory conditions in Chicago, Central European politics, Chinese porcelains or woman's status in the Orient. But some of the natives thought her gullible and deplored the scientific theories of her experts. In the midst of all the hubbub she would turn to the Florida Department of Agriculture or call up Edwards in the middle of the night to settle a point on water elevation. Mrs. Palmer was too diplomatic to override local opinion. She wanted seasoned advice, from whatever source, and then she drew her own deductions, but this did not save her from some grim mistakes. She brought in nearly every new machine and gadget turned out by the International Harvester Company. Some worked. Others were duds on her difficult land. She bought her own sawmill and hauled lumber.

Mrs. Palmer planned to own the largest grapefruit acreage in the world. She hoped to have tank steamers coming in the

Big Pass to haul fruit juices to Europe. She foresaw a winter resort at Venice along European lines and a race track on her property. She was determined to cultivate the indigenous crops, promote scientific methods and raise the status of the community. It was a two-way investment in real estate and human values—the old Palmer combination, to make money and help the community at the same time. Some of her plans went through. Others failed. The obstacles she encountered were formidable. She picked up large acreage for comparatively small sums, then sank a fortune in developing the land. She did not live to see great profits but her first eleven-thousand-dollar investment at Osprey has mushroomed today into the strong family inheritance of the Palmer First National Bank and Trust Company in Sarasota, the Palmer Florida Corporation, the Palmer Nurseries Garden Center and the Palmer ranch. Streets in the vicinity testify to the Palmer influence—Potter Street, Honoré Avenue, Palmer Boulevard, Adrian Avenue and D'Orsay Street.

By 1911 the work of clearing timber and landscaping was well under way. Mrs. Palmer had always had a taste for the outdoors and for horticulture. Her conservatory on Lake Shore Drive and her gardens in London and Paris had been more than ornamental appendages to her houses. She knew about flowers and plants and trees and now she extended this knowledge with concentrated study of the sort of vegetation that would do best in the Florida soil. Lawns and gardens were laid out, crossed by paths that were designed to follow the natural flow of the land. She particularly wished to save the more beautiful trees.

The remodeling and enlargement of the house presented problems. No carpenters were available, so local fishermen were called in to work under the direction of Thomas Reed Martin, an architect whom she brought from Chicago to direct operations. Like the other men who worked for her he found her money-wise and a hard-driving business woman, but just and open to reason in her dealings. Plants and shrubs were imported and fitted into the native setting. An artificial brook ran from the well on the hilltop, winding through the jungle and splashing over rocks at the bottom. The Duchesne Garden, better known as the sunken Blue Garden, was picturesquely framed by the shell mounds of the Indians. Another garden was devoted to roses and rare varieties were brought from all parts of the world. A pavilion fronted on Mirror Lake. Masses of mauve orchids stirred in the sea coast winds and the *Schizolobium excelsum*, a rare Brazilian flowering tree, grew in feathery masses. Visitors walked through rows of yellow acacias, past Chinese hibiscus, bougainvillaea and brilliant crotons. Mrs. Palmer never tired of the jade, amethyst and turquoise of sea and sky, of the dramatic sunsets and shifting winds, of the cardinals and mocking birds that darted through the jungle, of the laurel and resurrection trees that grew without her aid.

"The most wonderful thing in the world is a garden," she told a reporter at this time. "I have found my one talent, if I have any, at Sarasota Bay. It is to watch beautiful things grow and see flowers blossom as I plant them."

Vines shadowed The Oaks, which became famous for its beauties, both natural and contrived. The simple white-columned porch faced toward Midnight Pass. Indoors was cool and shadowy on the hottest day. Mrs. Palmer chose to call it her "beach cottage," but her art, her crystal, china and silver, the tall bisque figurines with which she adorned her dining table, and her entourage seemed luxurious enough to visitors. She presided with style and still wore Paris gowns for dinner, but her more striking jewels were never seen at The Oaks. She used chintz with some of her Louis XVI furniture brought from Chicago. A few of her favorite paintings hung in the house. She believed in enjoying her art as well as in owning it, and would often pause before her pictures and admire them. Her Impressionists looked particularly well in this setting of sunshine, color and the sea. One of Monet's haystacks hung over her eighteenth-century, French provincial, carved oak mantelpiece in the living room. Raffaelli, Degas and Cassatt, as well as Monet, were represented. After her death one of the downstairs rooms was converted into a miniature art gallery and The Oaks became a show place for the public.

Sea walls and docks were built along the shore front of her property. Her private dock fronted on Little Sarasota Bay. The Palmer family used speedboats and bathed at Crescent Beach, where a cabana stood on white sand, but Mrs. Palmer never lounged on the beach. Her energetic nature demanded ceaseless action. She was the executive every hour of the day. Her family gathered in strength around her. Her sons Honoré and Potter, by this time mature businessmen and executives of the Sarasota-Venice Company organized for her holdings, built a home named Immokalee at Sarasota. Her uncle, Benjamin F. Honoré, built The Acacias, a colonnaded mansion on top of an Indian mound, with a splendid view of the bay. Here he and his wife Laura held open house for the Honoré clan. Mr. Honoré, Adrian and Nathaniel came and went. Mrs. Frederick Grant stayed at The Acacias after her husband's death in New York in 1912.

The Chicago *Sunday Tribune* carried a full-page layout of Sarasota pictures. When her fellow townsmen learned that Mrs. Potter Palmer had invested heavily in the region a number followed her there, as Kentuckians had followed her father to Chicago. The little town, founded in 1886, came to life about the time of her arrival. A small electric plant was installed and two feeble street lights shed their beams on Main Street, which still had a stream running down its center and live oaks lining it at either side. Municipal waterworks and a sewage system were installed. Sea walls were built. A new bank was opened. The Yacht Club revived and the first motion picture Sarasotans had seen was offered in a tent show for ten cents a viewing.

Mrs. Palmer gave impetus to the town's development by establishing payrolls. She would demand three hundred men at a time. She told Blackburn to hire anyone who would work, but the local supply did not meet the demand, so she brought in workers from the outside—Italians, Negroes, men of different races. This invasion was not welcomed by the native homesteaders and her labor troubles began. However, she paid the highest wages along the seaboard and sparked Sarasota's business start.

Her thirteen hundred acres of citrus groves did well and soon she was shipping grapefruit to Chicago. She reclaimed an area of muck land east of Sarasota, had it drained and irrigated, and started vegetable crops. Here celery growing became a major local industry after her death. But her first big venture—the Bee Ridge development, designed to promote model farm development—came a cropper. She cut up seven thousand acres into ten- and forty-acre tracts and started a selling campaign. But the settlers were not happy. They complained that the land did not come up to expectations. The assorted types who arrived expressed dissatisfaction and Mrs. Palmer felt the chill winds of public disapproval.

As always when checkmated she moved on to other things. Her next step was to establish a model cattle ranch called Meadow Sweet Pastures in the Myakka River region, popular with hunters, anglers and campers. When she first toured this area by horse and carriage she was impressed by its lakes and towering palms, its giant oaks draped with Spanish moss and its rich pastures.

She was an enthusiastic sightseer and served the party with a picnic lunch she had brought with her. Recent rains had flooded the road and water soon lapped at the carriage floor. She refused to turn back. Instead the elegant Mrs. Palmer tucked her skirts firmly around her ankles and propped up her feet above the water line.

Her attention was drawn to the beauty of Shep's Island.

"There's approximately 6,000 acres in that tract and you can get it for about $75,000," Edwards told her.

"And much as if she were ordering a bag of peanuts, she said, 'Buy it for me,' " the real estate man recalled.

But she did much of the negotiating personally with Garrett Murphy, a cattleman better known as "Dink." He told her he would sell the land but must first dispose of his cattle.

"That's easy. I'll buy the cattle, too," Mrs. Palmer assured him.

In no time at all she was handing over to him a check for $93,000, while he moaned that he was giving up his life's holdings. However, when he walked into the next room where some of his rancher friends were waiting as this interesting encounter took place, he kissed the check with enthusiasm. Mrs. Palmer rounded up three separate ranches in all. The highest sum she paid for this land was four hundred dollars an acre; the lowest was eight dollars an acre. With the acquisition of three thousand head of cattle with the Murphy ranch she began an intensive study of the cattle business.

Meadow Sweet Pastures was eighteen miles from The Oaks, so she built a camp at the end of Upper Myakka Lake, largely for the benefit of her grandchildren. Potter D'Orsay was six in 1911 when she took up residence at The Oaks. Little Honoré was three. A year earlier Pauline and Potter had had their first son, who became Potter Palmer, III, so that when Mrs. Palmer settled in Florida, she had three grandchildren, and two of them bore her husband's name.

She installed an electric power system at the camp and set up a group of portable bungalows on the property. Colored lights were strung all through the palms and vines. She journeyed with her family and parties of friends to the camp, taking her butler, cook and a retinue of servants to make life comfortable for all concerned. This was her place of retreat and she enjoyed it. People came from far and near to try to catch a glimpse of Mrs. Potter Palmer roughing it in the woods. She chummed with the ranch workers but retired out of view at mealtime. She was not a stranger to this sort of life. She had often joined Honoré and his wife at their ranch in Oregon. Bertha was as adept in the wilds as in a Victorian drawing room.

Her days at Osprey were rich with enterprise and novelty. The men who managed her ranch and citrus groves got closer to Mrs. Palmer and stood less in awe of her than many of her friends in Chicago and Europe. If she had felt lonely at times in the social pastures of Newport and elsewhere she came closer to the average human being in Florida. True, she was still surrounded by a retinue of servants, secretaries and managers, but the men on her property could talk to her at firsthand as she rode around. They could bring their grievances to her and be heard.

She would tour every spot where work was under way—in the early days by horse and buggy, then in a Model-T Ford, finally in Cadillacs. "She was always a good sport and most wonderful company," Blackburn recalled. "As far as comfort or looks were concerned she would just as soon ride in a truck as a Rolls-Royce." The foremen would come up to her car and report on progress. At home or abroad she knew what everyone was doing, what money was being spent, what returns she was getting. If the news was bad she took it without a sign. Her letters expressed what she felt but in conversation she was cool, unruffled and polite, even under stress.

"She never fussed about anything—she was too sweet for that," Captain Frank Roberts, skipper of the *Betsy Roberts*, commented. She would be down at the dock at eight in the morning to meet his boat coming in. He brought in ice, mail, supplies of all kinds—her precious Monets, implements from the International Harvester Company, seeds from distant lands, rosebushes, caviar, Paris gowns. Once she served a "silver tea" on top of his boat. The butler set it up and Mrs. Palmer poured tea for the Captain as they rounded the point. For a time she let Captain Roberts' passengers tour her place during the brief stop his boat made at Osprey, but they did so much damage to her gardens and carried away so many souvenirs that she had to end this custom.

As she made her rounds, directing workmen and studying new growth, she wore simple tweeds, or plain linen skirts with batiste blouses, all beautifully fashioned to fit her still trim figure. She wore walking boots and used a cane. Friends who visited her in the afternoon recall her poised at lookout points with a wide-brimmed hat to shield her pink and white complexion from the sun, and a tall staff resembling a shepherdess crook that gave her a queenly air. She was now the lady of the land, running an agricultural empire. It was creative effort that she felt was good for the community and stimulating for her.

"She was constantly on the go," her Sarasota physician, Dr. Joseph Halton, recalled. "She was a natural born cruiser, mentally and physically. She left the rocking chair for other people to get into. She radiated influence and was a good listener. When you interviewed her you felt you were in a presence and you pondered your words. She was an engaging conversationalist herself and had a good sense of humor."

Dr. Halton was persuaded that Mrs. Palmer found her early years in Florida her best. She had seen much, experienced much. She was ripe on the bough and knew at last what she wanted. Her grandchildren were growing up around her and her family sense was unfailingly strong. She was aging gracefully, and felt that she had never been so useful. She refused to sell a foot of her land until the last few months of her life. When Edwards would propose a deal she would laugh it off. "Why, I wouldn't think of disposing of that beautiful piece of property. It's the apple of my eye."

She rarely told stories herself but she enjoyed a joke, and one of her favorite companions was a surveyor named Arthur Tuttle, who had an endless stock of anecdotes that genuinely amused her. She made helpful suggestions when a truck had to dig her car out of the mire. She did not complain when her alfalfa crop failed, her pheasants died, her tulips refused to grow in the native soil or her wild rice patch was flooded and had to be harvested from boats and fed to the mules. Daily there were disappointments that even money could not remedy.

Blackburn kept harping on the desperate need for drainage and she entertained a government engineer at a picnic on a sand bed under a bridge. She wanted him to build a canal from the Myakka to the bay.

"Madam, you are not properly coached," he told her. "You know, it's hard to get the government to dig a canal in dry land."

When T. Coleman du Pont dined at The Oaks, Mrs. Palmer had Blackburn join them to discuss drainage of the land.

"I make blasting powder," he reminded her. "I could blast it right through the county."

Mrs. Palmer took him up at once on this. "Let's have a canal," she said.

Operations were started and the first three or four shots blew some sand around.

"It seems as if this soil doesn't blast well," the experts finally agreed.

But her major farming troubles began with the ranch. She made the mistake of having silos built, like the cattlemen of the Midwest, not realizing that in Florida the cattle could graze all year on the ranges and pastures. Then she quietly imported a carload of seventeen Brahma bulls and turned them out on the range, cross-breeding them with the native cattle. She put up buildings for the ranch hands and had cement hauled by ox team to make vats for dipping the cattle, an innovation which was regarded at first with great suspicion but resulted finally in the disappearance of ticks. Some of the homesteaders sat around with rifles, sure that the process would kill their cattle.

They believed that the ticks came from within. In the end, when the good results were apparent, they all sought this boon.

Tick fever was wiped out. With her dipping vats, the fine grasses that she planted for feed, and the blooded cattle she bred, Mrs. Palmer was ahead of her time. But the value of these steps was not immediately recognized. The natives disliked her prize cattle and thought that they did not thrive on the Florida scene, but in later years her son Honoré and his wife continued to breed Santa Gertrudes, and ticks no longer plagued the rancher. Mrs. Palmer shipped the first trainload of cattle ever to go out of Florida. It went to Texas and brought in $25,300. She liked to think of herself as a rancher, in spite of all the trouble this title brought her.

"Before she died we had seventeen hundred of the best cows I have ever seen," Blackburn recalled.

The free range was traditional at this time and when Mrs. Palmer decided as a protective measure to fence in some of her property there was local indignation. She had done all that she could to propitiate the homesteaders and squatters. She gave barbecue roasts for the workers. She visited the wives of the original settlers and established friendly relations with them, avoiding the patronizing note and recognizing their native pride. The old families liked her, but woodsmen, squatters and hermits who were disposed to go out with wire clippers by the light of the moon cut down a stretch of her fences and killed many of her cattle one night. It became a habit with them to raid her property and plague her workers when she was away. The minute she turned her back mayhem broke loose. She was particularly outraged by the attacks on her Negroes and the shooting up of her property.

Echoes of these disturbances followed her to Paris, where she went in the spring of 1914. Another raid had taken place and she felt she could no longer tolerate the situation. She sent a warning to V. A. Saunders, who ran the local store at Osprey, that he had better let the men who gathered on his premises at night understand that she would turn the law on them if there was one more demonstration. These attacks had become notorious, not only locally, but in Tampa, Jacksonville and much further afield, she pointed out. No community could prosper with such a "gang of lawless desperadoes . . . allowed to go at large." She had every intention of protecting her property and her workers. She was not giving warning in "an unkind spirit" but she meant business. Mrs. Palmer came right to the point:

Since buying at Osprey I have been greatly annoyed by the annual criminal assaults on my place and on my innocent, unprotected, sleeping Negroes, by cowardly bands of armed men who came at night to shoot them up and drive them away. Every investor wants to know first of all about labor conditions, and to find a community away back in the atrocities of the lawless Ku Klux era finishes its case at once.

Mrs. Palmer wrote in the same vein to Blackburn on April 14, 1914:

What prospective buyer would invest there after learning how I was treated, I who have spent a large amount of money to show what the soil and climate can do and to create values. . . . What a horrid position I am forced into. It is disgusting. I should feel very badly to help put any man in the chain gang but perhaps it is our duty and thus make the country possible for honest, law-abiding citizens who are trying to develop it.

Aside from outside depredations there was mutiny among her own workers. William F. Prentice, her manager at The Oaks, was an Englishman who had taken out American citizenship. He was unpopular and although she had great faith in him she had to take him to task. She was informed on all sides that he was overbearing with the workers and too prone to criticize the Crackers. She did not like this, and she thought that he should do more for new workers coming in. "I want the Negro quarters fixed comfortably," she wrote. He was not to allow the men to shirk or neglect their work but he must treat them justly and kindly if they gave good service. If they did not, "I want them to go." She finished by telling him that she thought him a very good man, but that the discontent worked to her disadvantage, and he must pay attention to the points she raised.

Even while she was reprimanding Prentice she wrote vigorously to Blackburn in his defense, saying that he was a fixture and invaluable, while the men under him "passed to and fro like the tides of the sea." He and his wife were "trustworthy, capable, responsible people and I greatly esteem them, and will never let them leave me." Actually, Prentice's life had been threatened on four occasions and she let the word get around that "if a hair of his head were injured those at fault would pay dearly for it."

In the end she discharged everyone who had been disloyal to Prentice and he continued to report to her on every move being made at her place. At home or abroad Mrs. Palmer must be kept closely informed. She could follow almost from hour to hour what her workers were doing. She gave advice and directions by long distance. Did Hawkins go down deep in his search for the bulbs planted around the lake? How much did it cost to run the big engine for five hours? How long did it take a "faithful workman" to go over all the lawns with the mower? What experience had the new gardener had? Had he good references from his last place? "A good gardener is not like a day laborer, he leaves his record, good or bad, behind him," Mrs. Palmer commented. How were the roses doing, and the crepe myrtle hedge, and which vines fared best on the tall green poles?

Were the fire hoses all in order and were they kept near each house? "I do not want any smoking near the houses, or anything that might cause a fire." The rose garden and the Duchesne Garden must be weeded by hand and should be done by the head gardener. "One of the little hand cultivators might possibly be small enough to run between the rose plants, or else the gardener will have to use one of the 3-pronged weeders to get them out," she wrote.

It would not be necessary to commence with the flower seed before August and she would send him a list of what she wanted planted before then, she wrote to Prentice. No watering was to be done during the heat of the day. This had killed many plants during the rainy season. A most conscientious man was to have this duty—"otherwise it will do no good and he will only waste his time and the water." The best times were from five to eight in the morning and from four in the afternoon.

Mrs. Palmer told Prentice precisely how he should train the vines on the poles and enclosed a sketch done by herself to show what she wanted. She had studied many beautiful gardens in Europe and had not viewed them with her eyes shut. The privet hedges were to be trimmed. Expenses were to be cut to the bone. No one was to be hired without her permission until her return. But the gardeners were not to be restricted in any way.

On July 10, 1914, with the First World War a month away, Mrs. Palmer wrote to F. H. Guenther of Sarasota from the Rue Fabert, making it clear that she was tired of spending money on The Oaks when labor conditions were such that all the work done in winter, and the plants she put out, were lost in summer through her workers being driven off, plus the ignorance and laziness of gardeners. Things were to be kept down to the simplest planting, with only a few men caring for the place. She would no longer attempt to do what she had planned, since Osprey had become a "burden of work and care while I was there and a continual nuisance when absent." She had been forced to spend all her spare hours since reaching Paris writing back "to keep the peace and making plans and giving elaborate directions to have them carried out."

But Prentice continued to report cheerfully from The Oaks.

The rain was good after a drought. They had laid tile drains through the beach to the sea wall and had cut a road through the shrubbery without sacrificing any trees. They had cleaned out the cabbage trees and cut down the dead orange trees in two of her groves. The large sycamore tree was a "perfect picture." The terrace was being sodded. The roses were being cut back. The hogs were healthy. The pampas grass was in full bloom. When the teams finished plowing, harrowing and hauling, the shell work for the roads would begin. By ill-luck 125 feet of the South Road sea wall had collapsed in a heavy storm. The begonias, forget-me-nots, violets, mixed geraniums, bougainvillaea, poinsettias and spineless cactus were thriving. Men were working on the rose garden, The Oaks garden and the Bermuda lawn. The mule at the farm had died of old age. Prentice had been asked if Labor Day would be a holiday. He said no. The only holidays were Thanksgiving, Christmas and the New Year. "In conclusion, Madam," he finished, "I am pleased to report all going well."

In another letter he informed her that four men were working on the fence at the East Stable, teams and crew were busy on shell for the roads, one Negro was hoeing a grove, another was clipping a mule. Field day was coming up and the pavilion was installed on Mirror Lake terrace. The turkeys looked fine and all the chickens had been sold. What were her orders for installing the new laundry tubs? Would black-striped wallpaper be in order for her bedroom? Henderson's Sunny South seed had arrived and a fox had been killed on the place that morning.

Thus Mrs. Palmer in Chicago, in New York, London or Paris, kept track of every detail at The Oaks—the executive in full command. She watched the housekeeping bills closely as well as the larger expenditures around the place. No one would do anything or pay a bill without consulting her first when she was within reach. As time went on she acquired the feeling that everyone was out to make a little profit on Mrs. Potter

Palmer. Although too serious-minded to be subject to whims she thought nothing of having a lawn torn up and reseeded, or of changing her mind about what she wanted and pushing through an alternative plan, but she had a practical as well as an artistic sense where gardening was concerned. She was an inveterate walker and her gardeners never knew when she would sail into view and make knowing comments on their work.

Chicago saw less of her after she had settled in Sarasota for the long winter seasons, but her interests were still deeply imbedded there and old friends visited her in the South. In the year she first went to Florida she offered a gold medal with a thousand-dollar prize for the best picture by a promising young artist, for although she no longer bought paintings her interest in art never flagged. At the same time she gave the Art Institute of Chicago a large number of her Impressionist paintings for an exhibition that lasted for several months and was regarded as perhaps the best showing of its kind in the country up to 1910. In that same year she held an "art review" at the Palmer mansion, raising fourteen hundred dollars for the Chicago Woman's Club.

She was interested to note that in London the Impressionists were already virtually out of date. When the post-Impressionists were shown at the Grafton Gallery in 1910 the London *Times* commented: "Our dear old friends the 'Impressionists' are already démodés, and a younger and more audacious and more modern generation has raised the *dernier cri*." But Mrs. Palmer let them alone, and Chicago was not altogether prepared for the Armory Show that startled New York in 1913. The staff and students of the Art Institute staged a protest meeting as the work of the Cubists and Futurists headed west. They burned Matisse and Walter Pach in effigy. W. M. R. French, the director, left for California rather than cope with the *Nude Descending a Stairway* that was being discussed across the country. Meanwhile, traditional art was fetching staggering prices on both sides of the Atlantic, with Henry E. Huntington paying $505,440 for Gainsborough's *Blue Boy*.

There was much creative activity around the Art Institute and Chicago was astir with a fresh generation of gifted artists and writers. Many of them gathered at the Cliff Dwellers' Club to discuss current trends in the arts. Hamlin Garland had established this club in a penthouse on top of Orchestra Hall. Theodore Dreiser, Susan Glaspell, Robert Herrick, Edith Wyatt and Edna Ferber were turning out books that were causing talk. Harriet Monroe established the magazine *Poetry* in 1912 and began publishing the work of Edgar Lee Masters, Vachel Lindsay and the early poems of Carl Sandburg. Willa Cather's *O Pioneers* was a sensation in 1913 and her book *The Song of the Lark* got its title from Jules Breton's painting in the Institute, widely reproduced in calendars throughout the country.

Michigan Avenue, which Mrs. Palmer could remember as a garden spot, was now a parapet of buildings. The city was gracefully laid out with parks and sweeping boulevards. There were 300,000 pupils in the schools and two and a half million books were borrowed annually from the public libraries. The Chicago Opera Company was flourishing and the romance of its tenor Lucien Muratore and Lina Cavalieri, the Italian soprano who was popularly heralded as the most beautiful woman in the world at the time, was exciting public interest in 1913.

The Chocolate Soldier was the current rage. Irving Berlin was popularizing a new kind of jazz with "Alexander's Ragtime Band." The tango and one-step were taking the place of the waltz and two-step. The turkey trot was intriguing the young and shocking the old. The hobble skirt was tripping up the emaciated and slinky woman who had succeeded the buxom Gibson girl. The sculptured look was now the vogue. Hats had shrunk because of the motorcar but black aigrettes and white ospreys had a following of their own and bandeaux bound the hair. Turbans and tunics, harem skirts and bead embroidery had taken firm hold, and Paul Poiret pushed the Oriental influence. At this point Mrs. Palmer retained a touch of the Queen Mary look. She never quite abandoned the regal air, the stiff coiffure, or the natural dignity that became her.

Labor forces were steadily gaining ground in the community and in January, 1912, she offered the use of her home on Lake Shore Drive to August Belmont when she learned that the National Civic Federation was about to hold a meeting in Chicago. Belmont accepted her offer on condition that she act as hostess and temporary chairman in the current debate between capital and labor. The union men accepted, with the provision that they would not be expected to wear dress suits. They had read of the doings at the Potter Palmer mansion. But they also knew that Mrs. Palmer, for all her airs, had done a lot for the working woman. However, they walked into her home in a truculent way, determined not to be patronized. They looked around with some skepticism and there was the queen, warm, friendly and even casual in her manner. They could find no trace of condescension in her and left quite warmed by her common sense and natural hospitality. This was the year in which her old admirer, W. T. Stead, went down with the *Titanic*, as well as a number of her millionaire friends.

She was at her house in Paris when the war broke out in the late summer of 1914. She was caught by surprise, like everyone else, but went to work immediately, personally packing boxes, crates and chests with papers, printed matter she had picked up on her travels, and her particular personal treasures. She had furs, etchings and household effects valued at $224,104 put in storage in London and Paris before she left. This included 533 pieces of porcelain and jade, as well as tapestries and carpets, a Veronese (which later turned out to be a fake), 30 Whistler and 144 Pennell etchings, her favorite canopied satinwood bed with Wedgwood insets, silver, china, and in numerable objects of art. Her pearl and diamond dog collar, her most valuable tiara, and several of her more spectacular pieces of jewelry were in storage at Tiffany's Paris branch when the guns first roared. Leon Wannieck, the Polish dealer who had arranged many of her Oriental purchases, fled to the Spanish border with some of the jade and porcelain treasures that Mrs. Palmer had in the French capital. He brought them back at the close of the war.

It was a period of confusion and excitement but material possessions had ceased to matter as the war became a grim reality. Mrs. Palmer was devoted to France and its people. Sadly she left her house on the Rue Fabert when Paris was evacuated and headed in her Rolls-Royce for Cherbourg. She later turned over the property to the American Red Cross as a home for chaplains.

She left her car to rot on the dock and was back in the United States by the end of August. On her return to Chicago she went to work for the Red Cross, after a brief trip to Florida to see that things were moving ahead at The Oaks. Committees were waiting for her to steer them into action. "It's been a number of years now since I have been home in Chicago at Christmastime," she said, as she settled down to the work she did best—organization in an emergency. Her house again became a center for civic activity.

The war still seemed remote from the United States, but it was vivid to Mrs. Palmer, with her close European links and her fresh memories of what she had seen before she left. The Cantacuzène children had been brought home already from Russia for safety and now they were in the family circle, with Ida looking after them. The Prince soon was wounded in the fighting and in course of time both he and Julia returned to America and took up residence with the children at The Acacias. Now all of Mrs. Palmer's grandchildren played happily together at The Oaks and at camp, while she came and went and continued to develop her property.

On December 16, 1915, she sent King Albert of Belgium 11,700 francs for his stricken country, with an evocative note:

MAJESTÉ:
Will His Majesty be amiable enough to receive a small contribution for His Christmas charities which I send in memory of His Majesty's noble and gracious mother who was always so gracious and kind to me.
I venture to hope that His Majesty has not entirely forgotten the name of one whom he so greatly honored by His visit at Newport during His American tour. I deeply sympathize with the gallant Belgian nation upon whom unnumbered and undeserved sorrows and horrors have fallen and together with all of the civilized world join in admiration of her devoted and patriotic stand led by Her Heroic King whom luckily I had the opportunity of appreciating before he was called to His high mission.

In February, 1916, at a time when wartime benefits had become the social gambit, Mrs. Palmer went over to Palm Beach and appeared at a ball there in all her pre-Florida glory, winning the title of Queen of Jewels. She had plenty of competition that night. The jewels displayed at this ball became legendary. Mrs. O. H. P. Belmont had a chain of perfectly matched diamonds, seven and a half feet long, which had belonged to Catherine the Great, as well as her string of Marie Antoinette's pearls. Mrs. Hamilton Rice wore pearls that were reputed to be worth half a million dollars and Mrs. Edward Wentworth's diamond necklace was world-famous. Mrs. Palmer's jewels did not compare in value with these but their aggregate effect and the manner in which she wore them always caused a stir in any gathering. She had great delicacy of line, along with her proud carriage, and Mrs. Carter H. Harrison, who never failed to toss bouquets at Mrs. Palmer, found the general effect that of a "queenly personality."
Mrs. Palmer's family life and attitudes were clearly defined at Sarasota between 1914 and 1918. She had always known

how to create diversion within her own family circle and now she turned her attention to her small grandchildren as once she had done to their fathers, Honoré and Potter. She was natural and affectionate with children and she made many plans for them. D'Orsay was the liveliest of the younger generation, a boy who lived adventuresomely later on and used to surprise his grandmother's guests by leaping out at them from behind bushes. She would summon his governess and O'Orsay, always amiable however much in disgrace, would be removed from the scene.

She approved of the pioneering touch for small boys and encouraged them to enjoy the life at her camp. She had bought ponies for them to ride and brought a rancher from the Far West to teach them in the best manner. As in the case of her own two sons, she wanted them trained to do everything well. Although Honoré and Potter had grown tired at times of being dressed up and carted over Europe like little princelings, their mother had always combined with the luxurious touch her own zeal for their physical well-being and hardihood. Now she gave her grandchildren a succession of pets, chose books for them and had them report to her on their reading. She encouraged them to use their toolboxes and to take a zestful interest in their riding, boating and the outdoor life in general. The children did not stand in awe of her. They made Valentines for grandmother, and wrote her penciled notes, all of which she saved, along with the script of a play *Hiawatha* that they staged by themselves.

Little Honoré wrote to her from Sarasota on January 30, 1917:

Dear Grandmother, The rabbits have not come yet. You said you wished me to remind you of this when I reached home. I thank you very much for the twenty-five dollars you sent me at Christmas time. I have not spent it but you know how fond I am of books and I shall enjoy it very much later on. I send you 50 kisses and hope your cold is better now. Love from Honoré.

On December 16, 1915, she sent King Albert of Belgium 11,700 francs for his stricken country, with an evocative note:

MAJESTÉ:
Will His Majesty be amiable enough to receive a small contribution for His Christmas charities which I send in memory of His Majesty's noble and gracious mother who was always so gracious and kind to me.

I venture to hope that His Majesty has not entirely forgotten the name of one whom he so greatly honored by His visit at Newport during His American tour. I deeply sympathize with the gallant Belgian nation upon whom unnumbered and undeserved sorrows and horrors have fallen and together with all of the civilized world join in admiration of her devoted and patriotic stand led by Her Heroic King whom luckily I had the opportunity of appreciating before he was called to His high mission.

In February, 1916, at a time when wartime benefits had become the social gambit, Mrs. Palmer went over to Palm Beach and appeared at a ball there in all her pre-Florida glory, winning the title of Queen of Jewels. She had plenty of competition that night. The jewels displayed at this ball became legendary. Mrs. O. H. P. Belmont had a chain of perfectly matched diamonds, seven and a half feet long, which had belonged to Catherine the Great, as well as her string of Marie Antoinette's pearls. Mrs. Hamilton Rice wore pearls that were reputed to be worth half a million dollars and Mrs. Edward Wentworth's diamond necklace was world-famous. Mrs. Palmer's jewels did not compare in value with these but their aggregate effect and the manner in which she wore them always caused a stir in any gathering. She had great delicacy of line, along with her proud carriage, and Mrs. Carter H. Harrison, who never failed to toss bouquets at Mrs. Palmer, found the general effect that of a "queenly personality."

Mrs. Palmer's family life and attitudes were clearly defined at Sarasota between 1914 and 1918. She had always known how to create diversion within her own family circle and now she turned her attention to her small grandchildren as once she had done to their fathers, Honoré and Potter. She was natural and affectionate with children and she made many plans for them. D'Orsay was the liveliest of the younger generation, a boy who lived adventuresomely later on and used to surprise his grandmother's guests by leaping out at them from behind bushes. She would summon his governess and O'Orsay, always amiable however much in disgrace, would be removed from the scene.

She approved of the pioneering touch for small boys and encouraged them to enjoy the life at her camp. She had bought ponies for them to ride and brought a rancher from the Far West to teach them in the best manner. As in the case of her own two sons, she wanted them trained to do everything well. Although Honoré and Potter had grown tired at times of being dressed up and carted over Europe like little princelings, their mother had always combined with the luxurious touch her own zeal for their physical well-being and hardihood. Now she gave her grandchildren a succession of pets, chose books for them and had them report to her on their reading. She encouraged them to use their toolboxes and to take a zestful interest in their riding, boating and the outdoor life in general. The children did not stand in awe of her. They made Valentines for grandmother, and wrote her penciled notes, all of which she saved, along with the script of a play *Hiawatha* that they staged by themselves.

Little Honoré wrote to her from Sarasota on January 30, 1917:

Dear Grandmother, The rabbits have not come yet. You said you wished me to remind you of this when I reached home. I thank you very much for the twenty-five dollars you sent me at Christmas time. I have not spent it but you know how fond I am of books and I shall enjoy it very much later on. I send you 50 kisses and hope your cold is better now. Love from Honoré.

Three weeks later, on February 21, Honoré wrote that the goats had come. They were pretty and he liked them better than his rabbits. He was looking forward to going to Myakka, where he would have a horse on which to ride after the cows. On his last visit he had forgotten in his hurry to say how much he had enjoyed himself. He begged her pardon and looked forward to seeing her on Friday.

There were plenty of diversions at The Oaks and at the ranch for children and grownups alike. Mrs. Palmer at times went bird hunting. She was a good shot but gave this up when her health failed. Her family often did trap shooting in the morning and she would give valuable prizes, such as gold watches and chains, to the winners. She liked to talk to Charles W. Webb about the pelicans, cranes, kingfish, herons and even the flamingos that had haunted her property in earlier days. Her woods were alive with deer, quail, pheasant, wild turkeys, doves and hares.

Both Webb and Blackburn knew her well and saw her under trying conditions at times. Both men thought she had stamina, charm and courage. She always seemed to Blackburn to be happy in a boat but he never saw her catch a fish. She often talked to him about streams in which she had fished in different parts of the world and she was interested in listening to tales of the many species in local waters—the tarpon and stone crabs, the groupers, oysters and shellfish of all kinds. She would drive out of her way to watch the turtles nosing around, and she ordered all the alligators in sight killed. She had a goldfish pool at The Oaks and could not understand why recurrent crops of her fish disappeared, until the water was drained and it was found that they were being eaten by cottonmouth moccasins. She entered her speed boat *Flying Fish* in the local races.

Thanks to her influence Sarasota pushed ahead as a popular resort. The arrival of the Ringling brothers a year after her descent brought another type of dynamics into the area. Mrs.

Palmer shared in many community endeavors and initiated some. She felt that a woman's organization was needed and she worked with Mrs. F. H. Guenther of Chicago for the establishment of the Woman's Club in 1913. She gave them quarters and loaned them two thousand dollars to get started. The club promoted park improvements, tree planting and sundry plans to beautify the town. It supported the library, backed good causes and stimulated local enterprise.

But Mrs. Palmer's civic consciousness did not obscure her realistic sense of values. Her last great scheme involved the development of Venice as an attractive resort and sporting center, with facilities for shooting, fishing, sea bathing, boating, golf, tennis, riding and motoring. She planned a hotel on the Gulf front with an adjoining colonnade quadrangle where tea and coffee would be served. Shops would abut the colonnade and a walk would lead to the orange grove, where fruit, straight off the trees, would be served in a pavilion.

This was how Mrs. Palmer envisioned the resort, but when Charles Wellford Leavitt, a New York city planner and landscaping engineer, submitted his estimates to the Sarasota-Venice Company she was staggered by the costs. She pointed out to him that they would demand a greater outlay of capital, without any return, than even Mr. Flagler dispensed at Palm Beach. By this time she was somewhat disillusioned with community enterprise.

Leavitt had roughly blocked out a railroad station, civic square, town hall, market, church, school, stores, golf club, yacht club, docks, commercial hotel, residential colony, farm colony, a sporting hotel, orange parkway paths, with golf course, canals, roads, streets and parks. He suggested H. O. Milliken, an architect who had lived in Italy, to supervise the building operation.

His plans would work out charmingly, Mrs. Palmer wrote to him on February 26, 1916, if one had no regard for expense, but "we wanted to burden ourselves with as little work and expense as possible to get the best results." And why devote two and a half miles in the heart of her most valuable property to four civic centers? She went on:

> Why any civic center? We do not wish even one in our lovely countryside. Of what value are these civic centers and what helpful functions are they supposed to perform? . . . As the only object of the Company is to sell its lands and close up its business, we do not wish to undertake social service or civic schemes in this territory where they are not needed and which would entail on us not only the primary expenses of creating and equipping them . . . but also the trouble and expense of administering and maintaining them. . . . I myself would not consider for a moment your proposal to assess my personal holdings north of the Bay, for the benefit of the winter resort improvements to the south, when no improvements whatever accrue to my land. This you demand, but it is quite out of the question. I would not allow it.

But the *determining* factor, Mrs. Palmer added, was that they could sell their land in its primitive state at a much larger profit than he proposed when developed. In fact, some of her property on the waterfront, without improvements, had already fetched $875 an acre, giving her a profit of $800. Nothing came of the resort plan. This was the year in which her beloved father died at the age of ninety-three, with all his surviving children around him. He had never seemed old to her, or to anyone else, and it was he who had proposed the Venice development. Shortly before his death there had been a great Christmas gathering of the Honorés in Chicago to honor him. Twenty-two of his descendants assembled round the patriarch, who was still vigorous enough to go to his office and attend to his business interests.

Funeral services were held at his home on Lincoln Parkway in Chicago. His five children walked out of the house behind the coffin, followed by his secretaries and a little group of servants. After his death Bertha never ceased to miss the small, old-fashioned gentleman with the white beard and bright eyes behind spectacles whose advice had always been of the utmost consequence to her. He had only to suggest something and she would carry it through. Lockwood died soon afterward. Henry Hamilton Honoré, Jr., had died in 1911, five years after their mother. The Honoré family was breaking up.

And now it was Bertha's turn. Her radiant health began to fail shortly before her father's death. For the next two years she fought a losing battle with cancer. None but her immediate family knew until near the end what ailed her. Although beset by pain and discomfort she never showed a sign and continued to work and direct operations until within a few weeks of her death. But a mastectomy in New York had brought home to her the knowledge that she did not have long to live. When she no longer toured her property and her workmen saw no more of her the story was whispered about in Sarasota that Mrs. Palmer was dying of cancer. But she kept her grip on things to the end. Four months before her death she was ordering New Orleans roses from Pasadena and Japanese hop vine seed from Floral Park, New York. Six weeks before the end she wrote to Guenther saying that whenever a cow was butchered at the pasture for the commissary, she wanted to know about it and how much it brought.

One of her last callers from the outside was Blackburn, who had seen her constantly in these final years. He had never heard her raise her voice or make a fuss about anything, and she looked as serene as ever, still beautiful but quite visibly wasted, behind the canopies of her Louis XVI bed. Her great dark eyes shone against the pallor of her face.

"I will never go back to the ranch," she said. "I have gone there for the last time."

Then she told Blackburn that she was leaving the ranch to her brother Adrian, and that she was hastening to get the boys paid off. Mrs. Palmer was calmly facing the thought of death.

She died on May 5, 1918, within a day of the sixteenth anniversary of her husband's death. She was sixty-nine years old. Her sons and their wives, her sister Ida, her brother Adrian and the Cantacuzènes were with her.

Sarasota went into mourning and Mayor G. W. Franklin

lowered the city flag to half-mast. Her coffin was taken by horse and wagon to the railroad and her funeral was held from her home in Chicago. Hours before the cortege set out, Lake Shore Drive was jammed with people to whom she was more of a symbol than a person. All they could see was a simple funeral wreath on the front door that had opened so hospitably for so many years. Now she lay in the gallery where she had played so dazzling a role. A blanket of orchids from her sons covered her coffin. After it was in place Ernest Woods, her English butler who had been with her in London and Paris, came in with a wreath of orchids and placed it reverently at the foot of the coffin on behalf of the servants—their last tribute to Mrs. Palmer, who had done them many kindnesses and had always shown interest in their personal affairs. All around were the Bertha Honoré Palmer roses named after her.

The service was read by the Rev. James S. Stone, rector of St. James's Episcopal Church, of which she had been a communicant. He was assisted by three acolytes, and the Imperial Quartet sang "Lead Kindly Light," "One Sweetly Solemn Thought" and "Sleep, Beloved, Sleep," Bertha's favorite hymns. The pallbearers were old friends—Charles L. Hutchinson, Martin A. Ryerson, Herman H. Kohlsaat, John S. Runnells, James B. Waller, F. B. Tuttle, Watson F. Blair and Edward Blair. She was buried in a mausoleum at Graceland Cemetery beside Potter Palmer, and close to her parents and brothers. With her death an epoch in Chicago's history was closed.

Mrs. Palmer had drawn up seven wills in her lifetime and her last showed that her husband's estate had more than doubled in value under her stewardship. She left close to twenty million dollars, although fluctuating real estate values made it difficult to estimate the exact sum. The bulk of her estate was handed down in trust to her two sons, with complicated provisions for her grandchildrens' inheritance. This included the Palmer House, then valued at five million dollars and 150 pieces of property left by her husband. The mansion on Lake Shore

Drive, with all its contents, also went to Honoré and Potter, who made an amicable division according to their tastes. At the time of her death she had five grandchildren and a sixth was born within the year. Honoré's family consisted of Potter D'Orsay and Honoré, II. Potter had four children in all—Potter Palmer, III, Bertha (later Mrs. Oakleigh L. Thorne), Gordon Palmer and Pauline (later Mrs. Arthur M. Wood).

She left $100,000 each to her daughters-in-law, Grace Brown Palmer and Pauline Kohlsaat Palmer; real estate and personal possessions, including her canary diamond ring, to her niece Julia; and to Ida all the property she had acquired from the estate of their father and her interest in the Scammon trust, which he had created. Her personal estate was valued at $1,750,000. Her jewels were divided equally between her sons, to be given to their wives, except for some individual bequests. It was noted that a princess and a kitchen maid both figured in her will. Her Myakka Lake property went to her brother Adrian and other land in Florida was placed in trust with him for the benefit of her brother Nathaniel and her sister Ida. Adrian had always given her counsel in banking affairs, just as her brother Lockwood, a Circuit Court judge, had advised her in legal matters. The Honorés were a close-knit family and the outside world knew little of their corporate operations.

A total of $515,000 was bequeathed to various charitable organizations. Mrs. Palmer specifically asked her sons to select a group of her paintings equal in value to $100,000 to give to the Art Institute of Chicago. Her legacies to her servants aggregated $30,000 and she made additional provision for former employees serving their countries in the First World War.

Mrs. Palmer's Myakka Lake land today is part of a state park. In 1934 a large acreage was bought from Adrian C. Honoré's estate for this purpose. Immediately afterward Honoré and Potter donated 9,200 acres in memory of their mother. They also gave the Sarasota Memorial Hospital an X-ray machine, and a Mrs. Potter Palmer memorial room perpetuates her name at the hospital.

Shortly before her death *Hampton's Magazine* summed up Mrs. Palmer's place in the sun in an editorial entitled "The Social Leader of Chicago." The writer pointed out that in the course of a busy life she had found time to maintain her supremacy in Chicago, to establish a firm social position in London and in Paris, to encourage and take an active part in many charitable and philanthropic movements, and to manage her big estate with all the acumen of a well-trained businessman. *Hampton's* attributed the secret of her success to a rare gift for diplomacy and went on:

> When men have it they are called diplomats; when women have it they are called tactful. Occasionally there is a woman who possesses it in such superlative degree and quality that she is admitted to the ranks of the diplomats. All who know her admit ungrudgingly that Bertha Honoré Palmer (Mrs. Potter Palmer) is a diplomat. . . . If Mrs. Palmer were a man she would make an ideal ambassador. The same qualities that have made her so successful as a mother, as a wife, as a social queen and as a business woman, would make her a successful ambassador. She is democratic, cordial, frank, yet never says a thing she does not want to say and seldom a thing she should not say. Her mental vision extends beyond the present moment, and her keen insight into human nature enables her to tell far in advance what effect a certain speech or a certain act will have. Her poise is perfect.

Few knew more of the private lives and hidden scandals of Chicago's leading families than Mrs. Palmer. She had observed them closely for nearly half a century and had watched their climb to wealth and fame. But she kept her own counsel and never spread ill tidings. Those who knew her best recalled that hers had been an exceptional life from start to finish. Fortune had always been on her side. She had grown up in a harmonious home and had enjoyed the fruits of love and appreciation. A marriage that had looked at first like a mercenary alliance had turned into a solid, lifelong partnership. Her husband had worshiped her and had never tired of paying tribute to her. None could altogether fathom her feeling for him. Tales that she felt she had outgrown him and treated him badly on her upward climb plagued her from time to time. But she suffered the penalties of living in a glass cage and could scarcely escape the criticism that whirled around so dominant a social figure. She was flattered, admired, respected, and at times attacked or jeered at on both sides of the Atlantic but in the end she usually had her way. Her parents, sister, brothers, husband and sons loved and admired her, so that to all outward appearances her life seemed happy and fulfilled.

However, her buffered background was not the total answer. She was described as "the most elegant American woman of her day" but Bertha Honoré might have been a driving force in any generation or social stratum. She had strength and purpose, ambition and intelligence. Her decisions and choices were apt to be soundly made and she grew in political wisdom. She struck out for the best wherever she saw it and moved unswervingly to her goal. Her sister Ida, who knew her from early childhood, considered her ardent in spirit, a woman who never exhausted her forces on small things but let the fires of her life burn deep.

It was her good fortune that she seemed immune to crippling circumstance until her fatal illness set in. Thus she was able to enjoy life to the full. She was no Hetty Green with her millions but spent freely where she felt her money would do the most good. After her husband's death she looked more closely to returns. If she seemed a hedonist to many she balanced her personal expenditure with zeal for the public welfare. Her fixed ambition to push Chicago ahead controlled her actions for the better part of her lifetime. Those who thought her a schemer intent only on her own aggrandizement misunderstood her true nature, although unquestionably she enjoyed her distinction to the full. In the end this citizen of the world was known quite simply as Mrs. Potter Palmer of Chicago—a label that summed up a legend and a way of life.

>>>>>>>>>>>>>> *Notes*

Chapter 1 *A City in Flames*

Reminiscences attributed to Mrs. Potter Palmer, Chicago Historical Society. Alexander Frear, "The Full Story of the Great Fire: Narrative of an Eye Witness," New York *World*, October, 1871. Contemporary clippings in Palmer papers, Chicago Historical Society. Princess Cantacuzène to author. Chicago *Times-Herald*, December 3, 1899. Chicago *Herald-American*, March 24, 1940. Robert Allen Cromie, *The Great Chicago Fire*. Henry Justin Smith, *Chicago's Great Century*. Emmett Dedmon, *Fabulous Chicago*. Ernest Poole, *Giants Gone*. Bessie Louise Pierce, *A History of Chicago*, Vol. II. Louise de Koven Bowen, *Growing Up With a City*. William Carnes Kendrick, *Reminiscences of Old Louisville*, ms., New York Public Library. Kathleen Jennings, *Louisville's First Families*. Honoré Palmer to author. *Palmer, Honoré, Grant Allied Families*, The American Historical Company, 1929. Reminiscences of Mrs. Frederick Dent Grant, Palmer family papers. W. P. Greene, ed., *The Green River Country from Bowling Green to Evansville*, 1898. Frederika Bremer, *America of the Fifties*. Wincester Hall to Mrs. Potter Palmer, February 25, 1898, Palmer family papers.

Chapter 2 *Merchant Prince*

Records of Visitation Convent, Georgetown, 1865–1867. Bessie Louise Pierce, *A History of Chicago*, Vol. II. Milo Milton Quaife, *Chicago and the Old Northwest, 1673–1835*. Louise de Koven Bowen, *Growing Up With a City*. *Christian Science Monitor*, August 24, 1916. Mary Hastings Bradley, *Old Chicago*. Ernest Poole, *Giants Gone*. Emmett Dedmon, *Fabulous Chicago*. Augusta Prescott, 1893, Palmer family papers. Princess Cantacuzene to author. Chicago *Tribune*, July

29, 1870, and May 5, 1902. New York *Daily Graphic*, October 24, 1874. Chicago *Times-Herald*, December 3, 1899. Chicago *Herald-American*, March 17 and 24, 1940. Hubert Howe Bancroft, *The Book of the Fair*. Ruth McKenna, *Chicago: These First Hundred Years*.

Chapter 3 *The Innkeeper's Wife*

Potter Palmer to Charles B. Farwell, December 2, 1889, Chicago Historical Society. Potter Palmer to Charles Leland, August 26, 1876, Chicago Historical Society. Lady Duffus Hardy, *Through Cities and Prairie Lands*. Sir John Lang, *America in 1876*. Rudyard Kipling, *From Sea to Sea: Letters of Travel*. James Fullarton Muirhead, *The Land of Contrasts: A Briton's View of His American Kin*. Joseph Kirkland, *The Story of Chicago*. *Chicago Magazine of Fashion, Music & Home Reading*, August, 1875. Undated note signed by Tallmadge Ballard, Chicago Historical Society. Bessie Louise Pierce, *A History of Chicago*, Vol. III. Princess Cantacuzène to author. Chicago *Times-Herald*, December 3, 1899. Chicago *Tribune*, May 5, 1902, and October 21, 1945. *New York Times*, March 11, 1950. Chaperone in *Herald American* (Chicago Weekly), March and April, 1940. David Lester, "His Monument to Love," *Coronet*, February, 1957. Frank L. Davis, "An American Describes the Palmer Castle," Illinois Society of Architects Bulletin, January–February, 1947. George William Sheldon, *Artistic Country-Seats*. Aline B. Saarinen, *The Proud Possessors*. Mrs. John A. Logan, *Reminiscences of a Soldier's Wife*. Julian Ralph, *Harper's Chicago and the World's Fair*. Henry Justin Smith, *Chicago's Great Century*. Ernest Poole, *Giants Gone*. John Drury, *Old Chicago Houses*. Wayne Andrews, *Architecture, Ambition and Americans*.

Chapter 4 *Mrs. Palmer Invades Europe*

Mrs. Potter Palmer, *Addresses and Reports of Mrs. Potter Palmer*. London *Times*, July 13, 1891. New York *World*, July 14 and 26, 1891. New York *Sunday World*, July 26, 1891. Chicago *Evening News*, October 7, 1891. Reminiscences of Mrs. Frederick Dent Grant, Palmer family papers. Potter Palmer to Charles L. Hutchinson, May 16, 1891, the Newberry Library. Mrs. Palmer's addresses to board of lady managers of Columbian Exposition, April 8, 1891, September 2, 1891, and October 18, 1892. Grace M. Dodge to Mrs. Palmer, February 19, 1892, Chicago Historical Society. Thomas M. Waller to Mrs. Palmer, November 17, 1891, Chicago Historical Society. Mrs. Isabella Beecher Hooker to Mrs. Palmer, May 8 and June 17, 1891, Chicago Historical

Society. Mrs. Palmer to Mrs. Hooker, July 31, 1891, Chicago Historical Society. Mrs. John A. Logan to Mrs. Palmer, October 16, 1891, Chicago Historical Society. Julia Ward Howe to Mrs. Palmer, July 10, 1891, Chicago Historical Society. Mary Lockwood to Mrs. Palmer, September 25, 1891, Chicago Historical Society. Theodore Stanton to Mrs. Palmer, December 14, 1891, Chicago Historical Society. George Healy to Mrs. Palmer, December 17, 1892, Chicago Historical Society. Susan B. Anthony to Mrs. Palmer, April 11, 1893, Chicago Historical Society. Mrs. Margaret F. Sullivan to Mrs. Palmer, December 11, 1891, Chicago Historical Society. Sara T. Hallowell to Mrs. Palmer, August 22 and November 10, 1891, Chicago Historical Society. Mrs. Palmer to Miss Josephine P. Cleveland, July 12, 1892, Chicago Historical Society. Hubert Howe Bancroft, *The Book of the Fair*. Mrs. Palmer to Miss Josephine P. Cleveland, August 22 and November 10, 1891, Chicago Historical Society. Julia Ward Howe to Mrs. Palmer, July 10, 1891, Chicago Historical Society. Lloyd Lewis and Henry Justin Smith, *Chicago, The History of Its Reputation*. Bessie Louise Pierce, *A History of Chicago*, Vol. III. Princess Cantacuzène to author. Mrs. Palmer's address in Manufacturers Building, World's Fair, October 21, 1892.

Chapter 5 *World's Columbian Exposition*

Columbian Exposition: Dedication Ceremonies Memorial. Mrs. Potter Palmer's address at opening, May 1, 1893, and at closing, October 31, 1893. Program, *Hospitality and Ceremonies, Woman's Building*, Chicago Historical Society. *A History of the World's Columbian Exposition*, 4 vols. Mary Kavanaugh Oldham Eagle, ed., *The Congress of Women Held in the Woman's Building, World's Columbian Exposition*. Ripley Hitchcock, *The Art of the World Illustrated in the Paintings, Statuary, and Architecture of the World's Columbian Exposition*. *The Columbian Exposition Album*. Maud Howe Elliott, ed., *Arts and Handicrafts in the Woman's Building of the World's Columbian Exposition*. Chaperone, Chicago *Herald-American* (Chicago Weekly), March 3 and April 7, 1940. New York *American*, June 24, 1893. San Francisco *Chronicle*, June 11, 1893. Indianapolis *News*, June 14, 1893. Rochester *Democrat Chronicle*, June 15, 1893. Pittsburgh *Commercial Gazette*, June 15, 1893. Carmen de Diaz to Mrs. Palmer, September 12, 1893, Chicago Historical Society. Mrs. John A. Logan to Mrs. Palmer, July 3 and August 2, 1893, Chicago Historical Society. Henry H. Smith to Mrs. Palmer, September 20, 1893, Chicago Historical Society. Ida C. Craddock to Mrs. Palmer, August 13, 1893, Chicago Historical

Society. Sara T. Hallowell to Mrs. Palmer, September 2, 1893, Art Institute of Chicago. Marian Deering to Mrs. Palmer, August 29, 1893, Art Institute of Chicago. Anders Zorn to Mrs. Palmer, November 24, 1893, Art Institute of Chicago. Undated notation by Eugene Field, Palmer papers, Chicago Historical Society. Princess Cantacuzène to author. Carter H. Harrison, *Stormy Years: The Autobiography of Carter H. Harrison*. Julian Ralph, *Harper's Chicago and the World's Fair*. Lloyd Lewis and Henry Justin Smith, *Chicago, The History of Its Reputation*. Henry Justin Smith, *Chicago's Great Century*. Ernest Poole, *Giants Gone*. Emmett Dedmon, *Fabulous Chicago*. Hubert Howe Bancroft, *The Book of the Fair*. Russell Lynes, *The Tastemakers*. Chicago *Inter-Oceaan*, June 10, 1893, and other contemporary newspaper clippings for the summer of 1893.

Chapter 6   *The Nation's Hostess*

Julian Ralph, "Our Great West," *Harper's Magazine*, 1893. Frederic Whyte, *The Life of W. T. Stead*, Vol. II. W. T. Stead, *If Christ Came to Chicago!* W. T. Stead to Mrs. Potter Palmer, January 30, 1894, Chicago Historical Society. W. T. Stead, "My First Visit to America," *Review of Reviews*, January-June, 1894. John P. Altgeld to Mrs. Palmer, March 11, 1894, and October 6, 1895, Altgeld papers, Chicago Historical Society. Judge H. M. Shepard to Mrs. Palmer, December 29, 1894, Chicago Historical Society. Mrs. Penfield to Mrs. Palmer, December 29, 1894, Chicago Historical Society. Mrs. Palmer to Franklin MacVeagh, December, 1895, Chicago Historical Society. Joseph Medill to Mr. and Mrs. Potter Palmer, April 6 (year unidentified), Chicago Historical Society. Mrs. Palmer to Senator William Lindsay, January 28, 1896, Chicago Historical Society. Telegrams and correspondence on Potter Palmer appointment in Chicago Historical Society. John C. Black to Daniel S. Lamont, January 28, 1896, Library of Congress. George W. Ochs to President Cleveland, February 3, 1896, Chicago Historical Society. James H. Eckels to Mrs. Palmer, February 4, 1896, Chicago Historical Society. Joseph Medill to Mrs. Palmer, February 5, 1896, Chicago Historical Society. *Elite*, July 18, 1896. Chicago *Daily Journal*, May 6, 1918. Honoré Palmer to author. Reminiscences of Mrs. Frederick Dent Grant, Palmer family papers. Princess Cantacuzène to author. Princess Cantacuzène, *My Life Here and There*. Julian Street, *Abroad at Home*. Bessie Louise Pierce, *A History of Chicago*, Vol. III. Frederick Francis Cook, *Bygone Days in Chicago*. John William Tebbel, *An American Dynasty*. Emmett Dedmon, *Fabulous Chicago*. Ernest Poole, *Giants Gone*. Lloyd Lewis and Henry Justin Smith,

Chicago, The History of Its Reputation. Ray Ginger, *Altgeld's America.* Harry Hansen, *The Chicago.*

Chapter 7   *Conquest of Newport*

Elite, February and September, 1896, and January, 1897. John Hay to Mrs. Potter Palmer, June 24, 1897, Chicago Historical Society. Maurice Joossens to Mrs. Palmer, June 1 and 3, 1898, Chicago Historical Society. Cardinal Gibbons to Mrs. Palmer, June 7, 1898, Chicago Historical Society. Henry White to Mrs. Palmer, March 29, 1898, Chicago Historical Society. Chicago *Journal,* May 6, 1918. New York *World,* June 12, 19, and July 24, 1898. New York *Herald,* June 5 and July 31, 1898. Mrs. Carter H. Harrison, Chicago *Herald-Examiner,* February 19, 1922. Princess Cantacuzène to author. Princess Cantacuzène, *My Life Here and There.* Gordon Palmer to author. Comment on interview with Pope in Palmer papers, Chicago Historical Society. New York papers, September 26 and 27, 1899. Henry James, *The American Scene.* Mrs. John King Van Rensselaer, *Newport Our Social Capital.* Cleveland Amory, *The Last Resorts.* Elizabeth Eliot, *Heiresses and Coronets.* Maud Howe Elliott, *My Cousin F. Marion Crawford.*

Chapter 8   *Art Collector*

Jean Raffaelli to Mrs. Potter Palmer, 1896, Art Institute of Chicago. Daniel Catton Rich, *Half a Century of American Art;* ed., *Catalogue of a Century of Progress Exhibition of Paintings and Sculpture Lent from American Collections;* and "Chicago Pioneered in Paintings," *Vogue,* August, 1944. Stephen Gwynn, *Claude Monet and His Garden.* Charles Durand-Ruel, record of Mrs. Palmer's art purchases from Durand-Ruel et Cie, Paris. Catalogues and pamphlets in Art Institute of Chicago. Benjamin K. Smith, Chicago art dealer, to author. Oliver W. Larkin, *Art and Life in America.* Margaret Breuning, *Mary Cassatt.* Malcolm Vaughan, "Mary Cassatt, Pioneer Woman Painter," *Reader's Digest,* November, 1959. Charles Fabens Kelley, "Chicago: Record Years," *Art News,* summer of 1952. T.B.H. in *Art News,* November, 1947. Maud Howe Elliott, *John Elliott: The Story of an Artist.* Hans Huth, *Gazette des Beaux Arts,* April, 1946. Sara T. Hallowell to Mrs. Palmer, December 30, 1892, and March 17, 1893, Art Institute of Chicago. Mrs. Palmer to Charles L. Hutchinson, January 27, March 15, April 27 (years unidentified), the Newberry Library. Reminiscences of Mrs. Frederick Dent Grant, Palmer family papers. Princess Cantacuzène and Honoré Palmer to author. Notes correcting picture titles, Art Institute of Chicago. Henry Justin Smith, *Chicago's Great Century*. Ernest Poole, *Giants Gone*. Lionello Venturi, *Les Archives de l'Impressionnisme*. Daniel Catton Rich to author. René Huyghe, "Simple Histoire de 2,414 Faux Corots," *Amour d'Art*, April, 1936. David Rosen and Henri Marceau, "A Study in the Use of Photographs in the Identification of Paintings," *Technical Studies in the Field of the Fine Arts*, Boston: Fogg Museum, October, 1937. Chicago *Daily News*, February 4, 1950. Chicago *Tribune*, February 10, 1950.

Chapter 9 *The Paris Exposition*

Claire de Pratz, "Reine de Chicago," *La Fronde*, May 10, 1900. *Womanhood*, July 1890. Vance Thompson, "Paris, City of Beautiful Women," *Cosmopolitan*, November, 1902–April, 1903. Adolphe Cohn, "The Streets of Paris," *Cosmopolitan*, November, 1902–April, 1903. Walter Germain Robinson, "The American Colony in Paris," *Cosmopolitan*, October, 1900. "Paris Fancies and Fashion," *The Gentlewoman*, May 12, 1900. Jean Phillipe Worth, *A Century of Fashion*. Two undated letters written by Mrs. Palmer in the summer of 1900 from Belgium to her mother, Mrs. Henry H. Honoré, Chicago Historical Society. Mrs. Potter Palmer to Mrs. John W. Mackay, late 1900, Chicago Historical Society. *New York Times*, May 7, 1918. New York *World*, March 3, 1901. Chicago *Tribune*, May 5, 1902, and February 19, 1950. Mrs. Carter H. Harrison, Chicago *Herald-Examiner* (Chicago Weekly), April 7, 1940. *Munsey's Magazine*, October, 1900. Julia L. Cole to Mrs. Palmer, late 1900, Chicago Historical Society. William Gardner Hale to Mrs. Palmer, late 1900, Chicago Historical Society. Chicago *Journal*, May 6, 1918. Mrs. Palmer to Judge Lambert Tree, spring of 1901, the Newberry Library. Potter Palmer to Franklin MacVeagh, June 23, 1899, Chicago Historical Society. Mrs. Palmer to Charles L. Hutchinson, October 9, 1905, the Newberry Library. *Elite*, January 28 and March 25, 1905. Art sales to Mrs. Palmer, Raoul Heilbronner catalogues, Library of Congress. Honoré Palmer to author. Princess Cantacuzène, *My Life Here and There*. Ruth McKenna, *Chicago: These First Hundred Years*. Douglas and Elizabeth Rigby, *Lock, Stock and Barrel*. Sonia Keppel, *Edwardian Daughter*. Virginia Sackville-West, *The Edwardians. The Bookman*, June, 1908.

Chapter 10 *Edwardian England*

New York *World*, June 16 and 23, 1907. Chicago *Record-Herald*, March 31 and September 8, 1907. New York *American*, March 17,

1907. Princess Cantacuzène and Honoré Palmer to author. Princess Cantacuzène, *My Life Here and There.* Sir Sidney Lee, *King Edward VII.* Shaw Desmond, *The Edwardian Story.* Dorothy Constance Peel, *A Hundred Wonderful Years.* Virginia Cowles, *Gay Monarch.* Consuelo Vanderbilt Balsan, *The Glitter and the Gold.* Sir Frederick Ponsonby, *Recollections of Three Reigns.* Lillie Langtry, *The Days I Knew.* Frances, Countess of Warwick, *Life's Ebb and Flow.* Daisy, Princess of Pless, *What I Left Unsaid.* Princess Catherine Radziwill, *It Really Happened, The Royal Marriage Market of Europe* and *Those I Remember.* Cecil Beaton, *The Glass of Fashion.* James Laver, *Edwardian Promenade.*

Chapter 11   *Chaliapin Sings for Mrs. Palmer*

Feodor Ivanovitch Chaliapine, *Pages from My Life.* Princess Cantacuzène to author. *New York Times,* November 3, 1907. *New York World,* June 2, 19 and 30, 1907. *Chicago Record-Herald,* September 9, 13, 14, 15, 1907. *Chicago Inter-Ocean,* September 15, 1910. *Chicago Herald-Examiner,* March 17, 1940. *Hampton's Magazine,* October, 1911. Sir Lionel Cust, *King Edward VII and His Court.* Lady Gwendolen Cecil, *Life of Robert Marquis of Salisbury.* Sir Sidney Lee, *King Edward VII.* Virginia Cowles, *The Gay Monarch.* André Maurois, *The Edwardian Era.* Frances, Countess of Warwick, *Life's Ebb and Flow.* Daisy, Princess of Pless, *What I Left Unsaid.* Sir Frederick Ponsonby, *Recollections of Three Reigns.*

Chapter 12   *Back to Nature*

"The Social Leader of Chicago," *Hampton's Magazine,* October, 1911. Gordon Palmer, Honoré Palmer and Princess Cantacuzène to author. Princess Cantacuzène, *My Life Here and There.* Virginia Robie, "The Oaks, Osprey on Little Sarasota Bay," *The House Beautiful,* January, 1920. A. B. Edwards, "History," *The Look-Out,* April 1, 1960. Chaperone, Chicago *Herald-Examiner* (Chicago Weekly), April 17, 1940. Reminiscences of Mrs. Frederick Dent Grant, Palmer family papers. *New York Times,* May 7 and 18, 1918. Chicago *Tribune,* May 18, 1918, October 21, 1945, and August 26, 1914. Chicago *Daily Journal,* May 6, 1918. Chicago *Herald-Examiner,* March 17, 1940. Mrs. Carter H. Harrison, Chicago *Herald-Examiner,* February 19, 1922. James Laver, *Edwardian Promenade.* Henry Justin Smith, *Chicago's Great Century.* Charles Fabens Kelley, "Chicago: Record Years," *Art News,* summer of 1952. *The Spur,* September 1, 1916.

Recollections of A. B. Edwards, A. E. Blackburn, Charles W. Webb, Captain Frank Roberts, Dr. Joseph Halton, Benjamin H. Russell, Mrs. Walter J. Bryan and Mrs. Ralph Caples, all of Sarasota, as told to author. Information supplied by Miss Louise K. Higel and Mrs. Doris Davis, of Sarasota. Karl H. Grismer, *The Story of Sarasota*. Sarasota *Herald*, November 29, 1936. Mrs. Palmer to Albert Blackburn, April 14, 1914; Mrs. Palmer to V. A. Saunders, June 22, 1914; Mrs. Palmer to F. H. Guenther, July 10, 1914; William F. Prentice to Mrs. Palmer, September 5, 1915; Mrs. Palmer to Charles Wellford Leavitt, February 26, 1911. Mrs. Palmer's Sarasota correspondence, Sarasota County Historical Commission.

⤞⤞⤞⤞⤞⤞⤞⤞⤞⤞⤞⤞ Bibliography

ADDAMS, JANE: *Twenty Years at Hull House.* New York: The Macmillan Company, 1949.
AMORY, CLEVELAND: *The Last Resorts.* New York: Harper & Brothers, 1952.
ANDREWS, WAYNE: *Architecture, Ambition and Americans.* New York: Harper & Brothers, 1947.
———: *Battle for Chicago.* New York: Harcourt, Brace & Company, 1946.
ASQUITH, MARGOT: *An Autobiography,* Vol. I. New York: George H. Doran Company, 1920.
BALSAN, CONSUELO VANDERBILT: *The Glitter and the Gold.* New York: Harper & Brothers, 1952.
BANCROFT, HUBERT HOWE: *The Book of the Fair. Columbian Edition.* Chicago: The Bancroft Company, 1893.
BEATON, CECIL: *The Glass of Fashion.* Garden City: Doubleday & Company, 1954.
BEHRMAN, S. N.: *Duveen.* New York: Random House, 1951.
BENSON, E. F.: *King Edward VII.* London: Longmans, Green Company, 1933.
BICKEL, KARL A.: *The Mangrove Coast.* New York: Coward-McCann, 1942.
BOWEN, LOUISE DE KOVEN: *Growing Up With a City.* New York: The Macmillan Company, 1926.
BRADLEY, MARY HASTINGS: *Old Chicago.* New York: D. Appleton & Company, 1933.
BREUNING, MARGARET: *Mary Cassatt.* New York: Hyperion Press, 1944.
CANTACUZÈNE, PRINCESS: *My Life Here and There.* New York: Charles Scribner's Sons, 1921.
———. *Revolutionary Days.* Boston: Small, Maynard & Company, 1919.

CECIL, LADY GWENDOLEN: *Life of Robert Marquis of Salisbury*, 4 vols. London: Hodder & Stoughton, 1922–1932.

CHALIAPINE, FEODOR IVANOVITCH: *Pages from My Life*. New York: Harper & Brothers, 1927.

CHATFIELD-TAYLOR, HOBART: *Cities of Many Men*. Boston: Houghton Mifflin Company, 1925.

Columbian Exposition Album: Chicago: Rand, McNally & Company, 1893.

Columbian Exposition Dedication Ceremonies Memorial: Chicago: The Metropolitan Art Engraving and Publishing Company, 1893.

COOK, FREDERICK FRANCIS: *Bygone Days in Chicago*. Chicago: A. C. McClurg, 1910.

CORNWALLIS-WEST, GEORGE: *Edwardian Hey-Days*. New York: G. P. Putnam's Sons, 1931.

COWLES, VIRGINIA: *Gay Monarch*. New York: Harper & Brothers, 1956.

CROMIE, ROBERT ALLEN: *The Great Chicago Fire*. New York: McGraw-Hill Company, 1958.

CUSHING, MARY WATKINS: *The Rainbow Bridge*. New York: G. P. Putnam's Sons, 1954.

CUST, SIR LIONEL: *King Edward VII and His Court*. New York: E. P. Dutton & Company, 1930.

DEDMON, EMMETT: *Fabulous Chicago*. New York: Random House, 1953.

DESMOND, SHAW: *The Edwardian Story*. London: Rockliff Publishing Corporation, Ltd., 1949.

DRURY, JOHN: *Old Chicago Houses*. Chicago: The University of Chicago Press, 1941.

EDDY, ARTHUR JEROME: *Recollections and Impressions of James A. McNeill Whistler*. Philadelphia: J. B. Lippincott Company, 1904.

EDWARDS, W. H.: *The Tragedy of Edward VII*. New York: Dodd, Mead & Company, 1928.

ELIOT, ELIZABETH: *Heiresses and Coronets*. New York: McDowell, Obolensky, 1960.

ELLIOTT, MAUD HOWE: *John Elliott: The Story of an Artist*. Boston: Houghton Mifflin Company, 1930.

——: *My Cousin F. Marion Crawford*. New York: The Macmillan Company, 1934.

ESCOTT, T. H. S.: *King Edward VII and His Court*, Philadelphia: George W. Jacobs & Company, 1903.

FIELDING, DAPHNE: *Mercury Presides*. New York: Harcourt, Brace & Company, 1955.

FULLER, HENRY B.: *The Cliff-Dwellers.* New York: Harper & Brothers, 1893.
GINGER, RAY: *Altgeld's America.* New York: Funk & Wagnalls Company, 1958.
GREGORY, ADDIE HIBBARD: *A Great-Grandmother Remembers.* Chicago: A. Kroch & Son, 1941.
GRISMER, KARL H.: *The Story of Sarasota.* Sarasota: M. E. Russell, 1946.
GWYNN, STEPHEN: *Claude Monet and His Garden.* New York: The Macmillan Company, 1934.
HANSEN, HARRY: *The Chicago.* New York: Farrar & Rinehart, 1942.
HARDY, LADY DUFFUS: *Through Cities and Prairie Lands.* New York: R. Worthington, 1881.
HARRISON, CARTER H.: *Stormy Years: The Autobiography of Carter H. Harrison.* Indianapolis: The Bobbs-Merrill Company, 1935.
HITCHCOCK, RIPLEY, ed.: *The Art of the World Illustrated in Paintings, Statuary, and Architecture of the World's Columbian Exposition.* New York: D. Appleton & Company, 1895.
HOWE, JULIA WARD: *Reminiscences, 1819–1899.* Boston: Houghton Mifflin & Company, 1899.
HUTCHINSON, WILLIAM T.: *Cyrus Hall McCormick.* New York: The Century Company, 1930.
JAMES, HENRY: *The American Scene.* New York: Harper & Brothers, 1897.
JENNINGS, KATHLEEN: *Louisville's First Families.* Louisville: The Standard Printing Company, 1920.
JEWELL, EDWARD ALDEN AND CRANE, AIMEE: *French Impressionists and Their Contemporaries Represented in American Collections.* New York: Hyperion Press, 1944.
KEPPEL, SONIA: *Edwardian Daughter.* London: Hamish Hamilton, 1958.
KIPLING, RUDYARD: *From Sea to Sea: Letters of Travel.* New York: Doubleday and McClure Company, 1899.
KIRKLAND, CAROLINE: *Chicago Yesterdays.* Chicago: Daughaday & Company, 1919.
KIRKLAND, JOSEPH: *The Story of Chicago,* 2 vols. Chicago: Dibble Publishing Company, 1892–94.
LANGTRY, LILLIE: *The Days I Knew.* New York: George H. Doran Company, 1925.
LARKIN, OLIVER W.: *Art and Life in America.* New York: Rinehart & Company, 1949.
LAVER, JAMES: *Edwardian Promenade.* London: Edward Hulton, 1958.

LEE, SIR SIDNEY: *King Edward VII.* New York: The Macmillan Company, 1927.
LEWIS, LLOYD AND SMITH, HENRY JUSTIN: *Chicago, The History of Its Reputation.* New York: Harcourt Brace & Company, 1929.
LOGAN, MRS. JOHN A.: *Reminiscences of a Soldier's Wife.* New York: C. Scribner's Sons, 1913.
LUDY, ROBERT B.: *Historic Hotels of the World, Past and Present.* Philadelphia: David McKay Company, 1927.
LYNES, RUSSELL: *The Tastemakers.* New York: Harper & Brothers, 1954.
MAUROIS, ANDRÉ: *The Edwardian Era.* New York: D. Appleton-Century Company, 1933.
MCILVAINE, CAROLINE: *Chicago and Its Makers.* Chicago: F. Mendelsohn, 1929.
MCKENNA, RUTH: *Chicago: These First Hundred Years.* Chicago: Old Fort Dearborn, 1933.
MUIRHEAD, JAMES FULLARTON: *America the Land of Contrasts.* New York: Dodd, Mead & Company, 1898.
PALMER, BERTHA HONORÉ: *Addresses and Reports of Mrs. Potter Palmer.* Chicago: Rand, McNally & Company, 1894.
Palmer, Honoré, Grant and Allied Families. New York: The American Historical Company, Inc., 1929.
PEEL, DOROTHY CONSTANCE: *A Hundred Wonderful Years.* London: John Lane, 1926.
PENNELL, E. R. & J.: *The Life of James McNeill Whistler.* Philadelphia: J. B. Lippincott Company, 1911.
PIERCE, BESSIE LOUISE: *A History of Chicago,* 2 vols. New York: Alfred A. Knopf, 1940.
―――, ed.: *As Others See Chicago: Impressions of Visitors, 1673–1933.* Chicago: University of Chicago Press, 1933.
PLESS, DAISY PRINCESS OF: *What I Left Unsaid.* New York: E. P. Dutton Company, 1936.
PONSONBY, SIR FREDERICK: *Recollections of Three Reigns.* London: Eyre & Spottiswoode, 1951.
POOLE, ERNEST: *Giants Gone.* New York: McGraw-Hill Company, 1943.
QUAIFE, MILO MILTON: *Chicago and the Old Northwest, 1673–1835.* Chicago: University of Chicago Press, 1913.
RADZIWILL, PRINCESS CATHERINE: *It Really Happened.* New York: Dial Press, 1932 .
―――: *The Royal Marriage Market of Europe.* New York: Funk & Wagnalls Company, 1915.

Bibliography

———: *Those I Remember.* London: Cassell & Company, 1924.
RALPH, JULIAN: *Harper's Chicago and the World's Fair.* New York: Harper & Brothers, 1893.
RICH, DANIEL CATTON, ed.: *Catalogue of a Century of Progress Exhibition of Paintings and Sculpture Lent from American Collections.* Chicago: The Art Institute of Chicago, June 1—November 1, 1933.
———: *Half a Century of American Art. November 16, 1939—January 7, 1940.* Chicago: Art Institute of Chicago, 1939.
RIGBY, DOUGLAS AND ELIZABETH: *Lock, Stock and Barrel.* Philadelphia: J. B. Lippincott Company, 1944.
RUSSELL, WILLIAM HOWARD, ed. FLETCHER PRATT: *My Diary North and South.* New York: Harper & Brothers, 1954.
SAARINEN, ALINE B.: *The Proud Possessors.* New York: Random House, 1958.
SACKVILLE-WEST, V.: *The Edwardians.* Garden City: Doubleday, Doran & Company, 1930.
SHELDON, GEORGE WILLIAM: *Artistic Country-Seats,* 2 vols. New York: D. Appleton & Company, 1886.
SMITH, HENRY JUSTIN: *Chicago's Great Century.* Chicago: Consolidated Publishers, Inc., 1933.
STEAD, W. T.: *If Christ Came to Chicago!* Chicago: Laird & Lee, 1894.
STREET, JULIAN: *Abroad At Home.* New York: The Century Company, 1914.
TEBBEL, JOHN WILLIAM: *An American Dynasty.* Garden City: Doubleday & Company, 1947.
TENNEY, JONATHAN: *New England in Albany.* Boston: Crocker & Company, 1883.
VAN RENSSELAER, MRS. JOHN KING: *Newport Our Social Capital.* Philadelphia: J. B. Lippincott Company, 1905.
VENTURI, LIONELLO: *Les Archives de l'Impressionnisme.* Paris: Durand-Ruel, 1939.
WARWICK, FRANCES, COUNTESS OF: *Life's Ebb and Flow.* New York: William Morrow & Company, 1929.
WHYTE, FREDERIC: *The Life of W. T. Stead,* 2 vols. Boston: Houghton Mifflin Company, 1925.
WILLIAMSON, JEFFERSON: *The American Hotel.* New York: Alfred A. Knopf, 1930.
WORTH, JEAN PHILIPPE: *A Century of Fashion.* Boston: Little, Brown & Company, 1928.

⪢⪢⪢⪢⪢⪢⪢⪢⪢⪢ *Index*

Abercorn, Duchess of, 61
Abercorn, Duke of, 185
Aberdeen, Countess of, 61, 74, 84
Addams, Jane, 45, 105, 107, 110, 165
Ade, George, 169
Albani, Emma, 162
Albemarle, Earl of, 195
Albert I of Belgium, 126, 132–133, 245
Alexander, George, 198
Alexandra of England, 169, 190, 195, 196, 202, 208, 210, 211, 218, 219, 221
Alfonso XIII of Spain, 194, 214
Allen, Viola, 188
Altgeld, John P., 106, 107
Amato, Pasquale, 210
Andersen, H. C., 152–153
Anthony, Susan B., 92
Antrim, Earl of, 213
Armory Show, 241
Armour, Philip D., 51, 87, 105, 122, 177, 188
Arnold, Matthew, 61
Art Institute of Chicago, 148, 158–159, 241, 242, 252
Ashley, Edwina, 195
Asquith, Herbert H., 203
Astor, John Jacob, 52
Astor, Mrs. John Jacob, 191
Astor, Mrs. William, 127, 128, 129, 131, 133, 135, 137, 170–171, 178, 191
Astor, William Waldorf, 210
Atholl, Duke of, 212
Atwood, Charles B., 78

Balfour, Arthur, 218
Ballard, Artie, 41
Balsan, Mme Jacques, 214
Barrett, Lawrence, 162

Barrie, James M., 219
Barrymore, Maurice, 162
Bartholdi, Frederic, 72
Bartlett, Frederick Clay, 160
Bartlett, Paul W., 78
Barton, Clara, 67
Beach, Mrs. H. H., 84
Beatty, David, 118
Beatty, Ethel Field, 118, 190, 192
Beau Brummell, 188
Bedford-Fenwick, Mrs., 61, 84
Beecham, Henry, 208
Beerbohm, Max, 219
Bellew, Kyrle, 162
Belloc, Hilaire, 219
Belmont, August, 129, 190, 243
Belmont, O. H. P., 130, 135
Belmont, Mrs. O. H. P., 129, 130, 138, 245
Bennett, Arnold, 219
Beresford, J. D., 219
Bernhardt, Sarah, 38, 162
Bitter, Karl T. F., 78
Black, John C., 122
Blackburn, Albert, 224, 231, 235, 236, 238, 247, 250
Blaine, James G., 59
Blair, Edward, 251
Blair, Watson F., 251
Blanc, Baroness de, 171
Blatchford, Robert, 203
Blériot, Louis, 218
Bogelot, Mme, 61–62
Bonheur, Rosa, 177
Booth, Edwin, 38, 162
Booth, John Wilkes, 11
Boric, A. E., 36
Bowen, Louise de Koven, 7, 46, 110, 216
Brassey, Lady, 61
Brazza, Countess di, 93

Index

Bremer, Fredrika, 12
Breton, Jules, 242
Brin, Baroness de, 171
Brooke, Lady, 58
Browning, Robert, 61, 219
Bryan, William Jennings, 123, 124, 145
Buckingham, Kate, 160
Buffalo Bill, 38, 92
Bull, Ole, 161
Burdett-Coutts, Baroness, 61
Burgstaller, Alois, 137
Burnham, Daniel, 71, 77, 97
Butt, Clara, 198
Byng, Robert Cecil, 205

Caine, Hall, 219
Calvé, Emma, 161
Campbell, Colin, 118
Campbell, Mrs. Patrick, 162, 210
Candler, J. W., 71
Cantacuzène, Bertha, 201
Cantacuzène, Ida, 202
Cantacuzène, Julia Grant, 48, 49–50, 51, 63, 96–97, 109, 117, 123, 125, 126, 133, 135, 138, 140, 141 ff., 175, 183, 184, 193, 199, 200, 201–202, 208–209, 217, 225, 244, 252
Cantacuzène, Michel, 142 ff., 184, 201–202, 217, 244
Carnegie, Andrew, 177
Carnot, M. Sadi, 61
Carnot, Mme M. Sadi, 61
Carr, John, 14
Carr, Mary Dorsey, 14, 15
Carse, Matilda B., 45
Carter, Leslie, 87
Caruso, Enrico, 188, 198
Cassatt, A. J., 154
Cassatt, Mary, 63, 75–76, 150, 151, 186, 230
Cassel, Ernest, 194, 195, 218
Castellane, Boni de, 53, 171
Cather, Willa, 242
Caton, Arthur J., 116
Caton, Mrs. Arthur J., 113, 116, 188
Caton, John D., 105, 108
Cavalieri, Lina, 242
Cazin, Jean Charles, 149, 154, 155, 186
Chaliapin, Feodor Ivanovich, 206–209
Charity Ball, 28, 57, 111–112, 179, 185, 188, 215–216, 217
Charles, Prince (Stuart), 213
Chatfield-Taylor, Hobart, 89–90
Chatfield, Wayne, 117

Chesterton, Gilbert K., 219
Chetlain, Mrs. A. L., 188
Chicago *Evening Post,* 217
Chicago fire, 1 ff., 185
Chicago *Herald-Examiner,* 215
Chicago *Inter-Ocean,* 51, 53, 88, 215, 217
Chicago *Record,* 160
Chicago *Times-Herald,* 160, 217
Chicago *Tribune,* 20, 31, 224, 230
Choiseul, Marquise de, 171
Christian, Princess, 57, 60, 61, 196
Churchill, Randolph, 190
Churchill, Lady Randolph, 141, 190, 204
Churchill, Winston, 204
Cleary, Mother M. Augustine, 23
Clemenceau, Georges, 149
Clemenceau, Mme Georges, 171
Clémentine, Princess of Belgium, 172, 173, 174
Cleveland, Grover, 45, 82, 83, 107, 122
Cleveland, Mrs. Grover, 84
Cobb, Henry Ives, 53, 56
Codman, Henry Sargent, 77
Colebrooke, Thomas Edward, 205
Columbian Exposition, 59 ff., 82 ff., 106, 148
Comstock, Anthony, 95
Corelli, Marie, 219
Cornwallis-West, George, 204
Cornwallis-West, Mrs. George, 204
Corot, J. B. C., 148, 154, 155, 156–157
Couzins, Phoebe W., 67, 68, 71, 93
Craddock, Ida C., 95–96
Craven, Countess of, 204
Crerar, John, 117
Cromer, Lord, 138–139
Cunard, Mrs. Ernest, 209–210
Curzon, Lady, 204
Curzon, Lord, 118, 204
Cushman, Charlotte, 162
Cust, Lionel, 214
Custer, George A., 34
Custer, Mrs. George A., 36

Damrosch, Walter, 161
D'Arcy, *see* Dorsey
Darrow, Clarence, 108
D'Auvergne, Charles de la Tour, 214
Davis, Erwin, 152
Davis, Florence, 204
Davis, John H., 204
Debs, Eugene V., 107, 108
Deering, Mrs. Charles, 96

Index

Degas, H. G. E., 75-76, 148, 149, 151, 154, 230
De Gray, Lady, 207, 208, 210
Delacroix, Eugene, 148, 156
De Lasteyrie, Louis, 214
De Loma, Señora Dupuy, 84
Del Val, Merry, 141
Del Valle, Consuelo Iznaga, 193
De Pachmann, Vladimir, 161
Depew, Chauncey, 79, 133, 145
De Pratz, Claire, 167-168
De Reszke, Edouard, 161, 210
De Reszke, Jean, 38, 161, 210
Deslys, Gaby, 198
Devonshire, Duchess of, 205
Devonshire, Duke of, 218
Dexter, Wirt, 117
Dino, Duc de, 171
Dino, Duchesse de, 171
Dobyns, Fletcher, 179
Doggett, Kate Newell, 46
Dorsey, Edward, 14
Dorsey, Mary, 15
Dorsey, Sarah Wyatt, 14
Douglas, Stephen A., 20
Doyle, Arthur Conan, 219
Drake, John B., 4, 42
Dreiser, Theodore, 242
Drew, John, 162
Drexel, Marguerite, 192
Dudley, Countess of, 198
Dufferin and Ava, Marchioness of, 204
Duncan, Isadora, 188
Dunne, Finley Peter, 160-161
Du Pont, T. Coleman, 235
Durand-Ruel, Paul, 148, 150, 151, 153
Duse, Eleanora, 198
Duveen, Joseph, 147, 186

Eckels, James H., 122
Eddy, Arthur Jerome, 160
Eddy, Augustus, 117
Eddy, Mrs. Augustus, 117
Eden, W. S., 39
Edward VII of England, 20, 58, 59, 91, 103, 104, 129, 164, 186, 190 ff., 208, 209, 210, 211, 217-218, 219, 220, 221
Edwards, A. B., 222, 224, 225, 227, 232, 234
Elliott, Gertrude, 198
Elliott, John, 153
Ellsworth, James, 160
Elsie, Lily, 198
Endecott, John, 30
Eulalia, Infanta of Spain, 86-91, 214

Fairbanks, N. K., 117
Farrar, Geraldine, 208
Farwell, Charles B., 36, 38
Farwell, Field & Company, 22
Fawcett, Millicent, 61
Ferber, Edna, 242
Ferrier, Gabriel, 54, 120
Field, Ethel, 118
Field, Eugene, 94, 161
Field, Marshall, 5, 8, 22-23, 27, 87, 89, 104, 105, 108, 113-114, 116, 118-119, 160, 183, 188
Field, Marshall, II, 119
Field, Mrs. Marshall, II, 190
Field, Marshall, III, 190
Field, Nannie, 112, 116, 119, 215
Field, Palmer & Leiter, 22, 28
Field, Mrs. Stanley, 184
Fish, Stuyvesant, 129
Fish, Mrs. Stuyvesant, 127, 131
Fiske, Minnie Maddern, 162
Fitch, Clyde, 188
Flagler, Henry M., 226
Forster, E. M., 219
Foy, Eddie, 185
Franklin, G. W., 250-251
Franz Joseph of Austria, 218
Fremstad, Olive, 209
French, Daniel Chester, 78
Frick, Henry C., 186
Frost, Charles S., 53
Fuller, Henry B., 161
Fuller, Melville W., 122

Gadski, Madam, 188
Gage, Lyman, 83, 107-108
Gainsborough, Thomas, 242
Galsworthy, John, 219
Gardner, Mrs. Jack, 186
Garland, Hamlin, 160, 242
Gates, John W., 177
George I of Greece, 164
George V of England, 221
Gerry, Mrs. Elbridge T., 128
Gibbons, Cardinal, 79, 133, 145
Glaspell, Susan, 242
Goelet, May, 187
Goelet, Robert, 211
Goelet, Mrs. Robert, 211
Goncourt, Edmond de, 149
Gorman, J. C., 6, 11
Gould, Anna, 171
Grant, Jesse, 57
Grant, Julia, *see* Cantacuzène, Julia Grant
Grant, Frederick Dent, 33, 34-35, 36, 48, 50, 56, 63, 64, 96, 135, 141, 163, 170, 175, 183, 198, 218

Grant, Ida Honoré, 14, 21, 28, 33–34, 35, 47–48, 50, 56, 63, 64, 96, 97, 122, 135, 141, 146, 150, 162, 163, 170, 175, 182, 183, 230, 244, 252
Grant, Nellie, 34, 48, 57, 135, 143
Grant, Ulysses S., 21, 24, 33, 34, 35, 47, 48–49, 56–57, 126, 141, 170
Grant, Mrs. Ulysses S., 34, 36, 47–48, 49, 57, 69, 110, 143, 144, 163, 182, 183
Grant, Ulysses S., II, "Buck," 35–36, 57
Grant, Ulysses S., III, 50, 63, 144
Grazioli, Duchess, 141
Greece, Queen of, 123
Gregory, Addie Hibbard, 92, 114
Guenther, F. H., 239, 250
Guenther, Mrs. F. H., 248
Guthrie, James, 11

Haggard, Rider, 219
Hahn, Reynaldo, 210
Haldane, R. B., 203
Hale, William Gardner, 178
Hallowell, Sara T., 63, 76, 150–152, 153–154, 156
Halton, Jack, 224
Halton, Joseph, 234
Hamilton, Alice, 46
Hand, Johnny, 43
Hardinge, Sir Charles, 202
Hardinge, Lady, 202
Hardy, Lady Duffus, 39
Hardy, Thomas, 219
Harlan, John Marshall, 122
Harrison, Benjamin, 38, 56, 73
Harrison, Carter H., 86, 90, 98–99
Harrison, Mrs. Carter H., 46, 113, 138, 181–182, 245
Harrison, Mrs. Russell, 73
Harvey, Mrs. T. W., 188
Havemeyer, Mrs. H. O., 75, 150, 186
Hay, John, 138
Hayden, Sophia G., 74–75, 77
Hayes, Laura, 136
Haymarket riot, 57, 106
Healy, George P. A., 54, 72–73
Heilbronner, Raoul, 186
Hengelmuller, Baron, 145–146
Hengelmuller, Baroness, 145
Henrotin, Mrs. Charles, 93, 123, 188
Henry, Prince of Prussia, 145
Henry of Pless, Princess, 204
Herrick, Robert, 161, 242
Hichens, Robert, 219
Higinbotham, Harlow N., 83, 86, 117–118, 216

Hofmann, Josef, 161
Holmes, Oliver Wendell, 130
Honoré, Adrian C., 14, 145, 183, 187, 224, 230, 250, 252
Honoré, Benjamin F., 14, 230
Honoré, Eliza J. Carr, 2, 11–12, 13–14, 15, 16, 29, 30–31, 33, 146, 172, 183, 189
Honoré, Francis, 14
Honoré, Francis, Jr., 14
Honoré, Henry Hamilton, 2, 13–14, 14–15, 18, 26, 29, 30–31, 33, 80, 97, 144, 183, 189, 222, 226, 230, 249
Honoré, Henry Hamilton, Jr., 14, 43, 250
Honoré, Ida, *see* Grant, Ida Honoré
Honoré, Jean Antoine, 14
Honoré, Laura, 230
Honoré, Lockwood, 14, 250, 252
Honoré, Mary Ann, 14
Honoré, Matilda Lockwood, 14
Honoré, Nathaniel, 14, 230, 252
Hooker, Isabella Beecher, 67–68
Howe, Julia Ward, 68, 87, 89, 130, 153
Howe, Maud Elliott, 87
Hunt, Richard Morris, 75, 77–78, 119, 120, 130
Huntington, Henry E., 186, 242
Hutchinson, Charles L., 63, 111, 158–159, 160, 251

Inglis, James S., 154
Iroquois Theater fire, 185
Irving, Henry, 162, 198
Iselin, C. Oliver, 170
Iselin, Mrs. C. Oliver, 170

Jackson, Huntington, 117
James, Henry, 130, 153
Japan, Empress of, 65
Jenney, William Le Baron, 77
Jerome, Jennie, 204
Jeune, Lady, 61
Johnson, Andrew, 23
Jones, Lawrence, 225

Kauffmann, Angelica, 197
Keith, Mrs. Walter, 184
Kelley, Florence, 46
Kemble, Fanny, 34
Keppel, Mrs. George, 194–195, 199, 209, 218, 220, 221
Kerfoot, S. H., 8
Kimball, W. W., 116–117, 160
Kimball, Mrs. W. W., 116–117, 160, 188

Kinsley, H. M., 31
Kipling, Rudyard, 38, 39-40, 219
Knutsford, Lady, 61
Kohlsaat, Herman H., 217, 251
Kyril, Grand Duke, 142

Lafayette, Marquis de, 14
La Fayette, Comte de, 145
La Fronde, 168
La Grange, Baroness de, 171
Lamont, Daniel S., 122
Langtry, Lily, 162, 169-170, 210
Lathrop, Julia, 46
Leavitt, Charles Wellford, 248
Lebaudy, Pierre, 186
Lehr, Harry, 127
Leiter, Daisy, 118
Leiter, Levi Z., 5, 8, 22, 23, 27
Leiter, Mrs. Levi Z., 131
Leiter, Mary, 118, 204
Leiter, Nancy, 118
Leland, Charles, 43
Leo XIII, Pope, 141
Lincoln, Abraham, 20, 21, 22, 59, 105, 114, 123
Lincoln, Robert Todd, 59, 87, 111, 114
Lind, Jenny, 12
Lindsay, Vachel, 242
Lindsay, William, 121
Lipton, Thomas, 192
Lockwood, Mary, 68, 93
Logan, Mrs. John A., 62, 67, 68, 71, 93-94, 166, 167, 171
Londonderry, Lady, 205
Lord, J. H., 224, 225, 226
Lorillard, Mrs. Pierre, 170
Lynn, Bridget (Bridey) Mullarkey, 182 183

MacArthur, Charles, 216
MacDowell, Edward A., 161
Mackay, Clarence H., 180, 191
Mackay, Mrs. John W., 64, 170, 177, 187
MacMonnies, Frederick, 63, 76, 78
MacMonnies, Mary Fairchild, 63, 76
MacVeagh, Franklin, 44, 111, 116
MacVeagh, Mrs. Franklin, 116, 188
Manchester, Duchess of, 129, 192-193, 205, 210
Mandeville, Viscount, 193
Manet, Edouard, 154
Mansfield, Richard, 162, 188
Mantell, Robert, 162
Margherita of Italy, 64, 83, 132, 133, 137, 169

Maria Theresa, Archduchess of Austria, 73, 97
Marie Henriette of Belgium, 64, 91, 172, 173 *ff*.
Marlborough, Duchess of, 129, 191, 204, 219
Marshall Field & Company, 10, 16 *ff*., 22-23, 27, 44, 118-119
Martin, Bradley, 192, 204
Martin, Mrs. Bradley, 64, 138, 192
Martin, Cornelia, 204
Martin, Riccardo, 208
Martin, Thomas Reed, 228
Mary of England, 221
Masters, Edgar Lee, 242
Matisse, Henri, 241
May, Princess of England, 58
McAllister, Ward, 111, 127, 134-135
McCormick, Cyrus H., 7, 36, 44, 83, 116, 120, 211
McCormick, Mrs. Cyrus H., 116, 199
McCormick, Elizabeth, 188
McCormick, Mrs. Harold F. (Edith Rockefeller), 215
McCullough, John, 162
McDonnell, Schomberg K., 213, 214
McDowell, Mary, 46
McGrath, J. J., 105
McKee, Mrs. J. R., 73
McKim, Charles F., 77
McKinley, William, 56, 124, 145, 164
McVicker, James H., 52
Mead, William R., 77
Medill, Joseph, 5, 8, 20, 98, 105, 116, 117, 122
Medill, Mrs. Joseph, 116
Melba, Madam, 161, 210
Mellon, Andrew, 186
Merritt, General, 111
Metternich, Mme de, 169
Metternich, Princess, 64
Miles, Nelson A., 57, 79, 87
Mill, John Stuart, 115
Miller, Gertie, 198
Millet, J. F., 156
Milliken, H. O., 248
Minwegen, Alderman, 180
Mitchell, John H., 171
Mitchell, Mattie, 171
Mitchell, S. Weir, 110
Modjeska, Helen, 38, 162
Monet, Claude, 148, 149, 156, 230
Monroe, Harriet, 242
Montesquieu, Comte de, 149
Moody, Dwight L., 105-106
Moody, William V., 161

Index

Morgan, J. P., 164, 186
Morland, Charles, 187
Mountbatten, Lady, 195
Munster, Earl of, 212
Muratore, Lucien, 242
Murphy, Garrett "Dink," 232
Murray, Mrs. Ronald Graham, 204

Nevin, Robert J., 141, 143, 144
Newman, John Philip, 57
Nicholas II of Russia, 196, 218
Nickerson, Samuel M., 120
Nightingale, Florence, 177
Nilsson, Christine, 161
Nordica, Lillian, 64, 161
Normannia, 65

O'Brien, John, 170
Oelrichs, Mrs. Hermann, 129
Ogden, William B., 54, 105
O'Leary, Catherine, 2
Olmsted, Frederick L., 77
Orloff, Prince, 202
Orloff, Princess, 169
Owen, Phillip, 59, 159

Pach, Walter, 241
Paderewski, Ignace, 161, 210
Paget, Mrs. Arthur (later Lady), 97, 129, 191, 204, 210
Palmer, Bertha, 252
Palmer, Bertha Honoré
 and ambassadorship, 121–122
 and art, 75–76, 147 ff., 186–187, 229–230, 241–242
 at Bar Harbor, 109–111
 and Charity Ball, 28, 57, 111–112, 179, 185, 188, 215–216, 217
 and Columbian Exposition, 59 ff., 82 ff.
 death of, 250–251
 early days of, 10–15, 18–25, 29
 in Europe, 32, 58 ff., 108–109, 123, 138 ff., 164 ff., 190 ff., 206–211, 217–221
 and fashion, 35, 40, 62, 168–169, 199
 in Florida, 222 ff.
 and golf, 135, 193, 199
 as hostess, 56, 69, 94, 100 ff., 113–117, 132–134, 145–146, 165, 179–180, 197, 206–211, 215
 jewels of, 32, 49, 62, 79, 115, 126, 128, 136–138, 191, 245
 and Legion of Honor, 177
 marriage of, 29–31
 and music, 11, 18–19, 24–25, 64
 and Palmer Castle, 53–56

Palmer, Bertha Honoré (*Continued*)
 and politics, 20–21, 23–24, 48–49, 57, 121–124, 178–181
 and social work, 44 ff., 101 ff.
 and suffragists, 45, 60–61, 67–68, 74, 92, 203
 and temperance, 45, 102–103
 and women's rights, 45–47, 60 ff., 165–166
Palmer, Gordon, 252
Palmer, Grace Greenway Brown, 183–184, 188, 216, 233, 236, 252
Palmer, Honoré, 33, 35, 36, 48, 49, 50–51, 52, 55, 97, 124, 126, 135, 138, 139, 140, 143, 145, 158, 178–181, 183, 184–185, 188, 198, 199–200, 216–217, 230, 233, 236, 246, 251–252
Palmer, Honoré, II, 232, 246–247, 252
Palmer, Pauline, 252
Palmer, Pauline Kohlsaat, 158, 217, 232, 252
Palmer, Potter
 and art, 63, 150 ff.
 at Bar Harbor, 109–110
 and Chicago fire, 6–7, 8–9
 courtship of, 25–26, 29–30
 death of, 181–183
 early life of, 10, 17, 30
 and hotel, *see* Palmer House
 and social life, 114–117, 130–131
 store of, 16–18, 22–23; *see also* Marshall Field & Company
 See also Palmer, Bertha Honoré
Palmer, Potter, II, 40, 48, 49, 50–51, 52, 55, 97, 126, 138, 140, 141, 145, 157, 158, 181, 187, 198, 199, 200, 217, 230, 232, 246, 251–252
Palmer, Potter, III, 232, 252
Palmer, Potter D'Orsay, 188, 217, 232, 246, 252
Palmer, Walter, 30
Palmer Castle, 56
Palmer House, 1, 4, 9, 28, 29, 32, 33, 36, 37 ff., 52, 102–103, 251
Paris Exposition, 59, 61
Parkhurst, Emmeline, 203
Patti, Adelina, 161
Pavlova, Anna, 210
Peck, Ferdinand W., 44, 52, 83, 166
Peck, Mrs. Ferdinand W., 166
Peter of Serbia, 212
Pickard, Paul, 181
Pilar, Maria de, 84
Pinero, Arthur W., 198

Pissarro, Camille, 148, 149, 154, 157
Poiret, Paul, 243
Poole, Ernest, 115, 138
Pourtales, Countess de, 171
Porter, Horace, 170
Potter, Henry Codman, 143, 144
Potter, Mrs. James Brown, 162
Prendergast, Patrick, 98
Prentice, William F., 237-238, 239-240
Prince of Wales, see Edward VII
Proust, Antoine, 62, 72, 149
Pulitzer, Joseph, 110
Pullman, George M., 13, 44, 51, 87, 105, 107, 108, 188
Puvis de Chavannes, Pierre, 154

Raffaelli, Jean François, 149, 154, 186, 230
Ralph, Julian, 101
Rehan, Ada, 162
Reid, Jean, 190
Reid, Whitelaw, 190, 192, 197, 209, 210, 220
Reid, Mrs. Whitelaw, 197, 209, 210
Renoir, P. A., 148, 154, 155
Rice, Mrs. Hamilton, 245
Rich, Daniel Catton, 147-148
Richmond, Duke of, 190
Ringling brothers, 247
Ripon, Marchioness of, 169
Roberts, Frank, 233-234
Roberts-Austen, Mrs., 84
Roche, Jules, 62
Rochefoucauld, Duc de la, 145
Rochefoucauld, Duchesse de la, 171
Rockefeller, John D., 215
Rohan Chabot, Countess de, 171
Ronald, Mrs., 64
Roosevelt, Theodore, 218, 220, 221
Root, Elihu, 145
Root, John Wellborn, 77
Roseberry, Lord, 190
Rosenwald, Julius, 188
Rothschild, Albert, 210-211
Rothschild, Ferdinand, 210-211
Rothschild, Henri de, 186
Roxburgh, Duchess of, 129, 187
Rumania, Queen of, 73
Runnells, John S., 251
Runyon, Theodore, 121, 122
Russell, Lillian, 162
Russia, Empress of, 65, 84, 123
Ryerson, Martin A., 44, 155, 159, 160, 251

Sadanaru Fushimi, Prince of Japan, 145

Saint-Gaudens, Augustus, 74, 78
Saint-Simon, Louis de, 184
Salisbury, Lord, 59, 213
Salisbury, Marchioness of, 61
Sampson, Adele, 171
Sandburg, Carl, 242
Sargent, John Singer, 130
Sartoris, Algernon, 34, 143
Sartoris, Algernon, II, 135
Sartoris, Nellie Grant, 34
Saunders, V. A., 236
Schahowskoy, Princess, 84
Schreiner, Olive, 202
Schwartz, Charles, 117
Seillière, Baroness de, 170
Selfridge, Harry Gordon, 118-119
Sembrich, Marcella, 188
Seward, William H., 20
Shaw, Anna Howard, 74
Shaw, George Bernard, 190, 198, 219
Shedd, John G., 110-119
Shepard, Henry M., 106-107
Shepard, Mrs. Henry M., 114, 188
Sheridan, Philip H., 34, 35, 57
Sherman, William Tecumseh, 49, 57
Siam, Queen of, 84
Siegfried, Jules, 62
Simon, Jules, 62
Sisley, Alfred, 148, 154
Skinner, Otis, 162
Smith, Benjamin K., 150
Smith, F. Hopkinson, 87
Smith, Henry H., 94
Somerset, Lady Henry, 61
Sothern, Edward H., 162
Southerland, Duchess of, 220
Soveral, Marquis de, 195
Spencer, Albert, 153, 154
Spencer, Mrs. John Thompson, 133
Stafford, Countess of, 218
Stanton, Elizabeth Cady, 62
Stanton, Theodore, 62-63, 72, 87
Stead, W. T., 103-104, 105, 145, 219-220, 243
Stevens, Frederic William, 171
Stevens, Paran, 87
Stevens, Mrs. Paran, 129, 204
Stevenson, Adlai E. (I), 87, 89, 121, 122
Stevenson, Letitia Green, 121
Stewart, A. T., 18
Stewart, Anita, 192
Stone, James S., 251
Stotesbury, E. T., 191
Stradford, Earl of, 205
Street, Julian, 120
Suffolk, Earl of, 118

Suffragists, 45, 60-61, 67-68, 74, 92, 203
Sullivan, Louis H., 77
Sullivan, Margaret F., 74
Sumner, W. A., 224
Suriya, Phra Linchee, 84
Sutherland, Millicent, Duchess of, 204
Sweeney, J. S., 31
Swift, Gustavus, 51
Swinburne, Algernon C., 219

Taft, Loredo, 78
Tallmadge, Thomas, 56
Talleyrand-Périgord, Marquis de, 171
Teck, Duchess of, 58
Teck, Duke of, 58
Terry, Ellen, 162, 198
Thaw, Harry K., 170, 186
Thénier, Mlle, 64
Thomas, Theodore, 4, 84, 161, 188
Thompson, Frank, 154
Thorne, Mrs. Oakleigh L., 252
Titanic, 243
Tosti, Francesco Paolo, 198
Tree, Arthur M., 118
Tree, Ethel Field, 118
Tree, Herbert Beerbohm, 198
Tree, Lambert, 111, 179
Turin, Prince of, 133
Tuttle, Arthur, 234
Tuttle, F. B., 251
Twain, Mark, 49, 192

Uhl, Edwin F., 122

Vanderbilt, Alfred G., 191
Vanderbilt, Consuelo, 191, 214
Vanderbilt, Cornelius, 130
Vanderbilt, George W., 137
Vanderbilt, W. K., 186
Veragua, Duchess of, 83, 84, 85-86
Veragua, Duke of, 83
Victor Emmanuel, 126

Victoria of England, 8, 59, 60, 74, 186, 196
Voorhees, Daniel W., 122

Waller, James B., 251
Walpole, Hugh, 219
Wanamaker, John, 186
Wannieck, Leon, 244
Ward, Mrs. Humphrey, 219
Ward, Lady, 190
Warwick, Countess of, 58, 103, 104, 203, 220
Webb, Charles W., 247
Webb, John G., 225
Webster, Richard, 59
Wells, H. G., 219
Wentworth, Mrs. Edward, 245
Wentworth, John, 105
Wentworth, Moses, 117
West, Algernon, 212
Westminster, Duchess of, 205
Wharton, Edith, 130
Whistler, J. A. M., 149
White, Henry, 138-139
White, Muriel, 192
White, Sanford, 186
Whitney, Harry Payne, 135, 186
Wilde, Oscar, 198
Wilhelm II of Germany, 195
Willard, Frances E., 45, 61
Woman's Building, 59 ff., 84-85
Wood, Mrs. Arthur M., 252
Wood, Henry, 59, 87
Woods, Ernest, 251
Wordsworth, William, **219**
Worth, Charles, 169
Worth, Jean, 169
Wright, John, 28-29
Wyatt, Edith, 242

Yerkes, Charles T., 52, 80, 105, 160, 188
Yves-Guyot, Mme, 61

Zorn, Anders L., 87, 96, 145

THE LEISURE CLASS IN AMERICA

An Arno Press Collection

Bradley, Hugh. **Such was Saratoga.** 1940

Browne, Junius Henri. **The Great Metropolis:** A Mirror of New York. 1869

Burt, Nathaniel. **The Perennial Philadelphians.** 1963

Canby, Henry Seidel. **Alma Mater:** The Gothic Age of the American College. 1936

Crockett, Albert Stevens. **Peacocks on Parade.** 1931

Croffut, W[illiam] A. **The Vanderbilts.** 1886

Crowninshield, Francis W. **Manners for the Metropolis.** 1909

de Wolfe, Elsie. **The House in Good Taste.** 1913

Ellet, E[lizabeth] F[ries Lummis]. **The Court Circles of the Republic,** or The Beauties and Celebrities of the Nation. 1869

Elliott, Maud Howe. **This Was My Newport.** 1944

Elliott, Maud Howe. **Uncle Sam Ward and His Circle.** 1938

Fairfield, Francis Gerry. **The Clubs of New York** and Croly, [Jane C.] **Sorosis.** 1873/1886. Two vols. in one

[Fawcett, Edgar]. **The Buntling Ball:** A Graeco-American Play. 1885

Fawcett, Edgar. **Social Silhouettes.** 1885

Fiske, Stephen. **Off-Hand Portraits of Prominent New Yorkers.** 1884

Foraker, Julia B. **I Would Live It Again:** Memories of a Vivid Life. 1932

Goodwin, Maud Wilder. **The Colonial Cavalier.** 1895

Hartt, Rollin Lynde. **The People at Play.** 1909

Lehr, Elizabeth Drexel. **"King Lehr"** and the Gilded Age. 1935

Lodge, Henry Cabot. **Early Memories.** 1913

[Longchamp, Ferdinand]. **Asmodeus in New-York.** 1868

McAllister, [Samuel] Ward. **Society as I Have Found It.** 1890

McLean, Evalyn, with Boyden Sparkes. **Father Struck It Rich.** 1936

[Mann, William d'Alton]. **Fads and Fancies of Representative Americans at the Beginning of the Twentieth Century.** 1905

Martin, Frederick Townsend. **The Passing of the Idle Rich.** 1911

Martin, Frederick Townsend. **Things I Remember.** 1913

Maurice, Arthur Bartlett. **Fifth Avenue.** 1918

[Mordecai, Samuel]. **Richmond in By-Gone Days.** 1856

Morris, Lloyd. **Incredible New York.** 1951

Neville, Amelia Ransome. **The Fantastic City:** Memoirs of the Social and Romantic Life of Old San Francisco. 1932

Nichols, Charles Wilbur de Lyon. **The Ultra-Fashionable Peerage of America.** 1904

Pound, Arthur. **The Golden Earth:** The Story of Manhattan's Landed Wealth. 1935

Pulitzer, Ralph. **New York Society on Parade.** 1910

Ripley, Eliza. **Social Life in Old New Orleans.** 1912

Ross, Ishbel. **Silhouette in Diamonds:** The Life of Mrs. Potter Palmer. 1960

Sherwood, M[ary] E[lizabeth W.]. **Manners and Social Usages.** 1897

The Sporting Set. 1975

Van Rensselaer, [May] King. **Newport: Our Social Capital.** 1905

Van Rensselaer, [May] King. **The Social Ladder.** 1924

Wharton, Edith and Ogden Codman, Jr. **The Decoration of Houses.** 1914

Williamson, Jefferson. **The American Hotel.** 1930